City wildspace

Bob Smyth

Hilary Shipman
London

First published 1987 by
Hilary Shipman Limited
19 Framfield Road
Highbury
London N5 1UU

British Library Cataloguing in Publication Data
Smyth, Bob
  City wildspace.
  1. Nature conservation—Great Britain
  2. Cities and towns—Great Britain
  I. Title
  639.9′0941   QH77.G7

ISBN 0-948096-06-3
ISBN 0-948096-07-1 Pbk

Cover design by David Bennett
Data conversion by ImagePlus
Typeset in Oxford by Infotype Limited
Printed and bound by Biddles Limited
Guildford & King's Lynn

Contents

for
BFS

Acknowledgements

Specific thanks to those – council staff and urban
wildlife group workers or volunteers – who
contributed to the gazetteer are given in the
appropriate section of the gazetteer. For efficient
assistance over many years, I am indebted to the
Southwark libraries service and in particular to the
staff of Peckham Hill Street Library.
I am grateful to those who have read and
commented on various chapters, including Lyndis
Cole, Richard Robinson, Chris Rose and Allan Ruff,
as well as to Keith Corbett and John Newton for
their scrutiny of the London section of the
gazetteer. None, of course, should be taken as
necessarily agreeing with the opinions expressed.

The author

Brought up in Slough, where 'there isn't grass to graze a cow', Bob Smyth studied English at Wadham College, Oxford, where he was editor of *Isis*. Now a journalist with a special interest in environmental issues, he was co-founder of the London Wildlife Trust and its chairman from 1982 to 1986. Since 1983 he has been a member of the council of the Royal Society for Nature Conservation. From 1978 to 1983 he was a councillor for the London Borough of Southwark, and deputy leader from 1982 to 1983. As well as serving for five years on the planning and leisure committees, he initiated the creation of a leisure and recreation department.

1 | City wildspace

Urban nature conservation was until recently thought somehow frivolous, even ludicrous. It is certainly true that enjoyment of urban wildlife is inessential – but only in the sense that theatres or sports pitches are unnecessary. The usefulness of natural areas is tangible only as an educational resource, as places for study by pupils and students. By any other assessment, the natural or semi-natural environment is an ingredient as important as street trees or formal parks in making cities pleasanter places to live or work in.

This book is about the how, rather than the why of urban nature conservation. Other books – many of them published recently and listed at the end of the chapter – have evocatively described the variety of wildlife to be found in London and other cities and the pleasure to be derived from it. But how the sites came to be there, and what factors play a part in urban nature conservation, have not been so widely discussed.

As the next chapter demonstrates, concern for city wildspace is not altogether a modern preoccupation. Previous generations have fought to save their urban commons, both during the 19th century expansion of the conurbations and earlier. Among the first to discover, more recently, the value of what Richard Mabey christened 'the unofficial countryside' as an up-to-date version of commonland were younger members of the landscape architecture profession, as described in Chapter 3. Many of their colleagues remain unconvinced of the merit of such natural parks compared to those designed in text-book format. For landscape architects in the public sector there is little kudos in compiling a portfolio consisting of schemes where new fencing has replaced old corrugated iron but where the site has been otherwise left well alone. For those in private practice, the financial imperative is a stimulus to making projects as elaborate as possible. Set-piece designs for municipal parks or garden festivals attract healthy fees,

1

whereas if nature has already done much of the job for you it's difficult to justify large bills.

Local authorities have been similarly ambivalent in their attitude to the safeguarding of urban wildspace. The metropolitan county councils were enlightened planning authorities, as shown in Chapter 4, but were abolished before their green plans were either completed or implemented. Planners in district councils, like their landscape colleagues, worry about career development – and drawing up plans for techno parks is more likely to enhance their professional credibility than preparing schemes for nature parks. Some local councils have accepted that urban greening can assist a town's attractions to commerce, and thus contribute to job creation. Most disregard the amenity potential of wasteland sites, considering them better used for new houses or factories.

A counterbalance to unbridled commercial exploitation of land whether in country or town was the creation by the post-war Labour government of two quangos, the Nature Conservancy Council and Countryside Commission (to use their present titles). Each is constrained in its freedom of action by government control of its finances and management. When the last chairman of the Nature Conservancy backed efforts to protect the Somerset Levels from drainage by local farmers, for example, backbench Tory MPs ensured that his appointment was not renewed.

Nevertheless, both quangos have a creditable record of achievement – though they can also be criticised for not doing more. The Countryside Commission is commendably efficient in carrying out its remit to provide recreation facilities in the countryside and urban fringe. But the somewhat artificial division of responsibility between it and the Nature Conservancy Council is, regrettably, used to justify its attitude that nature conservation is peripheral to its activities.

The Conservancy, too, pays comparatively little attention to urban areas. Scientific staff, bred on the notion that conservation is about protecting botanical or biological rarities, tend to disparage the common and garden plants and animals characteristic of urban sites. They are also ill-trained to consider the human aspect of conservation. The traditional approach has been to keep human beings well away from sensitive areas. Urban conservationists, on the other hand, operate on the principle that wildlife is for people, a view that is fast catching on.

When the metropolitan county councils were abolished in 1986, the Conservative government was obliged to demonstrate that work on improving the urban fringe environment would continue. The result has been the creation of more local quangos – or qualgos – in the form of a new generation of Groundwork Trusts, which had originally been set up to work in the urban fringe, following an initiative by the Countryside Commission. Funded by private industry as well as public cash, these mulish creatures have the additional advantage from both a government and local council point of view that, unlike many voluntary sector conservation organisations, they avoid campaigning activities. In 1986, Home Secretary Douglas Hurd complained that 'one of the difficulties of our present system of government is the increasing role of pressure groups and interest groups . . . and the pressures which these groups exert on policy-making'. As Chapter 6 describes, the newly-formed urban wildlife groups, unlike many of their country cousins, operate as vigorous pressure groups. Rural county wildlife trusts are in many cases dominated by the squirearchy and reluctant to challenge the actions of landowners. The urban conservation movement, which attracts a younger and more radical membership, has the task of invigorating the conservation lobby nationally as well as within city limits.

Urban groups also face the problem of offending powerful landlords, these being the local councils who own the bulk of vacant land in most city areas. Groups are usually in pursuit of council funding for their activities and therefore dependent on the goodwill of town hall staff and councillors. And politicians of the major parties are unenthusiastic about voluntary sector organisations taking on the management of urban nature reserves. Labour's national policy on urban greening, as indicated in Chapter 7, is the most impressively detailed among all parties' environmental statements, but at town hall level many Labour councillors tend to take the view that: 'If a job needs doing, it ought to be done by direct labour.'

Conservatives, on the other hand, appear to think that if a job needs doing, it ought to be done for free. Conservative councils, while in theory supportive of the concept of voluntarism, fail to provide the pump-priming funds necessary if voluntary organisations are to function. At Conservative government level, the predominant philosophy has been that environmental work is a convenient way of reducing unemployment figures. Since 1979 the number of places on the Manpower Services Commission's Community Programme (or its earlier equivalents), which is largely concerned with environmental schemes, was, until 1987, steadily increasing. As well as being an inadequate substitute for properly paid jobs, the excessive use of untrained and under-supervised MSC workers can harm sites being worked on. Conscious of growing public interest in green issues the government has increased funds available to the Nature Conservancy Council, but little has trickled down to the voluntary organisations, rural or urban.

As will be apparent, this account of the history of urban nature conservation, the first in book form, is written from the standpoint of a lay conservationist. The strength of the urban wildlife movement is that it attracts the support of the hitherto uncommitted as well as those with a lifelong passion for natural history. Many become involved when a patch of land in their neighbourhood is threatened by commercial or council development. In my own case, the impetus derives from the early 1970s when the local council was intent on demolishing a terrace of listed buildings in order to construct a new road. The terrace still stands, the road is only half-built (and remains unopened) and a vigorous Civic Trust society came into being to fight other planning battles.

Direct contact with such issues brought the realisation that planners were still operating within a demolish-and-rebuild philosophy that most assumed had been discredited. It also revealed that few councillors had any interest in the quality of the environment. My passive interest in politics was converted into active participation as a councillor. Thereafter, membership of the council's planning and leisure committees meant, in particular, making decisions about park design and management. Interest in the potential of informal parks came later.

What I have tried to do in this book is to convey an impression of how urban nature conservation works in practice, rather than in idealised theory. Many may find the views expressed tendentious. I hope, indeed, they will provoke debate.

There is nowadays far greater awareness of the importance of city wildlife than in 1974, which is the year that urban nature conservation became a recognisably organised activity. Yet in early

1987 there are at least a dozen important wildlife sites under threat in London alone, their future to be decided by public inquiries. If the following pages sometimes appear impatient, this is one of the reasons why.

References and further reading

The Unofficial Countryside by Richard Mabey (Collins, 1973).
Country London by John Talbot White (Routledge and Kegan Paul, 1984; paperback 1986).
The Wild Side of Town by Chris Baines (BBC, 1986, paperback).
Wild in London by David Goode (Michael Joseph, 1986, paperback).
City Safari: Wildlife in London by Gavin Weightman and Mike Birkhead (Sidgwick and Jackson, 1986, paperback).
London's Parks and Woodlands by Andrew Crowe (Fourth Estate, 1987, paperback) is a magnificently thorough guide to London's open space, including due attention to areas of wildlife interest.

2 | Historical background

In a crowded public hall in south London, the leader of the local council, of aldermanic bulk, was savaging a representative of the borough's tenants' associations. The event was an evening session of a public inquiry, in early 1985, presided over by a DoE inspector. The subject under debate was Southwark council's plan to build council flats on a patch of Dulwich woodland. The politician bellowed that houses were more important than wildlife any day. Not necessarily, said the tenants' spokesman:

> There was a surprising degree of unanimity on this issue. We feel that counterposing the argument for better housing to that for open space is an artificial device. One of the greatest sources of grievance among council tenants is the general environment in which they are housed rather than the housing itself. The preservation of decent and pleasing environments is an essential part of any housing strategy.

The outcome of the inquiry is described later, but the statement was an indication of how far, by 1985, urban nature conservation had come to be accepted as an issue of concern not only to naturalists but to a much wider public. A decade earlier, urban ecology in Britain had been the interest of a handful of ecologists, landscape architects and planners. In the USA and elsewhere in Europe, notably Germany and Holland, its importance as an element in town planning had long been recognised. A combination of events in England in 1974, however, gave impetus to a movement that, in the 1980s, has become part of the social as well as the physical fabric of our towns and cities.

On television, Richard Mabey guided viewers around 'The Unofficial Countryside' of London which he had described in his book of the same title published the previous year. At a conference

6

in Manchester, landscape architects were exposed to the thinking of American and European colleagues about 'Nature in Cities', the proceedings later forming the basis of an important book of that title. Landscape architects were also discovering for themselves the urban wildspace being designed into Dutch cities and suburbs. In the six main English conurbations outside London – the West Midlands, South and West Yorkshire, Greater Manchester, Merseyside and Tyne and Wear – new metropolitan county councils were beginning their brief life, and were, along with some county and borough councils, appointing the first local authority ecologists. In the West Midlands, a regional officer of the Nature Conservancy Council (NCC), George Barker, commissioned a survey of Birmingham and the Black Country that produced, a few years later, an evocative portrait of its wildlife in *The Endless Village* by Bunny Teagle.

This increased attention to the natural environment was part of the reaction against the vast council estates and tower blocks created during the post-war redevelopment of Britain's cities. Yet, in various ways, citizens had been interested in the natural history of their towns for centuries. Their interest took three main forms which eventually combined to produce nature conservation as a distinctive activity, though it was not until after the last war that it became a movement with significant impact.

Firstly, there were naturalists – amateurs and professionals – who were (and are) relentless recorders of the plant and animal life of the areas where they work and live. Secondly, there were those who cherished the city's open space and fought for it when threatened. Finally, there was by the beginning of the 19th century a nascent opposition to cruelty to animals which grew into a wider concern for the protection of animals – especially birds – and plants.

Local natural history societies, such as the London Natural History Society formed in 1858, still survive around Britain, and, though often remote from the hurly burly of conservation battles, are repositories of wildlife lore whose origins are in Elizabethan times. William Turner, while physician at the ducal mansion of Syon House in West London, earned his sobriquet as 'father of British botany' from his *Herball* published in the years 1551-1566. At the end of that century John Gerard, superintendent of Lord Burghley's gardens at his Theobalds estate, produced his *Herball or General Historie of Plantes* in which Hampstead Heath features prominently. The area is also described by Thomas Johnson, whose 1629 account of a botanical ramble around the Heath is reprinted as an appendix in Richard Fitter's *London's Natural History*. The country's first botanic garden was established at Oxford in 1621, the Chelsea Physic Garden following in 1673.

Systematic botany was devised by the Swedish naturalist Carl von Linné who visited London a year after the publication of his *Systema Naturae* in 1735. It was London which benefited after his death by receiving his collections which, in 1788, formed the basis of the Linnean Society which remains natural history's pre-eminent academic forum. Home-grown botanists included William Curtis who published his *London Flora* between 1777 and 1798, set up botanical gardens successively in Bermondsey, Lambeth and Brompton – and who in 1977 gave his name to London's first modern ecological park. Even in those days, and earlier, pollution from the smoke of coal fires was a serious problem, and the Royal Botanic Gardens were founded in 1759 at Kew, safely to the windward of the city.

Best known of the early popular writers on wildlife is Gilbert White, whose *Natural History of Selborne* appeared four years before his death in 1793. In her delightful chronicle of *The Heyday of Natural History 1820-1870* Lynn Barber describes this national passion of the 19th century. The countryside was overrun by those collecting ferns for their drawing room display cases. The seashore seethed with collectors of shells, seaweed, anenomes and fish for parlour aquariums. Amateur geologists toured the country, hammers tucked into belts, to build up their samples of rocks and fossils. Rare flowers were pressed into books, butterflies pinned to specimen boards. Nests were energetically raided by egg collectors, and the birds themselves shot as fodder for the taxidermist's art.

Lectures by eminent scientists attracted large and adulatory audiences. Hundreds of local natural history societies flourished. Visits to zoos and exhibitions of natural curiosities were a popular leisure pastime. A flood of mass-produced literature covering the gamut of botany and zoology, geology and palaeontology was avidly bought by the reading classes. Almost the only innovative authors during this time were Charles Lyell whose *Principles of Geology* (1830-33) much excited Charles Darwin, and Darwin himself who issued his *Voyage of the Beagle* in 1839 but delayed his *Origin of Species* for a further 20 years. Yet books such as *The Romance of Natural History* by Philip Gosse (today more famous as the victim of his son's biography *Father and Son*) achieved best-seller status.

As Lynn Barber records: 'Most of the subsequent best sellers of the 1860s were written either by Frank Buckland or by the Rev J G Wood . . . yet neither [they] . . . nor any other popular natural history writer of the 1860s tried to discuss Darwinism or explain it to their readers.' It was the German zoologist Ernst Häckel who, as a follower of Darwin, coined the word 'ecology' in 1873 to describe the inter-relationship of living things and their environment which Darwin had observed and made the foundation of his theory of evolution.

In the later 19th century, writers such as Richard Jefferies, author of among many other titles *Bevis* (1882), and W.H. Hudson, whose prolific output included *Birds in London* (1898) and *A Hind in Richmond Park* (1922), recreated the Gilbert White tradition of combining good natural history observation with literary skills. Arguably the first of the modern writers, who were more aware of the scientific basis of their chosen subject, was Max Nicholson who published his *How Birds Live* in 1927. As seen below, his role in nature conservation has been diverse and influential in the 60 years since then.

Measures to save open space stretch back to feudal times. The main threat in pre-19th century times was enclosure rather than development, the issue being one of life and death for those whose livelihood depended on the land which was being taken from them. The history of the Great North Wood in south London is an example of an area still tussled over. The public inquiry into the future of the Dulwich woodland mentioned above is in line of descent from battles such as that which, in 1615, saved Dulwich's Westwood when a local vicar led 100 parishioners on a protest march to the king in London. Dulwich commoners lost, in 1787, the right of access to their common – on which, incidentally, Margaret Thatcher's house and Denis's next-door golf course are now built. But local people were more successful a century later when, in 1897, 50,000 congregated on One Tree Hill to block an attempt to include the hill in another new golf course.

Organised conservation societies emerged in Victorian times, perhaps the earliest being the Thames Angling and Preservation Society formed in 1838 and still functioning. Public pressure in the 1840s persuaded the government to construct the first of the public parks which in London supplemented the royal parks. Victoria Park, at that time on the urban fringe of the East End, opened in 1845. It was followed by Battersea, initiated in 1843, and others such as Birkenhead on Merseyside, opened in 1846.

The struggles to save Hampstead Heath (1829-1871) and Epping Forest (1865-1874) were the most publicised of the campaigns to protect the country's commons. The movement generated, in 1865, the Commons, Open Spaces and Footpaths Preservation Society and eventually led, in 1895, to the founding of the National Trust. While the Trust's image is of a rural organisation, its roots were in London. The Commons Preservation Society secretary, Robert Hunter, was initially supported in his efforts to establish a land-owning trust by Octavia Hill, a pioneer of good quality housing for the working classes. As part of her efforts to improve the quality of life in slum areas, she successfully fought to save areas of open space such as those which now form Deptford Park and Hilly Fields in south London. The Trust's third founding member, Hardwicke Rawnsley, was vicar in the notorious Seven Dials area near Covent Garden before moving to a living in the Lake District, where he arranged the acquisition of many of the Trust's earliest properties.

The present century saw the setting up of the Council for the Protection of Rural England (to use its presentday title) in 1925 and a massive growth in societies catering for outdoor recreations such as cycling or rambling. During the 1920s and 1930s access to the countryside became a live issue. The Pennines, in particular, became an unofficial country park for workers in the industrial towns west and east of the spine of northern England. Landowners' attempts to keep walkers out of the moorlands provoked the famous mass trespass on Kinder Scout in 1932. Three years later, the Ramblers' Association came into being as a federation of hiking clubs. Pressure from such directions resulted after the war in the passing of the 1949 National Parks and Access to the Countryside Act and the setting up of the National Parks Commission, now the Countryside Commission, and the Nature Conservancy Council.

Despite this widespread interest in nature and open space, it was animal welfare that provided the main impetus for wildlife conservation. The Royal Society for the Prevention of Cruelty to

Animals was under way as early as 1824 (gaining its royal imprimatur in 1840) with the aim of promoting legislation protecting wild birds. The Royal Society for the Protection of Birds was not established until 1904 but had its origins in earlier societies set up to halt the killing of birds such as the grebe and egret to obtain their exotic plumage as fashion accessories.

Gradually there was a realisation that species protection on its own was not enough. By 1910, as John Sheail relates in his seminal history of nature conservation up to 1975, *Nature in Trust*:

> The National Trust owned 13 sites of special interest to the naturalist [but] naturalists were worried at the almost random way in which potential nature reserves were acquired, with apparently little regard for the national significance of their plants and animals.

In 1912 Nathaniel Rothschild, father of the redoubtable entomologist Miriam Rothschild, was one of the founding members of the Society for the Promotion of Nature Reserves – which evolved into today's Royal Society for Nature Conservation (RSNC) and which, since 1976, has been the umbrella organisation for the county trusts which proliferated in the 1950s and 1960s. The Society prepared the first list of areas of nature conservation interest in 1916, but Nathaniel's premature death in 1923 limited the Society's effectiveness thereafter. By 1941 it had acquired eight important nature reserves, but conservationists' primary concern was not for habitats but with trying to outlaw practices such as egg collecting. As Sheail describes:

> It was not until the 1940s that the potential of the Society was fully realised, when naturalists began to recognise changes in land use and management as the main threat to wildlife; when they realised that the acquisition and management of nature reserves, rather than legislation, would be the most effective way of making the world safe for plants and animals.

The formal academic world, which might have been expected to be interested in urban ecology, by and large treated this area of study with disdain. The young Max Nicholson's survey of starlings in London during the 1920s was a pioneering effort. At the end of the last war Richard Fitter produced his masterly account of *London's Natural History* but it inspired few imitators. In 1974 John A. Burton produced *The Naturalist in London*, yet it was Mabey's *The Unofficial Countryside*, written in the amateur tradition of Gilbert White, that had the greater effect. It remains a feature of urban nature conservation that those most effective in supporting it are predominantly non-scientists. As Lyndis Cole, landscape architect and designer of the William Curtis Ecological Park, observes in her appraisal of 'Urban Nature Conservation' in *Conservation in Perspective*:

> Urban nature conservation may be despised by some conservationists as merely a 'popular' movement. This is precisely what it is, and rightly so – it seeks to bring the concept of conservation to the general populace. While some may wish to label it as a passing fad, the support which it now receives, and the continuing rise of this support in an exponential curve, suggests that this section of nature conservation forms an integral part of the total conservation scene. Our fast dwindling natural heritage will only be retained with popular support.

References and further reading

The Endless Village by W.G. Teagle (NCC, 1978).
London's Natural History by Richard Fitter (Collins, 1945), number 3 in 'The New Naturalist' series, is available in paperback (Collins, 1984).
The Heyday of Natural History 1820-1870 by Lynn Barber (Cape, 1980) deserves reprinting.
Nature in Trust by John Sheail (Blackie, 1976) recounts 'The History of Nature Conservation in Britain'.
The Naturalist in London by John A. Burton (David and Charles, 1974).
Conservation in Perspective edited by Andrew Warren and Barrie Goldsmith (Wiley, 1983).

Accounts of aspects of the history of countryside conservation include:
The Common Lands of England and Wales by W.G. Hoskins and Dudley Stamp (Collins, 1963).

Nature Conservation in Britain by Dudley Stamp (Collins, 1969).
The National Trust – Past and Present by Robin Fedden (Cape, 1974).
Freedom to Roam by Howard Hill (Moorland Publishing, 1980) is an account of 'The Struggle for Access to Britain's Moors and Mountains'.
Britain's National Parks edited by Mervyn Bell (David and Charles, 1975; paperback 1979) includes an introductory chapter on the origins of the Countryside Commission.

3 | Landscape and landscape architects

Landscape architects such as Lyndis Cole discovered the potential of city wildspace in the early 1970s. Municipal parks of the 19th century, following Nash's pioneering example of Regent's Park (laid out in 1811, opened to the public in 1841), imitated the 17th and 18th century rural parklands which were in turn clever pastiches of natural landscapes. By the 20th century the rustic features of public parks had become so attenuated that the specimens of the 1920s and 1930s were little more than greensward with scattered trees, flowerbeds and a fenced-off pond for ornamental ducks. In garden design, the prevailing fashion by the 1950s was for hard-edged treatments. Festival of Britain styles continued through the 1960s and 1970s, with the giant concrete flower pot the symbol of so-called 'soft landscaping' around new offices and flat blocks.

A contrasting approach germinated in the 1960s with the large-scale landscaping of industrial wasteland and the spate of new towns. The Aberfan disaster of 1966 demonstrated that refuse tips accumulated during two centuries of industrialisation were not only unsightly but dangerous. Derelict land grants were provided by the government, launching a massive facelift programme that continues today most conspicuously in the form of the garden festivals, so far held in Liverpool and Stoke-on-Trent, with others planned in Glasgow, Gateshead and Ebbw Vale.

Two of the earliest reclamation projects were in the Lower Swansea Valley and the Potteries of Stoke-on-Trent where it was quickly realised that the transformation of mountains of mine and industrial waste into grassy, wooded hillocks involved more than earth-shifting equipment and traditional nurserymen's supplies. Tips were not only unstable and poor in nutrients but in many cases poisonous. If anything were to grow, landscape architects and their civil engineer employers recognised that they needed advice from environmental technicians. Ecologists were in. No longer an esoteric research pursuit, ecology became a practical science.

On the Continent, the ecologist had been in business since the end of the war. Faced with the rebuilding of their devastated cities, Germany and other countries such as Holland had depended on ecological expertise for the creation of their new city greenspace. In Britain, Max Nicholson was one of the first to suggest the relevance of ecology to design of our towns. In 1962, while director general of the Nature Conservancy, Nicholson wrote in the *Journal of the Institute of Landscape Architects* (now *Landscape Design*) that:

> In a world of urban sprawl, landscaping should lean as far as practicable towards the natural rather than the contrived or artificial, and ecology could provide the basis for such a new landscape.

Few of his colleagues paid much attention. The British Ecological Society was disengaged from urban conservation as from conservation generally, and has remained so. Though the Society's learned journals contain each year many articles on detailed aspects of urban ecology, it is perplexing that this mass of scientific research is so unrelated to conservation in practical terms. When it comes to public inquiries into the future of valued wildlife areas, campaigners usually have difficulty in finding experts willing to testify on the ecological features of such sites. Few scientists take a sustained countrywide interest in urban sites under threat – except for those hired by British Rail or the DoT to seek to destroy the conservationists' case. As Charlie Pye-Smith and Chris Rose have commented on the Society in their book *Crisis and Conservation*, it is:

> An academic body which has undergone years of fierce internal turmoil and debate about its role in conservation. Critics point to its embarrassingly large profits and the small sums which it gives to conservation projects.

In contrast, Max Nicholson in characteristic fashion launched a project to put his ideas into effect. Leaving the Nature Conservancy in 1966 he formed a company, Land Use Consultants, to undertake environmental projects with an emphasis on the creation of naturalistic landscapes. One of its first commissions was as consultant for the Central Forest Park in Hanley, part of the massive land reclamation programme in Stoke-on-Trent and the Potteries, and the firm has been responsible for other pioneering schemes up to the present day.

Since Nicholson reappears several times in the following pages, the post-war activities of this remarkable man are sketched here. During his time as second director general of the Nature Conservancy (1952-66) he was influential in persuading the long-established Society for the Promotion of Nature Reserves to become more active as the voice of the voluntary nature conservation movement. At his urging, the Society sponsored the formation in 1958 of the Council for Nature whose National Conservation Corps was the origin in 1970 of the British Trust for Conservation Volunteers (BTCV). The burgeoning county nature conservation trusts assumed, at his instigation, increasing responsibility for the care of Sites of Special Scientific Interest (SSSIs), grants being provided by the Conservancy for their acquisition. He was among those contributing to the progress of the International Union for Conservation of Nature after 1948 and, as he describes in *The Environmental Revolution*, was active in founding the World Wildlife Fund as its voluntary sector equivalent.

As well as occupying leading positions on innumerable international committees, he initiated two 'Countryside in 1970' conferences, chaired by the Duke of Edinburgh in 1963 and 1965, and promoted the idea of National Nature Weeks, events which gained cover-page treatment in the mass circulation *Radio Times*. In education, he persuaded London's University College to establish, in 1960, the first post-graduate degree course in conservation of the natural environment. Most recent of his creations has been the Trust for Urban Ecology (TRUE), formed in 1979 as the Ecological Parks Trust to manage the William Curtis Ecological Park and other urban nature reserves.

While Nicholson's contribution to the *Journal*, mentioned above, was an early detailed exposition of the importance of ecological factors in landscape design, a few practitioners had been aware of the ecological dimension since the 1940s, and soil and ecology had been among the subjects on the Landscape Institute entrance exam syllabus from 1946. Chronicler of 'Ecology and Landscape Design' in the Institute's 50th anniversary history is Manchester University lecturer Allan Ruff, whose writings and teachings have had an immense effect on successive generations of students since the 1970s. He recalls that:

> During the 1960s conservation was still firmly wedded to the countryside and did not directly involve landscape architects. The events of European Conservation Year [1970] helped to change that and drew people's attention to the urban environment.

Those who had earlier been conscious of the role of ecology in design, Ruff has pointed out, included Ian McHarg, one of those preparing plans for post-war planning while the war was being fought and who later continued his career in the USA. Others were Sylvia Crowe, Brenda Colvin and Brian Hackett, their contribution to landscape philosophy and practice having been diverse in the decades since the 1940s.

It was, though, someone from outside the profession who provided the most fundamental reassessment of the potential of city and industrial landscapes. Nan Fairbrother, a writer and lecturer on landscape design and land use with the unusual qualification of a first degree in English, produced in 1970 *New Lives, New Landscapes*, a text given additional impact by posthumous republication by Penguin two years later. In it, she considered not only the conservation of the countryside but the natural environment within towns and the urban fringe.

John Sheail has recounted how, as early as the 1920s, there was awareness of the wildlife value of unmown roadside verges, derelict sites such as brickworks and protected areas within London's royal parks. Fairbrother preached in more coherent form that open space in the city should not all be managed in horticultural style and that appropriate areas should be allowed to develop in natural fashion. Her continuing inspiration was demonstrated when, in 1985, the urban wildlife groups chose the name of Fairbrother Group for their national association. In retrospect, however, it is curious she failed to mention continental examples of urban landscaping which provided the greenprint for the younger generation of landscape architects.

The continental contribution had been acknowledged by George Chadwick in his 1966 classic *The Park and the Town*. He showed awareness of a new approach to park design when he described the Amsterdam Forest (or Bos) Park created during the 1930s:

> An ecological study was undertaken to determine those species naturally associated with the habitat of the polder lands, and the design was based on the climax vegetation to be expected, not on exotics which would require constant interference with the natural succession of vegetation: the Amsterdam Bos is radically opposed to the later Victorian park, which relied more and more on exotic material (both permanent and temporary) and thus on continued, detailed maintenance.

He describes similar examples in Norway and Sweden, but it was the Dutch who in the years following the war had developed this naturalistic style the most fully, creating wild landscapes within the new suburbs in the form of small 'heem' or 'home' parks, planted with a profusion of native species.

First among those from Britain to explore them was Allan Ruff in 1973, who recorded his discoveries on this and subsequent regular monitoring visits in *Holland and the Ecological Landscapes* (1979). Making her first trip in the same year was Lyndis Cole, then an MSc student on the conservation course at Wye College. Three years later she co-authored an article on 'Dutch Techniques for the Establishment of Natural Communities' in *Landscape Design*, and Netherlands cities such as Amsterdam and Delft have remained a place of pilgrimage for landscape students ever since.

Yet it was the USA which was a more immediately effective source of new ideas. On a trip to the States in 1972 Ian Laurie, director of the Manchester landscape department, studied papers presented to a Washington conference of 1968 on the theme of 'Man and Nature in the City'. Back in Manchester he organised a 1974 symposium titled 'Nature in the Cities' addressed by German, Dutch, French, Swedish and American ecologists and landscape designers, as well as their British colleagues. The book of the conference included examples of large landscaping projects in the UK: Brian Clouston's scheme for the Tyne, Wear and Tees valleys; Rodney Beaumont's reclamation work in the Clyde, Kelvin and Cart valleys of Glasgow; and Adrian Rourke's plans for

Manchester's valleys on behalf of the newly created Greater Manchester County Council.

The setting up of this and the other metropolitan county councils in 1974 was, as seen in the next chapter, a boost for urban fringe improvement schemes. New town corporations were also beginning to recognise the desirability of nature conservation as a factor in their development plans, with various county councils sharing that recognition. *The Ecological Survey for Central Lancashire New Town* appeared in 1973, and though the 1970 master plan for Milton Keynes largely ignored nature conservation, an ecologist was appointed a couple of years later. An *Ecological Appraisal of West Sussex* appeared in 1973 and Cheshire County Council, which claims to have appointed the country's first local authority countryside officer, issued an *Ecological Appraisal of Cheshire* in the following year.

It was in the Cheshire new town development based on Warrington where the theory was most dramatically put into practice. Among the tasks facing the development corporation, formed at the beginning of the 1970s, was the reclamation of the 1,000 acres covered by the rubble of the former Risley ordnance factory. Rob Tregay, one of Allan Ruff's students and contributor of a trend-setting paper on 'Urban Woodlands' to the 'Nature in the Cities' symposium, was appointed as landscape architect to the planning team, which also included ecologist Duncan Moffat and planner Ian Parkin. In ten years, Tregay and his colleagues have transformed the Risley dereliction into the leafy suburb of Oakwood.

Oakwood featured in the 1987 BBC TV series *The Wild Side of Town* presented by the Birmingham-based landscape architect Chris Baines, another of Ruff's many now influential students. During a rain-induced break during the filming in November 1986 Baines and Tregay found time to exchange views on the Warrington achievement and the state of the landscape profession in general. Said Tregay:

What we did at Oakwood was to design and plant a forest park and put the houses and other buildings in this green framework rather than the other way round – putting bits of greenery around the houses. At the same time Ian Parkin set up a ranger service to involve the residents in the newly-created countryside.

As it's turned out we were right in thinking that you can't have the landscaping without the rangering. It's the human element that makes the landscape work. As the success of the concept was seen to work, the method spread outwards from Oakwood through the whole mid-Mersey region and eventually more widely still. Despite initial scepticism it's a philosophy now widely accepted elsewhere.

Baines's scepticism is more to do with the nature of landscape design as a profession:

The problem with landscape architects is that, unlike architects, they are very thin on philosophy. There's great intimidation by the hierarchy of the Landscape Institute on this score. Students say: 'We like your ideas, but we see what's written in the journal *Landscape Design*, and we notice that it's only those who design the best lighting bollard who get the design awards.' They also see traditional practices spending large amounts of money on schemes in short periods, and it's only when people like Rob get recognition for rather different techniques that they gain confidence in trying something new.

However, things are changing, as Tregay pointed out, and the Warrington experience is now finding its way onto exam papers:

Students are asked for a critical analysis of what has been achieved, so they find it worthwhile to come here and see the theories in practice. What we can now think about is more ambitious designing with nature, not just imposing ecology on an area. The old guard say: 'This sort of thing isn't design.' But in Sweden they are well used to structuring a wild landscape with components that are similar to walls and rooms, spaces and vistas.

As Baines gnomically summarised: 'We are rediscovering the picturesque: it's all park.'

The overall objective, Baines and Tregay believe, is to re-establish contact between people and nature. Baines points to the spontaneous discovery all over Europe of the importance of green in the city – exponents including Sukopp in Berlin and Helsenberg in Sweden. It was, he suggests, given strength by the reaction against the concrete jungle of the 1960s housing, 'so that architects too changed their styles and began building once again with bricks and timber, using warm colours and traditional shapes'.

But implementation of the theory is a slower and fallible process. As Baines pointed out, experience at Hanley Forest Park in Stoke-on-Trent, first project of Max Nicholson's Land Use Consultants, showed it wasn't enough to plant thousands of trees because a lot of them died. And in Runcorn, a new town dating from slightly earlier than Warrington, willows and poplars and other fast-growing species were planted which are now breaking up pavements and drains.

Baines and Tregay agree that in its marriage of the different ingredients involved in design based on ecology and community involvement, the William Curtis Ecological Park – and its designer, Lyndis Cole – were pioneers of the new craft. The park was, inevitably, a Max Nicholson idea. In *The Planner* in 1975 he had set out his ideas (with co-authors) on 'Urbanism in the Age of Ecology' (a title that could easily be reversed). The Queen's jubilee celebrations of 1977 presented the opportunity to put them into effect on a Thames-side site which was an interim lorry park pending redevelopment. Using his friendship with the site's owners, Nicholson was able to persuade them to allow the land to be used as a temporary park as part of the planned Jubilee riverside walkway.

Having joined Land Use Consultants, Lyndis Cole was allocated the project and a minimal budget. She used this to transform two acres of tarmac and rubble into a variety of habitats including grassland, pond and thickets. A prefab field study centre was installed, a warden appointed and the park opened to visitors every day of the year except Christmas Day. In the following years it was visited by planners, ecologists, educationalists, journalists, photographers – and even landscape architects – in addition to the local schoolchildren who were its regular users. It closed in 1985, when the land was required by the developers, but by then the Ecological Parks Trust was running three more reserves in the same London borough, Southwark, where their work could continue.

Cole's own perception of the process of educating her profession is that in the early 1970s designers were able to see in Holland the natural planting of the 1930s and the low maintenance planting adopted in the post-war estates. The lessons learnt from land reclamation schemes of the 1960s then began to converge, local authorities being forced to work with nature because traditional planting would be too costly:

> So as part of the Hanley Forest Park programme in Stoke, natural colonisation of the slag heaps was studied and used as a template for future plans. At the time there was a lack of ecologists involved in the handling of such projects. There was a wealth of scientific information but it wasn't being put into practice. Setting up William Curtis was thus very much a matter of trial and error.

Around the country reclamation schemes were handled with little regard for the varied habitats that had fortuitously developed on the soils thrown up by mining or in wetlands formed by quarrying. The objective was the removal of eyesores and, frequently, the creation of neat recreational open space. In the 1980s the government redirected grant towards schemes within built-up areas to release land suitable for industrial, commercial or housing development, but with little care for the conservation of valuable wildlife sites. As Lyndis Cole observes: 'There remains a mismatch between the scientists and the practitioners. The ecologists in their white coats are still not coming up with the goods.'

Among projects intended to foster urban regeneration were garden festivals, an idea borrowed from Germany by Michael Heseltine. The first, in Liverpool in 1984, was great fun to visit and a commercial success, but little survived for permanent enjoyment. The Stoke festival in 1986 was less successful, hampered by the noxious quality of the terrain and appalling weather during construction and the early months of opening. The exhibits too were widely criticised for their bijou character, arty rather than illustrating efficient use of resources. With work already under way for a Glasgow event in 1990, another in Gateshead in 1992 and a Wales festival two years later in Ebbw Vale, professionals have questioned the usefulness and methodology of the festival concept. The issues were aired at the Landscape Institute's 1986 conference and in the architectural

trade magazine *Building Design*. As Bristol landscape architect
Janie Thomas remarked:

> In Germany and America a long professional training produces
> landscape architects who are really competent in the relevant
> aspects of these matters [construction and cost control]. In
> Britain, a six-year course produces only somebody who thinks
> he knows. We are still an adolescent profession. We – and our
> Institute – need to grow up.

Allan Ruff offers the thought that one of the reasons for the
cosmetic character of many of the garden festival designs is
landscapers' sense of frustration. In many projects, when money
runs out it is the budget for external landscaping that is slashed,
and this can affect their approach:

> Landscape architects become like resting actors or pop stars
> – if they are given a new park or garden festival their
> suppressed creativity gushes out, not always with happy results.

The leading expert on reclamation techniques, Professor Tony
Bradshaw of Liverpool University, warned in his 1986 report,
Transforming our waste land: the way forward, that 'more money
is not the answer'. My own experience of how local authorities go
about urban landscaping projects, outlined in the next chapter,
confirms this view. Instead of assessing the wildlife resources of
a site – trees, shrubs, boggy patches and so forth – and building
their designs on this, landscape architects appear to prefer
completely rejigging the topography. Existing mounds are
flattened, with new contouring appearing elsewhere. Marsh areas
are drained, while new ponds are created in different parts of the
site. Useful calcareous rubble is carted away, useless topsoil –
which encourages a dominant growth of grass and rank weeds –
is imported. In the actual construction of the sites, contractors'
JCBs roam around with no on-the-spot guidance as to the pockets
of fragile habitats that need protecting.
   When I made these comments in *Building Design* in June 1986,
they provoked a response which suggested that the landscape
architecture establishment remains reluctant to accept the concept

of conserving natural features as part of an overall design. The immediate past president of the Landscape Institute, David Randall, wrote that:

> The landscape architect is trained to see both 'the wood and the trees' and to assess the value of what lies around a raw site for its potential in a new landscape but not to be hypnotised by it.

Referring to previous criticisms I had made of the handling of London's largest new park, Burgess Park in Walworth, he added:

> I well recall as a student going to see Abercrombie's original (1944) proposals for London and being amazed to see a new park proposed for an extensively bombed area not half a mile from where I lived, and wondering how long it might take to overcome local prejudice against it.

The gist of his reply appears to be that the creation of parkland is self-evidently such a good thing that its layout should not be queried by lay folk, only landscape architects being qualified to judge what ingredients should or should not be included. Younger professionals have jettisoned this elitist attitude in favour of involving the public in the design process. It is, after all, they who will be the users of the future open space.

References and further reading

Crisis and Conservation by Charlie Pye-Smith and Chris Rose (Penguin, 1984) includes an appendix succinctly describing the various national nature conservation organisations.
The Environmental Revolution by Max Nicholson (Hodder and Stoughton, 1970; Penguin 1972).
Fifty Years of Landscape Design 1934-1984 edited by Sheila Harvey and Stephen Rettig (Landscape Press, 1985) includes useful chapters by Ian C. Laurie on 'Public Parks and Spaces', John Parker on 'Just Keep Mowing for 300 Years' and Brian Hackett on 'Industrial Landscape and Reclamation'.
New Lives, New Landscapes by Nan Fairbrother (Architectural Press, 1970; Penguin 1972) remains in print in Pelican form.

The Park and the Town by George Chadwick (Architectural Press, 1966) is another classic from The Architectural Press deserving a paperback reprint.

Holland and the Ecological Landscapes by Allan Ruff (Deanwater, 1979, ringbound typescript).

Nature in Cities edited by Ian C. Laurie (Wiley, 1979) is subtitled 'The Natural Environment in the Design and Development of Urban Green Space'.

Ecology and Design in Landscape edited by Tony Bradshaw, David Goode and Ed Thorpe (Blackwell, 1986).

The Everywhere Landscape by Jane Brown (Wildwood House, 1982).

Nature in Cities by Herbert Sukopp and Peter Werner (Council of Europe, 1982), No. 28 in the 'Nature and Environment Series' produced by the European Committee for the Conservation of Nature and Natural Resources, is 'A report and review of studies and experiments concerning ecology, wildlife and nature conservation in urban and suburban areas'. 48pp of text are followed by more than 50pp of bibliography.

4 | The role of local authorities

The role of council planning departments in urban nature conservation has been as double-edged as that of landscape architects. Planners have had considerable power to encourage protection of the natural environment, but more often have chosen to be judged by their efficiency in facilitating housing, road or commercial development of open space. They have been, understandably, under pressure from their political masters to achieve such developments but, with some notable individual exceptions, have not as a profession had much sympathy with the concept of safeguarding the natural heritage.

A simple example of the reluctance of councils to treat urban ecology seriously is their failure to create more than a handful of Local Nature Reserves (LNRs), a title which indicates that they are protected and properly managed. Given the power to designate such areas of natural history importance in the 1949 National Parks and Access to the Countryside Act, 36 years later they had designated only two in London and some 120 in the country as a whole.

The creation of the six metropolitan county councils in 1974 (the Greater London Council having started life in 1965) did eventually benefit urban nature conservation, but not quickly or uniformly. Unencumbered by the statutory duty to provide person-to-person services handled by district councils, they were well placed to introduce a strategic approach to their regions' environmental problems. Responsible for structure plans, within which district councils drew up local plans, the metropolitan counties ought to have been able to include a comprehensive nature conservation strategy as a key element in these plans.

It didn't happen. When they were abolished 12 years later, only the West Midlands had published a site-specific strategy agreed with its local district councils. The GLC included an ecology section in its 1984 draft alterations to the 1976 Greater London Development Plan, but this was a general policy statement only, and was in any case quashed by the government as part of their abolition preparations. Greater Manchester rushed out a handsome but non-site-specific strategy in the last weeks before abolition – which, despite this drawback, won a Conservative Foundation award in 1987. Tyne and Wear produced a more detailed (but draft) document also at the last gasp. Plans in Merseyside and South and West Yorkshire included just a paragraph or so mentioning nature conservation.

An attempt to identify what the country's 500 or so county and district councils have achieved in the nature conservation field was recently made by David Tyldesley whose *Gaining Momentum* is subtitled 'An Analysis of the Role and Performance of Local Authorities in Nature Conservation'. He asked planners if they had 'forward plans' for nature conservation or site schedules that such strategies are necessarily based on. It is a tribute to planners' honesty that a majority admitted they had neither. There were inevitably a number over-charitable to themselves in declaring that a token mention of 'ecology' in a local plan amounts to a programme. Conservationists checking their own councils' responses (the book charts them in detail) are either amused or dismayed, depending on temperament, to see claims to have 'forward planning, published plans and routinely involved nature conservation bodies' when the authorities' procedures are in reality inadequate or even hostile.

An early assessment of the quality of ecological advice available to planning departments was undertaken by John Roberts (now running TEST – Transport and Environment Studies) and John Elkington (now a consultant to various environmental bodies including the Groundwork Foundation). Their report, in a three-part series of articles in *New Scientist* in 1977, followed a suggestion by Max Nicholson in the previous year that there ought to be a study of 'the ecology of ecologists'. The questions they raise about the relationship between planners and ecologists, and the training of future planners, remain valid ten years later. Having identified an 'ecology boom' in 1974/5 when the first few dozen local authority ecology posts were established, they nevertheless concluded that planning departments largely retained unchanged attitudes to the natural environment.

What the councils have achieved is best assessed by a look at different regions in turn.

Manchester

The most dramatic example of what could be achieved by sympathetic planning departments was the work of the Greater Manchester council (GMC) between 1974 and its abolition in 1986. The city and its satellite towns grew up on the Pennine rivers, running from north, east and south into the westward-flowing Mersey. The planning department recognised the rivers as 'green corridors' with great potential, 'like the spokes of a wheel, [traversing] every kind of area – urban, suburban and rural'. As early as 1975, the county council had secured agreement with the ten district councils to a comprehensive programme of restoration of blighted landscapes. Through partnership arrangements, as described in an admirably informative set of publicity leaflets produced during the campaign against abolition, 'major projects (such as a country park or river valley) are funded by the GMC, but are guided by a joint committee of members of the councils involved, the GMC itself and often up to three districts. The Water Authority is also a partner in many schemes.'

Projects were launched in the Croal/Irwell, Medlock, Tame, Mersey, Etherow/Goyt and Bollin valleys, and country parks created at Pennington Flash, Jumbles, Hollingworth Lake, Moses Gate, Daisy Nook and Werneth Low. As at Warrington, countryside rangers were an integral element in the various schemes, as described in the leaflets:

> Apart from sorting out day-to-day problems relating to access and trespass, damage to fences and stiles, protection for plant and animal life and so on, the wardens put on busy programmes of countryside events – guided walks (very popular in the main river valleys), talks, 'clean-up' campaigns, volunteer days, nature trails and much more. A number of river valley and country park newsletters and news-sheets are produced – describing what's going on in the area and the warden's plans, and including interesting articles about such things as geology or wildlife.

The county council was also one of the first to involve the voluntary sector in its work by setting up in 1976 a Wildlife Working Group

with representatives from the county nature conservation trusts
and local natural history societies. Their knowledge of the region
formed the basis of a habitat survey listing over 270 sites of wildlife
importance. Ray Gemmell, a young ecologist inherited from the
Lancashire county council by the GMC planning department, was
responsible for collating the survey (which is the basis of the
gazetteer on pages 176 – 190). As well as being treasurer of the
British Ecological Society, he is author of many papers on
landscaping technology notable for their pragmatism among a
technical literature which is frequently arcane to the point of
irrelevance.   It is a compliment to the achievement of Gemmell
and his colleagues that they survived GMC abolition and, as the
Greater Manchester Countryside Unit, are funded by all ten local
councils. Having moved to Tameside (otherwise known as Ashton-
under-Lyne) in 1987, the unit, though bereft of the resources
formerly available from the GMC, is able to continue its liaison
and advisory work, including a major input into the recently
initiated upper catchment area activities of the Mersey Basin
Campaign.

Merseyside

Here, the metropolitan county council formed in 1974 established
a county planning department with Audrey Lees as county planner.
Later becoming director of planning for Greater London, she
showed in both roles a well-developed consciousness of the
importance of the natural environment in urban planning. Though
she retired after GLC abolition, she remains a powerful member
of the Nature Conservancy Council and other bodies.

One of her early acts in Merseyside was, in 1975, to set up a
Natural Resources Unit responsible, like its Manchester
counterpart, for landscape reclamation in the county. As part of
the council's structure plan preparations the Unit's ecologist, Mick
Brummage, produced in 1983 a Register of Sites of Local Biological
or Geological Interest (which is the basis of the gazetteer, pages
190 – 196) identifying 70 such sites. Following the county council's
abolition, the unit survives in slimmed-down form as the
Merseyside Countryside Unit. Based at Sefton, it receives funding
from three of the five local district councils – Liverpool opting
out on the grounds of poverty and Wirral, across the Mersey, justly
claiming to have developed an excellent country park and ranger

system on its own account.

The Unit's role was supplemented by both voluntary and local council initiatives within the region. In Liverpool in 1975, a young geography graduate, Grant Luscombe, and two colleagues launched what is possibly the earliest of the urban wildlife groups, the Rural Preservation Association. Under its present title of Landlife, it and Luscombe continue their work on the creation of nature gardens in and around the city. Also intended to involve the community in environmental improvements was COMTECHSA (Community Technical Services Agency), set up in 1979 under Inner City Partnership arrangements. The Environment Secretary in the Conservative government elected that year was Michael Heseltine who was, after the Toxteth riots of 1980, to take a personal interest in Merseyside's environmental problems. Liverpool's dockland was chosen as the location for the first of Britain's garden festivals in 1984. In the same year the city hosted a 'Green Towns and Cities UK/USA' conference which, with Heseltine's backing, led to the establishment of a national 'think green' campaign.

A further Heseltine idea originating in this part of the country has since flourished. In the late 1970s the Countryside Commission, as part of its urban fringe improvements programme in areas of industrial dereliction, floated an Urban Fringe Experiment dubbed UFEX 80. Suggestions were invited from districts where co-ordinated environmental improvements could be undertaken with local authority and Commission funding, St Helens and Knowsley being the successful bidders. Touring the area following the election, Heseltine expressed dislike of a project based solely on public money. He proposed instead a partnership deal whereby industry would provide some of the money. The result was the first Groundwork Trust in St Helens, followed by five others in the North-West and, more recently, the setting up of the national Groundwork Foundation.

Yorkshire

The county council in South Yorkshire was, in 1974, unique in setting up an environmental department separate from a planning department. Those living in the region protest that while its image is of dead coalmines and widespread dereliction, 70 per cent of the land is agricultural and that the region includes many areas of high landscape value such as the Pennine uplands. To the visitor, nevertheless, the ex-industrial landscape has the strongest impact, despite the progress made by the department's Conservation and Community Projects Group in implementing over 70 farm landscape schemes, seven nature reserves, 1,500-plus small sites and more than 180 school projects.

The Group did not survive county council abolition and its staff are now scattered among the four district councils. Former county ecologist David Wood is now countryside planning officer in Rotherham's planning department, together with his former boss Roger Mitchell, who is now also chairman of the Yorkshire Wildlife Trust. The old department's small sites team continues at Barnsley, which thus has a fairly strong conservation potential.

Sheffield has, on paper, an admirable policy of support for urban greening and employs a city ecologist in the natural sciences section of the city museum. Local conservationists suggest that implementation of this policy is, however, hindered by a division of responsibility between no less than three council departments. Planning and recreation departments have a role in preparing and applying a nature conservation strategy but the exercise is co-ordinated by the museums service. In Rotherham, David Wood anticipates that it will be a couple of years before his council's three departments – also planning, recreation and museums – are able to formalise a nature conservation strategy. Countywide, it was hoped that some regional perspective might survive through a Nature Conservation Forum convened by the Countryside Commission and NCC regional officers, but by the end of 1986 no inaugural meeting had been held.

Post-abolition arrangements in West Yorkshire were similarly fragmented. Bradford continues to administer the Ecological Advisory Service, jointly funded by the five district councils on a per capita basis. In 1978, the unit was the first local authority organisation to undertake a habitat survey of its area, the project taking three years and costing £20,000. In 1986 it began a survey of the urban areas, funded by the NCC and planned to take three years. In Leeds it has identified 280 sites of interest, and next to be covered are Wakefield and Bradford. The latter has commissioned its own nature conservation strategy document from the Advisory Service, the intention being for the Service to produce similar documents for the other districts subsequently. As Jack

Lavin, head of the unit since its inception, comments:

> What I'd like to see is the integration of conservation and countryside work, bringing it right into town and involving local groups as well.

Leeds, Wakefield and Kirklees (better known as Huddersfield) operated a joint countryside unit based at Wakefield following abolition, but this was wound up in March 1987 and the boroughs are going it alone. Wakefield published in 1986 a prospectus titled *Lighting the Green Fuse*, which described an approach designed to make the district more attractive not only to residents but to industry and visitors. In Kirklees two landscape architects in the technical services department produced in 1981 *Natural Economy*, an innovative report on 'an ecological approach to planting and management techniques in urban areas.' One, Richard Brooker, has progressed to the post of assistant director of leisure services and the council is supporting a joint working party of relevant departments in producing a pragmatic conservation strategy. Together with his colleague Matthew Corder, he has recently produced a follow-up to their earlier report, *Environmental Economy*.

Leeds continues to co-ordinate the Tong-Cockersdale countryside improvement project between the city and Bradford and a similar scheme in the Kirkstall Valley. As will be seen in the next chapter, it is also setting up a mammoth Groundwork Trust to handle work in the Lower Aire Valley. As in neighbouring South Yorkshire, the Countryside Commission's regional office, based in Leeds, is nurturing a conservation forum which is described by Jack Lavin as 'not an activist organisation but a group of professionals discussing issues.'

North-East

Following the abolition of Tyne and Wear County Council, North Tyneside District Council appears well equipped to continue the conservation programme initiated by the metropolitan county council. Newcastle itself is only now working on a nature conservation strategy. The three districts south of the river – Gateshead, South Tyneside and Sunderland – are continuing to collaborate in the Urban Fringe Area Management (UFAM) scheme half-funded by the Countryside Commission. A regional perspective survives in a North East Environmental Network (NEEN), a forum set up with posthumous county council money but lacking any staff.

The Midlands

West Midlands County Council sponsored the ambitious habitat survey which in 1983 identified over 20,000 open space sites in the region. Two years later, having secured the co-operation of the district councils, it published its nature conservation strategy and in the same year established a Wildlife Records Centre. Since then, Dudley has inaugurated its own nature conservation working party, while Birmingham is contemplating a similar forum for liaising between the council and conservation bodies to complement the Nature Conservation Forum formed by local voluntary organisations in 1985.

London

Audrey Lees arrived in London from Merseyside in 1980 and, with the backing of the GLC administration elected the following year, introduced an ecology section headed by former NCC assistant chief scientist David Goode. The section eventually consisted of half a dozen ecologists and had money to spend on both internal and external projects. Most significant of these was a comprehensive London Wildlife Habitat Survey in which six ecologists employed by the London Wildlife Trust surveyed over 2,000 sites during 1984/5.

The section was also responsible, during an energetic four years' existence, for the creation of three important nature reserves, later described in the gazetteer: the showcase Camley Street Natural Park in Camden, established on an old coal wharf on the bank of Regent's Canal; Gunnersbury Triangle in Hounslow, purchased with GLC cash; and the Tump 53 reserve in Thamesmead, sited on a former ammunition dump. Its publications included the first instalment of *A Nature Conservation Strategy for London*, a handsome document covering sites in two boroughs and a couple of major habitats. It gave generous grants to voluntary bodies such as the London Natural History Society, Ecological Parks Trust and London Wildlife Trust and, as a parting gift to Londoners, set up a London Ecology Centre with premises in Covent Garden and King's Cross as a base for voluntary action. Following GLC abolition the section survives as the Greater London Ecology Unit (GLEU) funded by a consortium of 25 of London's 33 boroughs and managed by a London Boroughs Joint Ecology Committee (LBJEC).

Two councils – Leicester and Southwark

Among the non-metropolitan districts, Leicester was a pioneer in its support for ecological guidelines in planning and recreation provision. An Urban Ecology Working Party was established under the aegis of the city's Urban Studies Centre in 1979, and in the following years its small team of ecologists undertook a series of projects aimed at conserving and promoting Leicester's wildlife, many of them involving local schools. In 1983, with city and county council backing, the group set up an MSC scheme which, titled the City Wildlife Project, today has a staff of more than 40.

In partnership with the council, the Project has landscaped half a dozen and more nature areas. As well as working with over 70 schools, its rangers carry out a busy programme of guided walks, talks and public events. Most recently it completed a two-year-long Leicester Habitat Survey and acquired a degree of medium-term security through an Urban Programme grant of £160,000. Spread over four years, the grant provides for the employment of the project director and urban conservation officer, with a proportion allocated for the carrying out of landscape work. The survey data was used by the Project to draft a Leicester Ecology Strategy for the council, which was expected to approve the document in 1987. More common is the curate's-egg record of some councils, such as the London Borough of Southwark. Its topology is characteristic of many urban boroughs, with densely built-up neighbourhoods in the area nearest to the city centre and leafier suburbs further out of town. As early as 1977 it backed the creation of the William Curtis Ecological Park. In 1978 it extended its role by handing over Dulwich Upper Wood to the nascent Ecological Parks Trust (EPT) and commissioned the design and construction of the Lavender Pond Nature Park in the former Surrey Docks.

During these years, as a member of the council's planning committee, I supported these projects without, I confess, having much understanding of what they were meant to achieve or what they would involve in management terms. I recall arguing with fellow committee member George Nicholson, later chairman of the powerful GLC planning committee, over the go-ahead for the Lavender Pond project. My view was that since the government was providing 75 per cent of the costs of this and other regeneration schemes in the dockland area, it was a bargain. Nicholson thought it a luxury, preferring any council money to be spent on the decaying parks in the rest of Bermondsey. No officer explained at that time that capital expenditure always involves subsequent revenue spending, or that management of any open space is labour-intensive and highly costly. Planning departments are not an executive part of the council in that they do not have a responsibility for managing land or (with some exceptions) providing other services direct to the consumer. The gap between these departments and those responsible for land management – whether titled a parks department, borough engineer's or technical services – is a frequent source of problems. The Pond faced many difficulties in its early years and today, though decorative and a useful educational facility, is most popular as an angling pond – not a use envisaged in the original concept.

In 1982, as deputy leader of the council, I was in theory better placed to influence the authority's open space policies. In practice, the inertia of professional thinking and departmental conservatism made it hard to change attitudes. The planning department was happy to accept two proposed nature reserves at Benhill Road and Marlborough Grove in the local borough plans then in preparation. But the leisure department, a new creation that I had wished since 1979 to carve out of an old-fashioned borough engineer's department and which was eventually set up in 1983, continued to view the idea of wildlife areas with hostility.

In the face of officer resistance, it was agreed by the leisure committee to lay out three wasteland sites adjacent to existing formal parks in informal style. The landscape design team, unfamiliar with this approach, produced layouts which were only partially successful. Subsequent management by parks staff has also been clumsy. One site, at Bonar Road in Peckham, has been tidied up out of existence. Even so, it and the other areas at Consort Road and Snowsfields, have not produced the worst problems predicted by parks management – large-scale rubbish tipping, for example – and survive as interesting if botched experiments.

The council's achievements in the nature conservation field of activity have continued to be contradictory. The leisure committee agreed to fund a part-time field officer for the Southwark Wildlife Group, by now part of the London Wildlife Trust. The planning committee agreed to lease to the trust the borough's finest wildlife site, Sydenham Hill Wood. The leisure committee embarked on an environmental improvement programme, wherupon the planning committee successfully demanded a hike of half a million pounds in its budget and launched its own 'Operation Facelift'. A glossy booklet intended as electioneering propaganda for the May 1986 council elections appeared, slightly late, that autumn. Superbly designed, it describes the BMX tracks, allotments and community gardens created on many of the borough's wasteland sites. Symptomatically, it nowhere mentions the function of the Southwark Wildlife Group, whose 1982 survey of vacant land in Southwark provoked consideration of such sites.

The council's failure to understand the fundamental role of conservation in planning was revealed in the two local plans it prepared for the north and mid/south areas of the borough. The north Southwark plan contained scant mention of nature conservation and, at the public inquiry into the plan, the GLC pointed out the absence of an ecological policy. In his report the DoE-appointed inspector advised that an ecology statement should be included in the final plan. Since the council rejected almost all the inspector's recommendations, there was in the end no plan at all. The Environment Secretary called the plan in and, after unsuccessful court action by the council, quashed it in 1987.

The mid/south Southwark plan, though mostly uncontroversial, contained proposals for building council houses on the upper part of Sydenham Hill Wood. From the council's point of view, facing a desperate shortage of housing land, this was not unreasonable. In coming to this conclusion, however, the planning department disregarded a report by its own landscape team on the harmful effects of the development on the nature reserve on the lower part of the hill, which much embarrassed the department when it was leaked to London Wildlife Trust.

The landscape team's report advised that if the sites were built on, both the building operations and the finished development would pose a threat to the Wood. It concluded:

As the woodland environment in London is a rarity there is an excellent case for the retention of this site to form an extension to Dulwich Wood thus restoring some of the former extent of the Great North Wood.

Conservationists, hardly surprisingly, took the same view and mounted a vigorous campaign leading up to three days' presentation of evidence at the local plan public inquiry at which the report was produced as part of London Wildlife Trust's evidence. There the borough planner vehemently demanded its withdrawal. When this was refused by the inspector, he suggested, to general mirth, that the landscape team's advice should be disregarded since it was merely the product of a role-playing exercise: the department had merely attempted to anticipate the conservation case in order to be able to rebut it.

At the packed evening session the leader of the Labour-controlled council led the attack on the community witnesses favouring retention of the wood. These included not only the Conservative MP, Gerald Bowden, but also the Labour parliamentary candidate, Kate Hoey, who retorted that:

> Council tenants on every estate in the vicinity have signed in overwhelming numbers the petition against development. I resent the implication that you have to be an owner-occupier to appreciate the natural beauty of the wood.

In his report the inspector advised that the larger of the two council-owned sites, Fernbank, should not be built on but that the smaller, Lapsewood, was developable. The initial reaction of the council's leadership was to indicate that it would ignore the recommendation in the final version of the local plan. Two factors caused it to change its thinking. Firstly, it was likely that if this happened the conservationists would successfully persuade the Environment Secretary to call in the plan and amend it. Secondly, meetings of the local Labour Party at ward, constituency and borough level voted to support the conservationist cause. Reluctantly, the Labour Group accepted the verdict in case continued refusal jeopardised DoE approval of the entire plan.

In the wake of GLC abolition the borough's planning department gave more attention to conservation matters. It appointed its own ecologist, collaborated with the Greater London Ecology Unit in the preparation of a nature sites appraisal and organised a wildlife fortnight. More dramatically still, the department was involved in a sequel to the main Sydenham Hill Wood inquiry, which resulted in an inspector's report of great significance for future planning decisions. Dulwich College estates governors, owners of a small site on the upper edge of the Wood formerly occupied by a Victorian villa called Beechgrove, applied for development permission for two blocks of 36 flats. The council, arguing that this would be intrusive in landscape and wildlife terms, rejected the application, an inquiry being held in late 1986.

The inspector considered the site, the thrust of the DoE planning circulars, the previous inspector's comments in the local plan report and the ecological evidence presented by the London Wildlife Trust and the Greater London Ecology Unit. Dismissing the estates governors' appeal, he said:

> The need to preserve areas of existing natural woodland within the urban areas is of as much importance in preserving our heritage and improving the quality of the environment as that of preserving the countryside.

Parks

Parks departments have, in contrast to this and other planning departments, been generally slower to adapt their attitudes. Park managers are a conservative breed, with an Angus McAllister-like passion for flower beds and manicured lawns. ('Angus McAllister, extending a foot that looked like a violin-case, pressed it on the moss. The meaning of the gesture was plain. It expressed contempt, dislike, a generally anti-moss spirit.' *Blandings Castle* by P.G. Wodehouse.) They are burdened in addition by staffing arrangements which make it difficult for them to deploy the workforce in ways which diverge from the custom and practice enshrined in agreements with the manual trade unions.

Chris Baines has been one of the most effective propagandists for changing open space maintenance techniques. In the book of his latest television series he makes the point that:

> We spend well over a thousand million pounds each year mowing the municipal grasslands of Britain. That is an awful lot of public money to pour into suppressing nature, but that is what it amounts to. Of course there is a place for neat, mown grass,

and much of it is needed for football, hockey and other formal sports, but it really is a desert so far as wildlife is concerned.

During the summer drought of the mid-1980s it was depressing to see Southwark council gardeners mowing areas where no grass was growing, the weekly routine being immutable. Some authorities, Wirral among them, have sought to vary the terms of employment to allow for staffing of parks in more flexible fashion. In exchange they offer consolidation of existing overtime bonus schemes into a higher basic wage, as well as increasing the variety of work undertaken by park keepers and gardeners.

Probably the first to establish a team trained in conservation techniques was the GLC parks department whose Conservation Unit has worked at Hampstead Heath since 1978. In Birmingham, Chris Baines has advised on regeneration of its parks through the introduction of wildlife features, but conservationists are aghast at the insensitive management of outstanding wildlife areas such as Sutton Park. Manchester has introduced a conservation course for its middle managers, supervised by Allan Ruff, and horticultural colleges include ecology in their training. It was, however, a voluntary sector organisation, London Wildlife Trust, which produced the first guide to *Encouraging Wildlife in Urban Parks*, though shared credit is due to the borough, Lambeth, which commissioned the report.

It is clear from the above account that, despite some successes, the metropolitan county councils were only just getting their act together when they were scrapped. By 1986 all, rather than some, should have produced the package of elements making up a rudimentary nature conservation strategy. While the GLC-type survey is the ideal, Greater Manchester and Merseyside showed what could be achieved by improvisation. Equally, it would have been a simple task to produce a uniform listing of conservation policies, instead of the authorities labouring over their own individual versions. Finally, it would not have been difficult for each to have produced a broad-brush site-specific greenprint for that region in the style adopted by the West Midlands and Tyne and Wear.

It is unfortunate that the metropolitan boroughs were not bequeathed a stronger framework for action, as few of these or other district councils were well advanced with their own nature conservation plans. Wigan was probably the first to produce a nature conservation strategy (in 1982), and St Helens in 1987 issued *A Policy for Nature*. But others have not been so enlightened.

The year before the abolition of the metropolitan county councils the Association of Metropolitan Authorities published *Green Policy*, 'a review of green policy and practice in metropolitan authorities'. Its account of the greening activities of the seven counties and ten sample district councils was in many respects heartening. Boroughs were rightly proud of their new walkways on former railway lines and other open space schemes, such as Birmingham's river improvement programme. Yet nature conservation is predominantly described in terms which suggest it was still thought of as cosmetic rather than as part of the infrastructure of any urban area, a marginal aspect of urban greening. Wakefield's *Lighting the Green Fuse* is perhaps an example of this syndrome, whereby urban greening is an idea councils pay lip service to without much commitment to its implementation. As a local cynic said of this document: 'It's purely a public relations job. It doesn't mean anything in practice.'

As a supra-national authority the European Community has so far had little influence on UK urban nature conservation. In 1987 it launched its *Fourth Environmental Action Programme (1987-1992)* and the associated European Year of the Environment (EYE). The launch of the Year included among its aims support for urban greening. Previous European campaigns, such as the Council of Europe's Year of the Water's Edge have tended to be ineffective. Funding for the necessary organisational role was usually minimal, lead organisations having to undertake co-ordination without additional staff. EYE, in contrast, appears to have been treated seriously from the start, a proper secretariat being established and an efficient publicity operation functioning well before the official launch date of March 1987.

A valuable product of early publicity activity was that it provided, for the first time, detailed news of what local authorities and voluntary organisations were doing in the environmental field throughout Britain. As the EEC says in its own introductory literature:

The EYE, however, is not an end in itself; nor is it a Year that will cease to have impact once it is over. It must, according to the Commission, be seen as a launching pad for a new approach. The aim of the Fourth Programme is to spell out the measures that will be necessary at community level during the first part of this new phase in the development of the Community's environmental protection policy.

Whether this ambitious attempt to put the environment in the mainstream of central and local government thinking succeeds remains to be seen. But on the simplest level of providing a nationwide means of communication for those involved in city greening activities, its first efforts showed how feeble past arrangements have been.

References and further reading

The Nature Conservation Strategy for the County of West Midlands (West Midlands CC, 1984) is available from the NCC at their headquarters.

Ecology and Nature Conservation in London (GLC, 1984), Ecology Handbook No. 1, includes an appendix on 'Ecology Policies in the draft alterations to the Greater London Development Plan' and is available from the Greater London Ecology Unit, County Hall, London SE1 7PB.

Draft Nature Conservation Strategy (Tyne and Wear CC, 1986) is available from NCC (North-East), Archbold House, Archbold Terrace, Newcastle-upon-Tyne NE2 1EG.

Gaining Momentum by David Tyldesley (Pisces, 1986).

Urban Ecology edited by R. Bornkamm, J. A. Lee and M.R.D. Seaward (Blackwell, 1982), the book of the 2nd European Ecological Symposium in Berlin in 1980, includes papers by Ray Gemmell on 'The origin and importance of industrial habitats' and by Tony Bradshaw on 'The biology of land reclamation in urban areas'.

Green Towns and Cities UK/USA by Sandra Higgins (Dartington Institute, 1984, 160 pp ringbound) is an interesting 'Summary of supporting research for Congress Paper'.

Towards Community Uses of Wasteland by Jacqui Stearn (NCVO, 1982, 72pp ringbound).

Abolition and the Countryside (Countryside Commission, 1985), Volume I of the Consultants' Report being the 'Summary of Findings'.

A Nature Conservation Strategy for London (GLC, 1986), Ecology Handbook No. 4.

A Strategy for Nature Conservation (Wigan MBC, 1982).

A Policy for Nature (St Helens MBC, 1987).

Urban Wildlife – What Next – and How?, a booklet summarising the proceedings of a 1985 conference in Birmingham (available from the Birmingham Urban Wildlife Group) includes an entertainingly frank account by the Leicester Project's director of 'Developing working relationships with local authorities'.

Encouraging Wildlife in Urban Parks (LWT, 1985).

Encouraging Wildlife on Golf Courses (LWT, 1987).

Natural Economy by Matthew Corder and Richard Brooker (Kirklees MBC, 1981) has recently been supplemented by their *Environmental Economy* (Spon, 1986), consisting of contributions by various authors on aspects of naturalistic management of landscape.

Green Policy (AMA, 1985).

The Sydenham Hill Wood File (178pp looseleaf) is available from LWT.

Brightening Up Your Neighbourhood (LB Southwark, 1986) is the – partial – story of the Southwark Environment Programme.

Wildlife in Southwark by Chris Rose (Southwark Wildlife Group, 1982, 60pp stapled) is 'a survey of the ecological potential of vacant land'.

5 | Quangos and qualgos

The main government agencies concerned with conservation are the Nature Conservancy Council and the Countryside Commission, both funded by the Department of the Environment. In recent years the Department has also supported the British Trust for Conservation Volunteers and, in the 1980s, created a new type of environmental qualgo – or quasi-autonomous local government organisation – in the shape of Groundwork Trusts.

NCC involvement in urban nature conservation was, initially, almost accidental. George Barker, now the Conservancy's urban adviser, describes how in the 1960s he and colleagues in its southern region embarked on a survey of wildlife sites in the area, but only in the countryside:

> The urban sites were too finely grained and we didn't know enough about urban factors, so we drew lines around the towns and left them out.

By the 1970s he was based in the West Midlands when he was approached by the newly formed West Midlands County Council, which needed advice about sites as part of its structure plan preparations. Realising he could give little useful guidance without a record of the territory, he decided to use some of his meagre funds on a survey of Birmingham and the Black Country. A potential surveyor suggested himself when Barker was attending a conference in Manchester:

> I was spending the evening in the bar with, among others, the naturalist Bunny Teagle. He very much brought himself to my attention by tipping my pint of beer into my lap with one of his usual dramatic conversational gestures.

43

Following this libation, Teagle went on to conduct a year-long survey, for which the fee was £400. Barker recalls this was criticised at the time as extravagance. Urban ecology was not high on the list of NCC priorities, or indeed on that of other conservation organisations.

Teagle wrote the survey report in a form which he and Barker hoped might tempt a Birmingham publisher by its local subject. Coincidentally the Conservancy was about to produce its second forward plan and was looking for a novel theme to launch it. The then director-general, Bob Boote, recognised the curiosity value of the survey and also reckoned its topic might interest one of the DoE ministers, Birmingham MP Denis Howell. The NCC's publications department asked Barker if he had any material suitable for immediate publication, and *The Endless Village*, a perennially enjoyable read, was thus published under an official imprint. As one critic observes: 'If they hadn't wanted it overnight it would have been translated into NCC officialese.' Instead it attracted widespread media coverage. Newspapers, radio and television were intrigued by the idea of, for instance, rare spiders living under Birmingham's notorious Spaghetti Junction.

Delighted by the response, the Conservancy followed up its success by commissioning further urban projects. Lyndis Cole was sent to discover what had been happening elsewhere in Britain, and Barbara Mostyn was asked to find out if, and why, urbanites appreciated wildlife areas.

Cole's report, *Wildlife in the City*, came out in 1979 and provides a useful conspectus of the state of urban ecology at the start of the 1980s. London and Birmingham account for 19 of the 27 projects described, these representing almost all the instances of urban conservation work at that time. In London, volunteers had taken Highgate Cemetery in hand; local societies had inspired conservation programmes in municipal parks at Hampstead Heath, Holland Park and Wanstead Park; and educational projects were under way in Newham and at Wimbledon Common. London's earliest nature reserve, established by the Selborne Society at Perivale Wood in 1905, had been declared a Local Nature Reserve in 1957. In 1973, neighbours of the Brent Reservoir had launched a campaign against proposed housing development around the lake.

In the Midlands, education projects had been introduced at the Botanical Gardens and on sites next to a number of the city's schools. Local pressure had ensured the safeguarding of sites at St Mary's Hospital and Peascroft Wood in Walsall and Moseley Bog in Birmingham. Elsewhere, a small site in Newcastle-upon-Tyne is mentioned as an example of the school reserves being created by regional branches of the BTCV, and in Milton Keynes the development corporation had formed a junior conservation corps to work on sites in the new town area. Cardiff provided an example of what could be achieved on a small site within a densely populated housing estate and, in another part of the city, the Glamorgan Canal had become the spine of a 17 ha reserve. St Martin's Pond in Nottingham was designated as a Local Nature Reserve in 1977. Most ambitious of the greening projects were the reclamation schemes in the Lower Swansea Valley and at the Hanley Forest Park, together with the network of school nature reserves in South Yorkshire.

The additional survey by Barbara Mostyn reported that wildlife appealed to all types of people but that they needed to identify with a site before they felt a sense of benefit from it. Nature parks were seen as valuable informal play areas for children, and as a means of enabling adults to escape from the stresses of the built environment and to re-establish contact with nature. Social benefits such as meeting people while engaged in site maintenance were also important. The converse was that many volunteers were depressed by vandalism of sites and public apathy.

A third document issued by the Conservancy in 1979 was the policy statement *Nature Conservation in Urban Areas: Challenge and Opportunity*. As a declaration of intent it was magnificent:

> For the most part the attitude of urban society towards its wildlife has at best been one of benign neglect. Nature has given us a second chance to prove that we are not oblivious of its value and it is time to take that chance by planning positively for the conservation and enhancement of nature and natural resources, in order to help our towns and cities become more interesting and enjoyable places to live or work in.

As a plan of action it was a flop. As early as 1982 the newly formed London Wildlife Trust was complaining that:

> On the one hand NCC is creating a high level of expectation by making general statements and taking general initiatives in

'urban conservation', yet on the other hand there is no clear, specific or coherent attempt to apply or interpret the statutory powers in a way which will help meet such expectations or sustain initiatives.

Individual NCC regional staff were frequently helpful behind the scenes, encouraging, for example, the formation of new urban wildlife trusts in 1980 and 1981. But while the Conservancy provided part-funding for these emergent organisations, it otherwise put little effort into urban work. George Barker became a one-man urban department, keeping in touch with regionally based staff through an Urban Habitat Network and with other urban practitioners through the launch in 1984 of a bulletin *Urban Wildlife News*.

Barker's budget was adequate for the commissioning of various urban research projects and city surveys, but the Conservancy's overall spending on urban work was small. In 1986/7 it secured from the government a doubling of its total budget to £32m (a further £4m increase being promised for 1987/8) to enable it to speed up its renotification of Sites of Special Scientific Interest. The urban allocation within 'Creative Conservation', the Conservancy's curious title embracing urban conservation, remained a paltry £300,000. Similarly, though one of the two main aims set out in the council's corporate plan is 'to support the NGOs [non-governmental organisations], largely through increased grant aid and closer consultation', only £0.6m was available for posts and projects in the entire voluntary sector.

In 1987/8 £2.2m was available as grant aid, half of this to be spent on land purchase. Of the remainder, £0.7m was already committed expenditure as a contribution towards the funding of some 100 posts around the country. The surplus would only provide part-funding for some 15 new posts, and the only organisations to receive support would be 'new and poor'. The estimate of one NCC officer was that the amount provided was 'only one tenth of what is needed'.

The urban budget is doubling in 1987/8 but remains inadequate in post-abolition circumstances. The metropolitan counties were spending £16m capital and £9m revenue on countryside and recreation projects each year. As the NCC's England director, Brian O'Connor, admitted in a letter to the county wildlife trusts a month after abolition:

> The NCC hopes to be able to expand its urban-based conservation programmes in the forthcoming year. Meanwhile we will do what we can; but the voluntary organisations will have an especially important function in keeping nature conservation to the forefront of the minds of councillors and officers of the local authorities during this transitional period. The direct help we can give to you this year is limited. However, do not hesitate to contact us if you feel that we can be of assistance.

The NCC's impotence at this important time is puzzling. Instead of taking the opportunity to step up its urban involvement, it said – in a report on the consequences of abolition sent to the DoE in 1985 – that it needed no extra money. This strange stance was later explained by one observer as being the result of a trade-off with the DoE: 'They told the NCC: 'Don't ask for money this time around and we'll see you alright next year.' Whatever the reason, the Conservancy, making up for lost time, agreed in spring 1987 that in consultation with other conservation organisations, the preparation of an Urban Programme statement could usefully be launched in mid-1988.

The main beneficiaries of abolition were the Countryside Commission and, through it, the Groundwork Trusts (GTs). Having been established in 1949 as the National Parks Commission, the Countryside Commission might easily have been wound up when the national parks were established. Instead it has skilfully identified new roles for itself – the creation of long-distance footpaths and country parks, for instance – and deployed its relatively small resources (in 1986 around £12m pa and 100 staff) very effectively. Reconstituted as the Countryside Commission for England and Wales in 1968 (the Countryside Commission for Scotland having been established a year earlier), it became a fully fledged quango in 1982. On that occasion it launched a prospectus, *Countryside Issues and Action*, which described its impressive record of achievement in urban fringe improvements. It also referred to its support for:

> The establishment of a London wildlife trust which will promote public interest in conservation within and around the nation's capital, and action to protect endangered sites.

Two years later, it halted the London Wildlife Trust's grant with the explanation:

> It is felt that your wildlife conservation bias, while worthwhile, is peripheral to the interests of the Commission.

This sudden disavowal of any interest in nature conservation was followed in 1986 by a clarification of the Commission's attitude towards urban areas, by the Commission's director, Adrian Phillips:

> We readily accept the principle that some things can be done for the countryside only by bringing the conservation message to urban residents rather than waiting for them to go to the countryside. But the focus must always be the countryside, not urban nature conservation.

In view of this lack of concern for both towns and nature conservation generally, its initiative in highlighting the threat to urban nature conservation during the passing of the metropolitan county council abolition legislation was welcome. Jointly with the National Farmers' Union, it successfully sponsored a Lords motion which demanded:

> The Secretary of State shall before the abolition day lay before Parliament a report on the steps he will take to secure the full adoption by the councils to which functions are transferred by this section in Greater London or a metropolitan county of those facilities, services and responsibilities for the protection and enjoyment of the countryside and areas for urban nature conservation which serve the continuing needs of Greater London or that county and neighbouring populations.

At the DoE's request, the Commission then commissioned a survey, *Abolition and the Countryside*, produced in 1985. Though a useful account of the work being done by the county councils in the urban fringe, its recommendations took little account of the urban nature conservation issue referred to in the Lords resolution. Nor did it take into account the part councils played in funding the voluntary associations on whose work so much urban nature conservation depends.

The consequence was that when Environment Secretary Kenneth Baker reported to Parliament in February 1986, his only additional financial allocation was a total of £2.4m intended mainly to finance the creation of new Groundwork Trusts. While Baker recognised that 'in some areas voluntary bodies will be a powerful driving force behind environmental improvement or conservation schemes,' no new money was made available to assist them. Groundwork Trusts, with their lack of campaigning tendency, were much more attractive.

Urban wildlife groups were, by coincidence, meeting that weekend to form a national association. In the first statement issued by the new Fairbrother Group, they protested:

By allocating additional funds to the Countryside Commission for urban conservation with no additional support for voluntary groups, he is ignoring the work already being done by the voluntary sector throughout Britain. And in encouraging the setting up of new Groundwork Trusts he is in danger of undermining the many existing wildlife groups.

The first Groundwork Trust had been launched in St Helens in January 1982, five others following in Wigan, Macclesfield, Oldham and Rochdale, Salford and Trafford and Rossendale. Director of the first Operation Groundwork in St Helens and Knowsley was John Handley, former head of Merseyside's Natural Resources Unit and a much respected figure in urban nature conservation. Heseltine's successor as Environment Secretary, Patrick Jenkin, decided the Groundwork concept could usefully be extended around Britain and in 1985 encouraged the setting up of an independent Groundwork Foundation. The three main partners in the Foundation were the Countryside Commission, Nature Conservancy and BTCV, and its objective was 'to provide a catalyst for co-operation between the public, private and voluntary sectors as a means of improving the environment'. In the summer of 1986 it set up shop in Birmingham with John Davidson from the Countryside Commission as director and John Iles from BTCV as director of trust development. Their aim was to establish five or so new trusts each year for the next few years. John Davidson added his view, in the booklet *Groundwork – The Environmental*

Entrepreneurs, that:

> Over the next five to ten years I see us developing as an enabling service for all kinds of environmental jobs that industry wants done. As environmental entrepreneurs, our aim is to build up a network of small businesses which earn their income by helping solve some of Britain's most pressing problems.

The Foundation also resolved the difficulty inherent in Heseltine's original concept, whereby at the end of five years each Trust was supposed to become self-supporting. As the St Helens Trust approached the end of its first five years, during which time it, like the other trusts, was receiving 50 per cent state funding on a declining basis, it was clear that it needed a further subvention if it was to continue in existence. The Groundwork Foundation duly provided the necessary amount and will presumably bankroll the other Trusts as their initial five year period ends.

By 1987 new Groundwork Trusts were agreed for West Cumbria, Merthyr Tydfil, East Durham, South Leeds, the Colne Valley and Hertfordshire, with those in the pipeline including prospective GTs in Belfast, Cardiff, Bristol and Avon, and Sandwell. Existing conservation organisations in several of these areas protested that the GTs were being set up without any consultation with bodies already carrying out conservation work. There were also complaints that the Groundwork Trusts were in some instances carrying out schemes with harmful environmental effects. The anxiety of urban wildlife groups increased when Leeds City Council announced its intention of setting up a South Leeds Groundwork Trust with a staff of 500 – 400 of them labourers – and a five-year budget of £14m. £12m of this was to be provided by the Manpower Services Commission (MSC) and only £1m each by the council and Groundwork Foundation. As a mechanism for obtaining cheap labour the scheme, proposed by a Labour council, could hardly be more blatant.

When the Foundation's chairman, Christopher Chataway, met one of the county trust critics he asked: 'Why don't you like us?' The answer, in addition to the above complaints, was that the Groundwork Trusts were being presented as voluntary organisations when, as the Leeds example starkly illustrates, they were solidly part of the state machinery. Unlike true NGOs, their management committees were selected by the Groundwork Foundation rather than elected by a membership, yet the government was claiming that their funding represented support for the voluntary sector. The first draft of the DoE advisory circular on nature conservation circulated in 1986 included in its section on 'The Voluntary Conservation Movement' a laudatory paragraph on the role of the Groundwork Trusts. After protests, mention of the trusts was omitted from the final version. John Iles, sensitive to the anxiety of the NGOs, later confirmed that:

> Groundwork Trusts are not part of the voluntary sector. They are environmental businesses.

The largest sources of income for the GTs are in the form of grants from the Countryside Commission and government for individual landscaping projects and money from the Manpower Services Commission for Community Programme (CP) workers employed by the Trusts. The conservation industry is a large scale consumer of MSC labour, but its use poses serious problems for employing organisations. The MSC's special employment measures originated as a job creation programme devised by the Labour government in the 1970s, the idea of it being that it provides the unemployed with useful training which will help them find permanent jobs. The Conservative government increased the number of places on the Community Programme to almost a quarter of a million by 1986. In recent years, almost all the environmental organisations – who are major participants in the Community Programme – have become concerned about many aspects of the Programme, both in practice and in principle.

The attraction of MSC to employers is that it provides free staff and running costs of up to £440 for each person employed, enabling many organisations to pay a large proportion of their core costs, such as office rental, from this source. CP's appeal to the government is that it is a mixture of job creation, training and a means of carrying out environmental work at low cost. The benefit to participants is a rate of pay that is higher than the dole, useful experience and job satisfaction if they are in posts that suit them.

The disadvantages are manifold, both technically and philosophically. Coping with MSC paperwork is, everyone agrees, 'a nightmare'. Setting up a team so that pay for key jobs is adequate to attract decent applicants is tortuous. The average pay per post is £67 a week, so to pay qualified staff £100 a week means taking on a larger number of part-time workers at £40 or so. Supervising a team of part-timers is awkward, and since the job is only for a year, competent people have to be laid off when they are becoming most useful.

Project supervisors are paid at market rates and are allowed to stay for a couple of years, but also have to be chosen from the unemployed. Good supervisors are much in demand but are forced into a curious cyclical employment pattern. One ecologist offered a full-time job, but with no guarantee that funding would be renewed at the end of the year, responded: 'I'd like to take it, but I don't want to lose my unemployed status.' His meaning was that he would qualify for a supervisor's job only if he were on the dole.

There is also widespread anxiety about the quality of work carried out by inexperienced or badly supervised teams. While recognising that much CP work is very valuable, the authors of the 1983 report *The Livable City* summarise the difficulties thus:

> There are other problems associated with MSC programmes – for conservation and for employment. The schemes are temporary, individuals work usually for no longer than a year and while a great deal of good work has undoubtedly been accomplished, a constantly changing labour force and one which (it is acknowledged) has not always been well enough trained or supervised, is not necessarily the most efficient way of tackling conservation tasks. Those who have been through job creation schemes can rarely look forward to more permanent work in the same field. There are simply not the jobs yet available to absorb all the many young people emerging not only from MSC schemes, but from college and university environmental courses.

A paradoxical result is that new graduates, lacking jobs, may spend several years on MSC schemes run by polytechnics – such as the North London or Thames polys in London – or other educational institutions – such as the urban studies centres. A circular effect is created whereby there is little pressure to create full-time posts because the work is being done, often very well, by the very people who would be employed if the permanent jobs had been established.

One of the most fundamental objections to the use of MSC work is that sometimes more priority is given to keeping projects going than to ensuring that their work on the habitat is appropriate. The report of a seminar on MSC organised by the Volunteeer Bureau in autumn 1986 quoted Mike Marshall, Heritage Coast Officer in Suffolk, who identified a danger that arises when organisations which are sizable users of MSC labour, such as Groundwork and BTCV, discover a lack of projects to keep their teams occupied:

> The experience of the use of MSC schemes in public sector environmental work was 'failure followed by disaster'. The direct use of SEMs [Special Employment Measures] on the Coast has meant that the LA [local authority] officers have been forced to spend more and more time looking for work to keep teams busy. There have been difficulties in finding appropriate work.

A consequence of this is that a proportion of management work carried out by MSC teams exceeds what is necessary in nature conservation terms and is harmful to the natural history value of habitats.

There is, too, concern about the effect MSC teams have on the host bodies. An organisation with a small core staff can be swamped by the larger numbers of CP workers. The role of volunteers can also be eroded, as described by Mike Marshall:

> As the input of MSC teams has increased over time, and staff resources have been concentrated on managing those teams, the time and resources devoted to volunteers has declined, and volunteer input to the project has declined. In 1980, 1,500 days of work had been undertaken by volunteers. In 1986, only 500 days of work had been completed by volunteers.

Somewhat on the principle of Gresham's law, whereby bad money drives out good, this substitution can affect the basic structure of an organisation as well as volunteer participation in the work being carried out. Landlife in Liverpool, for example, employs a large CP team but, until recently, did not bother much about attracting a formal membership. Similarly, the Urban Wildlife Group in Birmingham operates an impressively professional MSC scheme but is the only county conservation trust which takes the view that a large membership is unimportant. In such cases, they become vulnerable. A blow to all organisations with MSC CP schemes was the news, in early 1987, that the number of placements was to be cut back. A new scheme, the Job Training Scheme (JTS), was being set up to cater for under-25-year-olds, with a target for some 250,000 placements. CP funding was being reduced accordingly.

A similar imbalance between volunteer and MSC labour has become apparent at the British Trust for Conservation Volunteers (better known by its initials, BTCV, than by its full title). BTCV's original aim was to enable volunteers to carry out countryside management work, a role which continues, to the great benefit of volunteers and the sites worked on. From the late 1970s, however, the Trust became an increasingly large employer of MSC labour, receiving government aid for this purpose. The result has been that the Trust's enhanced staff became progressively dominant, with some volunteer activists unhappy at their own diminished influence on the Trust's affairs.

The scale of its operation is seen in its accounts for 1985/6. Of an income of £1.3m, £782,000 was derived from central government, £258,000 came from local and statutory authorities, and a similar sum from charities and industry, while membership fees produced only £32,000. The average number of MSC employees was 600, an increase on the 246 in 1985. At the Volunteer Bureau seminar Peter Thompson, manager of the BTCV's MSC schemes, described the Trust's guidelines:

> The BTCV has a policy of limiting the financial scale of its involvement to an equivalent of the BTCV's non-SEM finances. The schemes in which it is involved are almost all geared to finding work for volunteers or working with volunteers. Few are direct labour teams.

These do nevertheless exist, as in the case of its East Sussex Woodlands Project which is thought by some to be an inappropriate form of management, being attached to no bona fide nature conservation organisation. But BTCV still sees itself as having the interests of the voluntary sector at heart, as Peter Thompson went on to say:

> The BTCV is also a national agent for MSC schemes operated

by various county nature conservation and Groundwork trusts. The BTCV has a strong commitment to volunteer involvement and policies which allow no work to be done by paid staff if it could be done by a volunteer and that volunteers are not involved in practical tasks on sites which could be commercially developed. Through its commitment to MSC schemes the BTCV core staff has grown – from 20 in 1983 to over 100 in 1986. The BTCV's experiences of working with volunteers and Community Programme schemes indicates that where CP and volunteers work together the results are better than where CP schemes work alone.

During 1986 BTCV launched a programme to increase its individual members, the target being 50,000 within four years. Previously the Trust had relied on a degree of creative accounting to boost its output and income. When boasting of its 'healthily expanding network of over 350 local groups of conservation volunteers', it does not make clear that many of these are groups of other organisations which affiliate to BTCV in return for discounts on tool purchase and so forth. In the same manner it includes in its total of workdays (250,000) those of members of these independent groups (90,000) when they are working on a BTCV-supervised task. In early 1987 BTCV had less than 7,000 members.

The Trust was also garnering some extra income from tasks carried out by its MSC workers by charging a small sum for the work done. MSC blocked this practice in 1986 and BTCV now requests donations from the benefiting organisations, most being happy to contribute. In addition to its practical work, BTCV provides an immensely valuable service to other conservation organisations through its training schemes, both for practical conservation and management techniques.

Among the earliest BTCV organisers was John Iles. While working in industrial relations during the 1970s he started, together with Mike Wilde, the Don and Dearne Action Group in South Yorkshire, for which he later secured MSC funding as a full-time organiser. During the next few years the pair organised volunteers in three or so environmental projects each weekend – which, says Iles, was more than were being organised by BTCV groups elsewhere. In 1978 he and Wilde joined the BTCV staff and took over the running of the Trust's northern region:

> We spent the next years organising smaller and smaller regions.
> We had a healthy urban bias from the start, believing that things
> should start on people's doorsteps.

In 1982 he launched BTCV's national MSC agency but, watching
the growth of the Groundwork Trusts in the North-West, changed
his allegiance:

> I saw Groundwork as the next stage of development. BTCV was
> limited by the lack of sufficient finance, structurally and
> constitutionally. It has good relations with local authorities, but
> in a master-servant relationship rather than as partners.

In 1984 he was seconded to the Groundwork Foundation, the aim
of which, he explains, is not only to set up trusts in the urban fringe
but to cover city centres as well:

> John Davidson [Director of the Groundwork Foundation] went
> to see Kenneth Baker in March 1986 to try and get the
> Groundwork brief extended to cover urban areas, because in
> future we want to start in towns looking out, rather than on the
> fringe looking in. We aim to be urban from April 1st 1987. We
> could already set up a trust in an urban area, but apart from
> Urban Programme money we wouldn't get any grants for
> projects of the kind provided by the Countryside Commission.

Director of the Commission Adrian Phillips was asked by London
Wildlife Trust about the Commission's attitude to this extension
of Groundwork's remit. He commented that:

> So far as the Commission is concerned, we welcome the
> Foundation's wish to become more involved in urban projects.
> If this receives government approval, we believe it would not
> be appropriate for the Commission to remain Groundwork's
> principal source of funding. But we intend to remain a partner
> and continue to support Groundwork projects in urban fringe
> locations.

As an experienced practitioner, John Iles echoes the universal criticisms of MSC weaknesses, with the addition that he and BTCV colleagues have had some success in securing a reappraisal of the rules:

> We have been saying to government that we could out-turn more CP places if the rules were changed or there were more waivers. The main constraint is that MSC funding is on a year-by-year basis, hence the one-year limit on contracts, but we could achieve more if schemes were agreed for a longer period.

While Iles was with BTCV, the Trust commissioned the Dartington Amenity Research Trust to produce a report, *Work and the Environment*, surveying the scope of volunteer and MSC environmental involvement. Published in 1986, its recommendations included the setting-up of a National Environmental Work Scheme. Retitled UK 2000 and headed by entrepreneur and businessman Richard Branson, the organisation established later that year was sponsored by seven national environmental bodies including BTCV and RSNC.

UK 2000 is intended to achieve various objectives, the central aim being to improve the quality of projects carried out by MSC labour. To this end UK 2000 provides additional cash and a better disposition of MSC-funded staff. Branson and his staff are seeking to raise funds from industry and charities for allocation to schemes awarded a UK 2000 'kitemark'. The organisations carrying out the kitemarked schemes will also be allowed a higher proportion of supervisors in their MSC teams – one to six rather than the standard one to ten. Participating organisations will also receive a share of additional CP placements being made available by the government, and there are likely to be dispensations allowing key staff such as supervisors a longer term of employment than the customary maximum of two years. Finally, there is the hope that the scheme will try to ensure that some jobs secure permanent funding. While the RSNC's UK 2000 co-ordinator, Richard Woolnough – formerly conservation officer of the Suffolk wildlife trust where he ran a 100-plus MSC team and now on the staff of the Groundwork Foundation – commented:

> In Suffolk there has been little success in the development of

permanent jobs as a result of CP or VPP [Volunteer Placement Programme], but the potential for this was felt to be considerable. The Trust will be looking to UK 2000 for the development of schemes leading to permanent jobs, for example, in woodland management.

The potential contribution of UK 2000 to the improvement of the urban environment was strengthened by the setting-up of a permanent secretariat in spring 1987 and the appointment of Brian Lymbery, formerly at the Civic Trust, as director. Even before his arrival, staff had worked with remarkable swiftness to provide additional resources to dozens of schemes around Britain. The initial goodwill they elicited from the wildlife trusts demonstrated that quangos can be effective when they operate on a partnership basis, rather than trying to supplant existing groups. The Countryside Commission's principle of applying 'leverage', whereby other organisations are encouraged to handle the spadework, strengthens both parties.

An example of how quangos may fail if they do not cultivate a solid relationship with other organisations is 'think green'. Having been set up with DoE money after the 1984 Green Towns and Cities conference to foster local green campaigns around Britain, in the following two years it achieved only modest success. Photographs in its newsletter showed its distinguished directors, who included John Davidson, David Goode and David Wilcox (an environmental journalist turned environmental consultant). But, it turned out, the organisation had never been formally constituted and the directors were such in name only. By late 1986, 'think green' had almost crumbled.

In early 1987, however, the campaign resurrected itself, acquiring a new chairman and director, and offices in Birmingham instead of London. The future cannot be predicted but its history is a caution that quangos with shallow roots are dangerously liable to wither away.

References and further reading

Wildlife in the City by Lyndis Cole (NCC, 1979) is 'A study of practical conservation projects'.

Personal benefits and satisfactions derived from participation in urban wildlife projects by Barbara Mostyn (NCC, 1979).
Nature Conservation in Urban Areas: Challenge and Opportunity (NCC, 1979).
Nature Conservation in Great Britain (NCC, 1984).
The Livable City by Joan Davidson and Ann MacEwan (1983) is one of seven reports produced by a Programme Organising Committee, a consortium of quangos and NGOs, as a UK response to the World Conservation strategy.
Work and the Environment is available in a summary leaflet from BTCV.

6 | The rise of urban wildlife groups

In the spring of 1981 a gaggle of conservationists ambled round Clissold Park in Hackney, London, led by the bearded and plump but bustling figure of Chris Baines. As parks go, Clissold Park is well cared for and attractive; Baines pointed out that it could be a lot more interesting if looked after in a different style. Since those days Baines has become a familiar media figure through frequent television appearances and book authorship. But at the time, his message was revelatory:

> Look at those trees, clinically pruned so that all the dead branches have been lopped off. But it's in those branches where insects live which birds feed on and where birds such as woodpeckers nest. Obviously you don't want chunks of timber falling on passers-by, but away from the paths why not keep the deadwood – either on the trees or on the ground – as part of the ecosystem that would develop in a natural woodland?

Across the close-mown grass only a few pigeons and crows pecked around, as Baines continued:

> Why don't we leave the areas under the trees to grow a bit longer to provide food and shelter for a greater variety of birds? And if parks staff spend a lot of time on the flower beds in the more formal parts, why can't they create wildflower meadows in some of the more remote areas?

Of the ponds, teeming with ornamental ducks, he commented:

> See the concrete edges and the lack of undergrowth on the island in the middle. If you made it a bit more like a natural lake you would have rare ducks flying in for free.

The tour was part of the 'Nature in London' weekend conference which launched the London Wildlife Trust (LWT). Elsewhere Bunny Teagle was giving a slideshow on the wildlife of Birmingham, only marginally handicapped by a defunct projector ('. . . and here you would have been able to see the glorious summer flowering of an old gas works site').

Dignitaries such as John Davidson and Frank Perring, representing the Countryside Commission and RSNC, were present to legitimise the proceedings. Yet the creation of the new trust was a symptom of the spreading challenge to conservation attitudes still mainly orientated towards the countryside.

The message that nature conservation was as important in towns as in rural areas was most powerfully preached by the Urban Wildlife Group in the West Midlands. The early running had been made by the Birmingham group of Friends of the Earth whose Pete Byfield headed an MSC team which combined surveys, campaigns for site protection and popular publicity in its work during the late 1970s. Paralleling this activity was a revolt by mainstream conservationists, unhappy at the lack of interest shown in the West Midlands by the existing county conservation trusts. As one activist recalls:

> There was a West Midlands consortium with representatives of the three trusts – Warwickshire, Staffordshire and Worcestershire – on it, but it didn't address the issues while sites were being lost.

Wanting to emphasise its difference from the old county trusts, the conservationists forming the organisation set up at a workshop in 1980 called it the Urban Wildlife Group. Its first chairman was Roger Hammond, who was succeeded in later years by Chris Baines, Peter Shirley and Alison Millward. All, including Baines, would acknowledge that Baines was the star who gained them widespread attention. Until then he had pursued an orthodox career as a landscape architect, but a Saul-on-the-road-to-Damascus experience altered his perspective. His practice was handling fairly big projects in the UK and Middle East, landscaping around airports and hotel complexes which Baines now describes as 'pretty superficial and cosmetic'. Then, in 1979, he attended a conference on land reclamation where, he recalls, most people said it was best to dig everything up and start again. On his way home his car skidded and Baines woke up in the intensive care unit of a Sussex hospital. 'Subconsciously this experience very much changed my attitude to what I was doing.'

He had already been working on inner-city housing estates such as Milton Court in Deptford, a problem estate where a poor environment was one of the problems. His approach had been to involve tenants in redesigning their surroundings and participating in the work, with children planting trees and so forth. After the car crash, he became more interested in making this approach work.

As a part-time lecturer to post-graduate landscape design students at Birmingham Polytechnic he also happily admits he came under pressure from them to consider the natural landscape more fully. So he wound up his practice to concentrate on his new role as a campaigner:

> There was, and is, in the landscape profession an artificial conception of what the landscape should be. The things that attract attention are new materials, new techniques, new lamp-posts. But the bit people enjoy is the old railway cutting where they walk the dog each evening. They are called 'derelict' but they are often the most heavily used. It was the threatened loss of this unofficial countryside that decided me to use my communication skills – writing and later television – until people understood what it was about. It takes publicists to make things happen.

He cites the case of Queslett Quarry as an instance of people's growing sense of deprival. The site had been chosen by the county council for landfill, and in 1980 tipping destroyed most of the quarry, including the nesting place of 200 breeding pairs of sand martins. The council was eventually persuaded to revise its plans but, as Baines remembers:

> There was no support from sources such as the Nature Conservancy Council or RSPB, because their attitude was: 'There can't be anything of interest there because it's in a city.' The council for their part weren't doing it from malice but simply through ignorance.

The battle to save Queslett Quarry was one of several similar campaigns the Urban Wildlife Group supported in following years. Other major combat areas included the Woodgate Valley, Plants Brook Reservoirs and Stubbers Green Road Bog, as described in the West Midlands gazetteer (pages 156 – 171). Baines concludes that the lessons learnt from their first skirmishes were threefold:

> We found we needed to be very organised. We also realised we had to tackle things through official channels, so from the start we employed planners and ecologists to influence the council professionals. Finally, we recognised we had to change the attitude of the nature conservation organisations, which were very middle class in their composition and attitudes.

The UWG's current chairwoman, Alison Millward, adds that the Group also realised the importance of influencing politicians. Local councillors interested in nature conservation are fairly rare, and the West Midlands was fortunate in having David Sparks as chairman of the strategic planning committee. His planning team included Ian Collis, who prepared the 1984 *Nature Conservation Strategy for the West Midlands*. Following the abolition of the county council, Sparks survives in local politics as a councillor in Dudley and Collis is grappling with Derby's extensive dereliction.

The UWG does not actively seek a general membership. Baines argues that the main objective is to persuade councils to look after their wildspace and parks properly, and the Group can then wither away. 'God forbid', he says, 'that we should be doing the same things in ten years' time as we've been doing up to now!'

The three other urban trusts set up in 1980/81 do not share this philosophy. In the new county of Avon, the Somerset and Gloucestershire county trusts magnanimously encouraged the formation of the Avon Wildlife Trust. By clever use of an MSC team, it quickly built up a membership approaching 3,000 by turning a Nelsonian blind eye to counter-productive rules preventing MSC staff being used for fund-raising or membership recruitment. On Teesside, the Durham trust was happy to relinquish former territory in the new Cleveland county and, though the Yorkshire trust initially objected, a Cleveland trust started life in 1981.

Greater London, largest in area of the metropolitan counties apart from West Yorkshire, had by far the largest population: 6.7m out of a total of 18m in the seven English conurbations. It was only partially covered by the four county wildlife trusts surrounding the GLC area: Kent (formed 1958), Surrey (1959), Essex (1960) and Hertfordshire and Middlesex (formed 1965, though the latter county had disappeared in the reorganisation of local government in London that year). These participated in the London Nature Conservation Committee which sought to cover central London as well as the suburbs, but, as with the West Midlands forum, operated mainly as a talking shop rather than as an effective instrument for action.

The impetus for a new Greater London trust developed from a row within the Hertfordshire and Middlesex trust. Its council decided to buy a permanent headquarters in St Albans. A minority took the view that any available money would be better spent on practical conservation, especially in the urban fringe of north and west London where sites of key importance were under threat. Most active in suggesting that the trust was misdirecting its efforts was Chris Rose, a young ecologist who, having been brought up in West London, was very conscious of the danger to sites in the Colne Valley, the major valley through which the Thames formerly ran to the North Sea before taking its present course. As one of the most effective young turks in the conservation movement his career so far is worth noting.

While on the University College London (UCL) conservation course he and others had founded, in 1979, the British Association of Nature Conservationists, an intermittently radical organisation for thinking conservationists. Now an international campaigner for the World Wildlife Fund in Geneva, he was previously countryside campaigner for Friends of the Earth, co-authoring the trenchant *Crisis and Conservation*.

In the early months of 1981 he set about contacting other London conservationists to explore the possibility of a new London trust. He recruited Lord Melchett, active in many areas of the conservation movement, as patron of the new trust and Richard Mabey as president. Among others he also enlisted were Richard Robinson, a leading light in BTCV for some years, and myself, who had formed the Southwark Wildlife Group in 1980 after having been introduced to the concept of urban nature conservation while reporting on a BBC *Open Door* programme describing

Birmingham's wildlife initiatives. Several others with much longer experience of urban nature conservation were also actively involved, but such is the volatility of urban life that, six years later, we two are the only survivors from the trust's initial executive.

The idea of a trust for Greater London was tacitly backed by the NCC's local staff but upset some of the county trusts around London, fearful of a loss of membership and an erosion of territory. An influential figure in calming these anxieties was Surrey trust chairman John Montgomery, who had chaired the London nature conservation committee and continued this role as first chairman of the new trust's conservation committee. Pete Byfield was brought in to assist in preparations for the 'Nature in London' workshop, mentioned at the beginning of this chapter, at which the London Wildlife Trust was launched. Six years later, by spring 1987, the trust had 16 permanent staff, a 40-strong MSC team, and a membership of over 5,500, placing it in the top ten of the league table of RSNC trusts.

The RSNC had begun the decade with an interest in urban conservation that later waned. Its 1980 biennial conference (an event subsequently discontinued when the Society got into difficulties) was on the theme of 'Nature Conservation Goes to Town'. The papers presented there included an exhortation and warning from John Davidson, then with the Countryside Commission:

> If you wish to take on wider duties, now is the time to make your voice heard. Your movement would become more relevant to, and gain the support of, people who live in cities and are anxious to improve their local environment and who would like to see wildlife as a more important part of their local government. If you should decide for whatever reason against growing in that direction I would not be surprised to see other bodies being set up to fill the gap.

As it turned out, Davidson shrewdly judged the county trusts' limitations. Whereas membership of other national environmental organisations such as the National Trust and RSPB was rocketing, and new bodies such as the Woodland Trust boomed, the county trusts' membership increased at only some 5 per cent each year. Many of the trusts' councils were dominated by the upper middle class, usually middle-aged or older. By extension, this also applied to the RSNC's council. By 1985 this gap between the rural trusts and the urban trusts, with their more youthful and progressive membership, almost led to a parting of the ways.

The late and much-lamented *Vole* magazine as early as 1981 had pointed to a difference in attitude between the urban and rural trusts:

> One is quiet old rural conservation. Tired and toothless, it is obsessed with ingratiating itself with the powerful land lobbies and progresses as much by default as by design. The other is urban conservation – ill-defined but venting steam and vehemence from every orifice, it is unfettered by the dogmas that bind its rural counterpart. Though the urban conservationist's primary concern is on his own doorstep, he is also a powerful voice in arguing the nature conservation case beyond the city walls.

The growth of the urban trusts was followed in the mid-1980s by the emergence of smaller urban wildlife groups in towns and cities around Britain. Of three general types, they included groups that were town branches of rural county trusts (as in Reading and Nottingham), associations of other conservation organisations (as in Plymouth and Glasgow) or independent groups formed as a reaction to the rural bias of the older trusts (as at Norwich, Leeds, Sheffield and Manchester). Perhaps inevitably it was the two oldest trusts, Norfolk (founded 1926) and Yorkshire (founded 1946), that provoked the strongest reaction. The Norwich Wildlife Group was formed in 1984, followed by two new city groups in Yorkshire.

The Yorkshire Wildlife Trust, based in York, appeared to take little interest in the major cities of West and South Yorkshire. Nor did it pay much attention to the general public. At the trust's 1985 AGM, a Countryside Commission representative warned that their grant would be withdrawn if support for education and interpretation activities did not improve. The trust disregarded the signs of disaffection, and the AGM in the following year became an occasion when, for the first time, a county trust's linen received a thorough public laundering. On the morning of the meeting on 18 October 1986, *The Guardian* published an article, under the heading 'Trustworthy?', which dissected tensions within the organisation:

> Some naturalists working for the trust allege that its organisation is too outmoded and parochial to cope with this amount of responsibility. . . Critics of the trust say that the remaining council is composed largely of amateur naturalists who are afraid of upsetting local farming interests even when they damage wildlife.

Later that day, a number of rebels were elected to the trust's council and Roger Mitchell, the Rotherham planner, became the new chairman. Trust staff facing disciplinary action for the 'crime' of writing to a local MP urging the strengthening of the 1985 Wildlife and Countryside Act were left unmolested and the new council appears to be more prepared to collaborate with the two new urban groups.

Much of the pressure for change came from activists who had formed the Leeds Urban Wildlife Group, their stimulating effect being duplicated in Sheffield. Christine Bradley, a young lecturer in Sheffield University's landscape design department (and yet another of the lively graduates from the UCL course) was inspired by the 1984 Green Towns and Cities conference to organise action within the city. Co-founders of the Sheffield City Wildlife Group included her colleague Oliver Gilbert, an expert on urban eco-systems; Mike Wild of the city polytechnic's department of environmental and recreational studies; and Dennis Patton, now with the city's recreation department. Bradley was later appointed as director of the Shropshire Trust for Nature Conservation but her collaborators remain active in what is currently England's third largest city district (after Birmingham and Leeds).

On the other side of the Pennines in Greater Manchester a Manchester Wildlife Group emerged in 1986. By that time, however, the Lancashire county trust was beginning to develop its urban activities. Ted Jackson, conscripted as the trust's chairman at the beginning of the 1980s, remembers that 'when I became chairman the trust had no interest in urban sites, none whatever'. As manager of visitor services at Liverpool's Croxteth country park he was very conscious of the importance of communicating with urban populations. The trust now has a members' group in Croxteth and manages the Seaforth nature reserve at the northern tip of the Liverpool docks. Until recently it employed a field officer covering Greater Manchester and hoped for further workers in Liverpool and the towns of north Lancashire. Also in the north of the county, a Lancaster branch of the Liverpool group Landlife works closely with schools in the old county capital (the council offices now being located in Preston).

North of the county border, the Cumbria nature conservation trust has intelligently arranged MSC schemes to establish urban wildlife groups in Barrow, Workington, Whitehaven and Carlisle. East of the Pennines the Northumberland trust, though based in Newcastle, is fairly inactive in the city area. South of the Tyne, the Durham trust has produced an impressively thorough survey of wildlife sites in the Tyneside districts.

In Scotland, Glasgow suffers in conservation matters, as in other respects, from the hegemony of Edinburgh. Of all county trusts, the Scottish Wildlife Trust is the most patrician. As its development officer John Crichton comments on the difficulty in operating in Edinburgh, where the Trust is located: 'Those you may be opposing during the day, you know socially in the evening.' The elitist approach is in part responsible for problems it has encountered in recent years. The Chairman's Review in the NCC 1985/6 annual report states that:

> Our policy is to encourage the voluntary bodies to take on work appropriate to their strengths and to support them in this as best we can. Generally speaking this is working well, although the enthusiasm of individuals in the voluntary movement in Scotland and Wales cannot disguise an underlying weakness in members and resources.

Active members of the Trust's 'support groups' in Glasgow claim that, despite the size of Strathclyde compared to Lothian (2.3m population to 744,000), they are poorly supported by the Edinburgh headquarters. As one critic says:

> In the last ten years Glasgow has lost a significant proportion of its wildlife habitats, but we have had to fight our battles on our own. Other organisations such as the National Trust for

Scotland and RSPB are setting up local groups at meetings which are attended by between 100 and 200 people, which the trust isn't trying to match.

In explanation John Crichton comments:

There hasn't been an enormous amount of general interest in these areas until the last few years. Urban conservation is more something for the future.

Perhaps because of this vacuum, an MSC project sponsored by Edinburgh's Environmental Resource Centre was launched in 1986 as the Lothian Urban Wildlife Group. On the basis of the project, a membership organisation is now being contemplated.

In Glasgow, the Glasgow Urban Wildlife Group is a forum for organisations such as Scottish Conservation Projects, the north-of-the-border equivalent of the BTCV, but is not itself a membership body. In spring 1987, there were moves to create a Scottish equivalent of the Fairbrother Group under the title of the Geddes Group, taking its name from the early-20th century architect and landscape architect Patrick Geddes.

In Wales the story is brief. The Glamorgan trust covering the three Glamorgan counties has its roots in West Glamorgan, and in particular the Gower Peninsular, and has little strength in the more populous counties of Mid Glamorgan or South Glamorgan or in the capital of Cardiff.

It was within this nationwide context that urban wildlife activists met in November 1985 to form the Fairbrother Group as an urban conservation forum. The number of urban groups was increasing each year, but most of the county trusts still regarded cities only as a source of members, and the urban natural environment as having little conservation importance. At national level, the RSNC council and executive were similarly uninterested in urban activities. There was no representative of any urban trust on the executive, nor even on the conservation and scientific committee.

At their conference in Norwich, the Fairbrother delegates therefore decided they would set up independently of RSNC unless the latter mended its ways. Acting with unusual speed RSNC's executive, prompted by general secretary Frank Perring, agreed to set up an Urban Steering Group on which Fairbrother could nominate the bulk of places. Fairbrother's reconvened conference in March 1986 welcomed this move and, in constituting itself as the Association of Urban Wildlife Groups, declared its intention of working 'in association with RSNC'.

The formal setting up of the Fairbrother Group marked the coming of age of urban conservation. Its members included over 40 wildlife groups from all over Britain. Its conferences provided the means for a transfer of information between groups and the opportunity to formulate views on current urban issues. Through its participation in the RSNC urban steering group it shares responsibility for the Society's urban development officer. As the Fairbrother treasurer Richard Robinson, also chairman of LWT, observes: 'It is important to sustain an independent Fairbrother Group in case of RSNC backsliding.'

RSNC, umbrella organisation for the county trusts since 1976, ought to be the most powerful campaigner for the national nature conservation movement but has been handicapped by its federal status. Unlike the National Trust or RSPB it has no direct membership itself. Instead it relies for its core funding on a levy on the trusts' 170,000 or so membership, which is inadequate to sustain the size of staff appropriate for the country's main voluntary sector nature conservation watchdog. Hoping to augment its income through a sale-of-goods operation, it saw this collapse in the early 1980s and was bailed out by a DoE grant. While now more securely based, it suffers from the reluctance of its constituent trusts to increase their capitation contribution.

An additional problem arising from the Society's federal structure is its cumbersome decision-making process. All 47 trusts are represented on its 60-strong council, and each expects to be consulted in advance on policies and decisions before these are promulgated or implemented. When the bulk of trusts are themselves conservative in their attitudes, the prospect of vigorous action is limited.

Philip Lowe and Jane Goyder in *Environmental Groups in Politics* describe the environmental organisations as being predominantly 'open oligarchies'. By this they mean that they are run by a group of people who are to an extent self-perpetuating. While in formal terms they are democratically elected by the membership, in practice the governing body is self-selecting. At the same time, the organisation is 'open' in that it will not only allow, but actively encourage, the participation of newcomers who show they are keen and competent.

The RSNC operates a modified form of oligarchy, newcomers to its executive being encouraged only cautiously. Election procedures were, indeed, highly obscure until, in 1987, the executive issued a 15-page explanation of them in response to questions posed by LWT. The urban wildlife groups also function as open oligarchies, but are careful to pay attention to the 'open' element of the system.

The dangers of not doing so were dramatically illustrated by the near collapse of the Trust for Urban Ecology (TRUE) in spring 1987. After some years of neglecting to keep its membership in good repair, or to ensure that enough activists were recruited to its governing body, it faced financial difficulties. A rescue operation was successfully mounted by David Goode of GLEU, who became chairman of TRUE while Max Nicholson was elected president.

A falling out within the county trust movement also showed the risks of an organisation failing to adapt to changing circumstances. By 1986 the Leicester City Wildlife Project, whose genesis has been described in Chapter 4, had decided to become a more closely integrated part of the Leicester and Rutland Trust for Nature Conservation. The move was encouraged by Jenny Owen, chairwoman of the Project's management committee and an active figure in conservation circles. On the Leicestershire Trust's council, she also serves on RSNC's conservation committee and the Fairbrother executive, and has published several papers on urban ecology. Her husband, Denis Owen, is author of what is probably still the best guide to the wildlife of *Towns and Gardens*.

The merger progressed painfully. When the Project's bulletin was included in the Trust's newsletter, members complained they weren't interested in urban topics and found them intrusive. Members of the Trust's council were unsympathetic to the project's priorities, particularly its emphasis on education. Unhappy with the loss of their former freedom of action, the Project submitted a plea to the council for greater autonomy. The council refused, and so in 1987 the Project started the process of disentangling itself from the Trust.

In fairness to the county trusts it should be added that they have supported without complaint the principle of one trust, one vote. Regardless of the discrepancy between the Essex trust with its

10,000 members and the Birmingham Urban Wildlife Group with its 500, each has the same voting strength at RSNC's Council. Similarly, while the London trust has a respectable tally of members, its proportion of members to its catchment population is far less than almost all the other trusts. In compensation, the urban trusts are reaching a membership that the older trusts were failing to reach.

A portrait of the new type of city trust member is conveniently provided by a survey, carried out by Steve Micklewright as a UCL thesis, of the membership of the Avon and London trusts. Micklewright's findings were that urban trust members were predominantly middle-class and mostly in service, welfare and creative jobs. Not previously members of other county trusts, even where there was a former rural trust covering the area, they had joined to support conservation rather than to participate in it. Most had a recreational interest in wildlife rather than the solemn interest of a dedicated amateur naturalist, preferring the common and everyday wildlife around them as opposed to rarities. With a sophisticated understanding of current conservation issues such as threats to wildlife, they believed their trusts should engage in campaigning as well as in more traditional activities such as the establishment and maintenance of nature reserves.

A complement to this portrait of conservation as primarily a middle-class concern is the survey by Alison Millward and Barbara Mostyn, to be published in 1987, into public usage of urban nature reserves. One of the sites researched was Gillespie Park, close to the Arsenal football ground, where responses from this non-yuppie neighbourhood indicated widely accepted appreciation of this wildlife facility, both for its educational usefulness and as a local amenity. Despite this approbation, it was discovered before the report's publication that even such a well-established site was not secure. Islington Council had leased the land from British Rail and, though four years of the lease were outstanding, BR was putting this and adjacent land up for auction. At the time of writing, a campaign was under way to safeguard this borough's only significant area of wildspace – an example of the need for urban wildlife groups to act as local environmental watchdogs.

The role of urban wildlife groups, operating in areas where 80 per cent of Britain's population resides, is, however, already more than parochial. Alison Millward in her capacity as chairwoman of the Fairbrother Group and the RSNC urban steering group envisages a 'rejuvenation' of countryside conservation as a result of the input of the urban conservationists. As one experienced observer of the conservation scene commented:

> The urban groups operate rather like the Tribune or Bow groups in politics – a bit ahead of their respective parties.

References and further reading

How to Make a Wildlife Garden by Chris Baines (Elm Tree Books, 1985).
Nature Conservation Goes to Town (RSNC, 1980): these unpublished papers remain interesting and deserve to be made more widely available.
'Urban Conservation' by Chris Rose and Charlie Pye-Smith (*Vole*, January 1981).
Environmental Groups in Politics by Philip Lowe and Jane Goyder (Allen and Unwin, 1983).
Who Are Our Members? by Steve Micklewright (University College London, 1986, unpublished; digest in *Ecos*, spring 1987).
People and Nature in Cities by Alison Millward and Barbara Mostyn (NCC, 1987).
Towns and Gardens by Denis Owen (Hodder and Stoughton, 1978) is part of 'The Natural History of Britain and Northern Europe' series.
The Conservation Review (Webb and Bower, 1985) consists of a useful resumé of the various UK conservation organisations, plus accounts of projects entered for that year's Conservation Foundation awards scheme. The book includes what is possibly the most convenient list of conservation addresses, even if by now somewhat out of date.

7 | Politics and policies

A cameo of the relationship between politicians and pressure groups was provided by a meeting in a House of Commons committee room in mid-1986. On the one side was David Clark MP, Labour spokesman on conservation issues, supported by Labour Party researchers responsible for producing Labour's environment policy statement as part of its general election manifesto. On the other were leading environmental campaigners invited by the Green Alliance to offer advice to Labour's joint policy committee on the environment. Clark, indicating the committee's thinking, asked towards the end of the proceedings: 'Why do you give the Conservatives a good press when Labour has the better ideas?'

The answer was given by Robin Grove-White of the Council for the Protection of Rural England, a dynamic campaigning organisation despite its somewhat Edwardian title. Why, he asked, should they be grateful to Labour when, while in power up to 1979, its ministers had paid little attention to green issues? Green campaigners were not uncritical of the present government but, yes, they were naturally gratified when some ministers were receptive to ideas put to them. Good intentions, whether expressed by Conservative, Labour or other parties, were not enough. The good intentions – or otherwise – of the parties are here examined, beginning with the smallest party.

The Green Party 1986 manifesto, *green politics: fact and fiction* (greens appear to prefer lower case to capitals), is understandably aggrieved that the other parties have caught them bathing and walked away with their clothes. A feisty document, it rubbishes the other parties' green credentials before setting out its own wares. It swiftly dismisses the Conservatives thus:

> It has to be said from the outset that there is no substance to
> Tory claims even to be conservationists, let alone green. There

is not even an official publication of good environmental intentions from the Conservative Party proper. The greenest straws in the Tory wind come from an American university and a researcher in the Bow Group.

Of the Social Democratic Party it says:

A cheeky passage in the SDP's *Conservation and Change* says 'Labour in power has shown little interest in environmental problems'. In fact, the current leaders of the SDP were senior members of the Labour governments in question, so they can take little credit from the misplaced jibe.

It bats Liberals out of the window with the comment that:

What was said about the SDP's green pretensions in economic matters can be seen to apply to Liberals too.

Of the nationalist parties it observes that:

The SNP and Plaid Cymru might be regarded as single-issue political pressure groups with a set of policies tacked on to complete the picture.

Turning to Labour, it quotes Robin Cook MP admitting in *New Ground*, the magazine of SERA, the Socialist Environment and Resources Association, that:

If we are to be frank, Labour's record on ecological issues is wretched.

Its own policy on the environment it summarises as being the 'preservation and enhancement of the urban and rural environments, seeking a maximised balance [sic] between beauty, ecological diversity and public amenity.' Of the urban environment it adds that its aim is: 'To make inner cities greener through the provision of more allotments, gardens and city farms.' And, one hopes, wildspace. The problem for British greens is that, unlike their counterparts in West Germany and elsewhere who benefit from an electoral system involving proportional representation, they seem unlikely to win more than the occasional seat on a local council somewhere in the West Country.

As for the Social Democratic Party, even hardened political observers gasped when spokesman Bill Rodgers, notoriously hostile to environmentalists when Labour's transport minister, announced he may have got it wrong. The party's *Conservation and Change* spells out its urban conservation policies in somewhat superficial fashion, as though only half-briefed. The relevant section proposes more trees and gardens on council estates, and that 'derelict land should be reclaimed and in some cases used as allotments, in other cases protected as an ecological park'. It adds that 'canals, waterways and derelict railway lines should be used for leisure or other purposes.' This does not suggest a very informed awareness of how wildlife areas relate to each other, or that canals and railway lines – derelict or not – are important green corridors which ecological parks should ideally link into.

The voluntary sector is addressed in similarly chinese-meal style:

> The roles played by statutory non-governmental organisations and voluntary bodies in protecting the environment are considerable. We would not envisage such organisations being transformed by our proposed changes to the structure of government, although we would hope that their roles would be enhanced by the greater prominence that would be attached to environmental issues.

The document does not specify how it will assist this enhancement.

An Environment for the Future, the Liberals' discussion paper published after the Green Party diatribe, includes a recognition that:

> The greening of our urban areas is an important target. Such programmes would extend well beyond the conventional municipal flower beds and parks, for the aim should be to encourage a diversity of natural environments for wildlife to flourish and people to enjoy. In implementing this planning authorities should produce programmes for improvements to be carried out by any reasonable means available, including the use of grants to support local groups. We would also make available a fixed proportion of the rates or other local taxes being used

by parish/neighbourhood councils (or even by approved civic societies or tenants' association) for environmental improvement schemes chosen by them.

Simon Hughes MP, Liberal spokesman on the environment, is an eloquent platform speaker who is consistent in encouraging community groups to bully local politicians into protecting valued wildspace. In his own Bermondsey constituency, however, it can't be said that was very effective in preserving the Bricklayers Arms Sidings. Though the site was identified by the GLC ecology unit as one of London's half-dozen most important wasteland wildlife areas, British Rail gained permission to develop the land following a public inquiry which Hughes did not attend.

The report of Labour's policy committee, *The Environment*, is an impressively detailed document of some nine closely printed pages. Its paragraph on 'Planning and the environment' in the section on 'The urban environment' is a good blend of general principles and specific comments:

> Labour believes in the importance of nature conservation in cities as well as the countryside. Our aim is to safeguard urban wildlife habitats, to protect and enhance the natural environment, and to increase opportunities for people to enjoy the natural environment and the wildlife it supports.
>
> Nature conservation should be an integral element of the planning process rather than an optional extra. We will therefore:
>
> - Encourage local authorities to carry out surveys to identify land of wildlife and recreational value, include nature conservation policy statements in local and structure plans, and employ professional ecologists.
>
> - Ask all councils to consider setting up nature reserves in their areas.
>
> - See that government planning advice includes a presumption against the destruction of sites which have existing natural history value.
>
> - Encourage the creation of small nature gardens and larger natural parks.

In a fundamental respect, however, the statement is alarming.

While proposing a massive growth in state activity at national and local level, it virtually ignores the role of the voluntary sector. The Conservative government at least recognises this, though cynics may attribute this to the fact that volunteers are cheaper, in their statement *Conservation and Development*:

> The voluntary movement has experienced tremendous growth in the past few years. It has contributed much to the recent popularity of the environment as an issue of public and political debate; it has exercised increasing influence on the development of environmental policies; and it has become a major instrument of practical conservation. It would now be unthinkable to imagine environmental policies without the contribution of this voluntary movement.

Not for Labour, it wouldn't be. In its 10,000 word statement the word 'voluntary' appears twice. The role of the environmental NGOs is mentioned twice, one reference being only by inference ('Environmental representatives should be included on the boards of socially-owned industries.'). There is, to be sure, much talk of 'consultation' and even formal machinery as in: 'We will discuss with interested parties the possibility of setting up community environment councils, similar to community health councils, to ensure community involvement in environmental policy making.' These are weasel words, as the following paragraph reveals:

> We envisage a partnership between the different tiers of government and local voluntary groups. For example, if the local authority fails to set up nature reserves in its area, local groups could be given the resources to do so.

The reality is clear: only in the last resort will voluntary groups be allowed to manage nature gardens or nature parks. Otherwise nature reserves will be municipalised, becoming part of the parks manager's empire.

In my own submission to the joint policy committee I suggested that:

> In previous governments, and in local government still, Labour has too frequently viewed this area of activity (and others) as

a matter for legislation, bureaucratic machinery and DLO [direct labour organisation] implementation. Labour must in future accept a pluralist approach which allows people a role in planning and managing both the built and natural environment.

The statement in *The Environment*, while including many valuable specific recommendations as in the urban paragraph quoted above, is depressingly corporatist rather than pluralist. In Liverpool the consequences of such a statist philosophy have already been seen, where the city council withdrew support from the voluntary sector and refused funds for housing associations in its area. Those with direct experience of some Labour councillors' hostility to voluntary action, whatever their manifestos may promise, will fear their attitude will be regressive rather than progressive.

The dichotomy within different sectors of the Labour Party emerges in other documents. The *Green Policy* produced by the Labour-dominated Association of Municipal Authorities recognises that:

Self-management schemes are an objective in themselves . . . Wherever it is possible to increase the involvement of residents in the management and organisation of facilities, whether they be parks or tennis courts, the identification between people and their environment is strengthened and this is bound to be beneficial . . . The facility under their care is no longer something provided and run by others over which they have little control, and it becomes possible to build a much richer relationship between the residents, the facility and the local authority.

These are admirable sentiments, and, as seen in preceding chapters, some pragmatic Labour councils are happy to go a stage further and use all the free MSC labour they can get. In others, the idea that the public should be allowed a role in managing any municipal facility is anathema.

For their part, Conservative councils can be as reluctant to allow devolution of power to the grassroots as any doctrinaire Labour administration. In Tory Barnet local conservationists spent three years campaigning for proper care of Coppetts Wood and the nearby Glebelands, preparing a detailed plan for their future management as a county trust nature reserve. In late 1986 the council announced it accepted the management plan, but that it was going to run the Wood and common itself.

Various other documents produced by the Labour and the Conservative Parties illuminate their current thinking about particular aspects of conservation and the role of the voluntary sector. Southwark Council produced in 1986 the report *A Working Community*, launched by the Labour Party nationally in late 1986 as a blueprint for its plans to create one million new jobs within two years if elected as the next government. The creation of some 6,000 jobs within this borough was proposed: 4,400 as town hall employees, the rest in the private sector. The voluntary sector as a current or potential employer was nowhere mentioned. At a conference in January 1987 Labour's employment spokesman, John Prescott MP, was asked about this omission. His reply was:

> It would not be the policy of a future Labour government to aid the voluntary sector.

An additionally alarming aspect of the plan from a conservation point of view was its proposal for an environmental task force consisting of 20 workers and costing an annual £300,000 in wages and overheads. Given the poor record of existing parks staff in care of the natural environment, the prospect of a hit squad tidying up wasteland sites is not reassuring. It is depressing, too, to note the discrepancy between the sum of £0.3m which the council would like to spend on environmental improvements and the paltry amount (£8,000 pa) it allocates to the voluntary organisation within the borough, the Southwark Wildlife Group, which has been carrying out such work since 1981.

The chairman of the committee which produced Labour's statement was Tom Sawyer of the National Union of Public Employees, which represents town hall manual workers. Presenting the document at the Party's national conference he described 1986 as 'the year Labour discovered the environment'. Those involved in NGOs may hope that Labour will eventually recognise the existence and value of the voluntary sector.

The Conservatives, as pointed out by the Green Party pamphleteer, until 1986 had no formal environmental policy, successive Environment Secretaries making up policy on the hoof.

Michael Heseltine dreamed up Groundwork Trusts. Patrick Jenkin thought it a good idea to relax development control in the metropolitan green belt, and got clobbered by his own party's suburban MPs for his temerity. Kenneth Baker wasn't around long enough to do much except commission the report that led to the setting up of UK 2000. Nicholas Ridley arrived from the transport ministry as a noted 'dry', but with 'damp' William Waldegrave being given control of a mini environment ministry within the Department.

Protecting the Environment, produced by the Conservative Research Department, includes scant reference to urban nature conservation. The only other document which (at the time of writing) is effectively a Conservative policy statement is the already mentioned *Conservation and Development: The British Approach*. This glossy document was billed as the United Kingdom Government's Response to the World Conservation Strategy, and was presented to the 1986 Ottowa conference discussing progress in implementing the World Conservation Strategy.

It frankly recognises that:

> As will become apparent to the reader, there is no single British Environmental Policy . . . However, it should become apparent that running through the collection of policies set out in the subsequent chapters of this report, there is a common, unifying theme . . . 'development without destruction'.

As a pull-together of information about conservation since the war it is useful. As a guide to future action it is almost worthless. While the two environmental quangos, and in turn the NGOs, receive funding after an annual assessment of corporate plans, the Conservatives have produced no such forward programme.

A chart in *Conservation and Development* shows the scale of DoE support to the NCC since the election of the first Thatcher administration. Static in real terms for the first four years, it has doubled in the last four years, mainly to allow for the Conservancy's SSSI renotification workload. Yet, as described earlier, the amount allocated to the voluntary sector for core costs remains puny. The Conservatives would argue that funds reach the NGOs through other channels such as MSC and Urban Programme, but this is not an adequate basis for building a long-term conservation structure. As a NCC staffer comments: 'Our system of three-year grants is absurd when everyone knows there is a need for permanent aid.' Worse, early in 1987 the NCC announced that in future it would not be funding core posts, and that grant money would be directed towards projects. Coupled with the unexpected reduction in MSC CP places following the introduction of the Job Training Scheme, the effect is likely to be serious.

The chapter in *Conservation and Development* called 'Involving the Community: Voluntary Action and Public Enjoyment' begins with a statement presented by a Conservative government working party to the UN Conference on the Human Environment at Stockholm in 1972:

> Volunteering is fast ceasing to be an activity practised by a small minority for the benefit of the majority but it is becoming the means whereby the majority of citizens may become involved in their own community, whether in the form of pressure groups, whether by physical work in their immediate environment or in other ways.

Updating the picture, it continues:

> The numbers of people involved in some way in voluntary environmental groups runs into millions. Bodies ranging from the small neighbourhood community group concerned about the conservation of local amenities such as trees, through the local nature conservation trusts and civic groups, to large, well-funded, national organisations all have a contribution to make . . . Many are active leaders in environmental education, and some contribute significantly to law enforcement. As already noted, it was the voluntary movement which, in association with the statutory conservation agencies, took up the call in the World Conservation Strategy to produce a Conservation and Development Programme for the UK in 1983.

Despite this reliance on the voluntary sector, there is no mention in this section of future funding arrangements other than a business sponsorship scheme. Having boasted of its support for new Groundwork Trusts, which have little to do with the voluntary sector, the buck is passed elsewhere with the facile suggestion that 'even closer links between the business community and the voluntary movement are both desirable and necessary if levels of spending on conservation are to keep on rising steeply.'

Though the Conservatives effusively recognise the work of the voluntary sector, it is worth noting a speech in the autumn of 1986 made by Home Secretary Douglas Hurd which revealed the traditional Conservative view of voluntary action as ideally conforming to the 'vicar's wife' style of do-gooding:

If you believe, as I do strongly, that one of the difficulties of our present system of government is the increasing role of pressure groups and interest groups, then one has to be a little wary of changes which would in practice add still further to the pressures which these groups exert on policy-making, pressures which do not necessarily add up to the general good. Pressure groups interpose themselves between the executive on the one hand and Parliament and the electorate on the other. That constitutional relationship should not be distorted, nor the executive's proper accountability weakened. If freedom of information simply means freedom for pressure groups to extract from the system only those pieces of information which buttress their own cause, then conceivably the result might be greater confusion and worse government.

However, in what was perhaps a form of backtracking from this vehement attack on the role of pressure groups, Hurd made a further speech early in 1987 which was more characteristic of the 'wet' wing of the Conservatives. He warned the Party and its supporters living in the suburbs and shires that they ignored the inner cities at their peril. To his Bow Group audience he suggested that a harmonious community could only be built 'through bringing volunteers together as active citizens'.

Though Douglas Hurd bewails the unduly prominent role of the voluntary sector, the evolution of the new DoE circular on nature conservation illustrates very precisely how useful outside advice can be. Until 1987 the main planning guidelines were in the DoE advisory circular 108/77, *Nature Conservation and Planning*. In 1986 a draft of its replacement, *Nature Conservation*, caused dismay throughout the conservation movement. Its vapidity was summed up in the Department's own covering letter which states that 'this circular is not considered to have any significant expenditure and manpower implications for local planning authorities.' Though a hefty document of over 20 pages its key sentence, to be quoted at planning committees and public inquiries, was actually weaker than that in its predecessor which read:

> The Secretaries of State look to local authorities to take full account of natural conservation factors both in formulating structure and local plans, and in the consideration of individual planning applications.

In the new 1986 draft, this was diluted to:

> Nature conservation may be a material consideration in the determination of some planning applications, to be weighed along with other planning considerations, including the provisions of the development plan for the area and relevant national policies as set out in planning circulars.

The circular in its final draft, issued in early 1987, remained weak but, in presentational terms, was a great improvement. It was written in English, whereas its predecessor was turgidly convoluted. It contained full recognition that nature exists in towns as well as the countryside. And the key sentence now read:

> The Secretaries of State also look to local authorities to take full account of nature conservation in the consideration of individual planning applications.

Organisations submitting their comments had included Wildlife Link, the national consortium of conservation organisations, which produced a detailed report *Local Authorities and Wildlife*. Its proposals, together with those of David Tyldesley in *Gaining Momentum*, will remain valid as an informal Circular whose philosophy is:

> The government should encourage the LAs to accept a considerably increased role in conserving and enhancing wildlife on their own estates and throughout their area.

More useful and forward-looking than many political documents is *The Livable City*, a report by Joan Davidson and Ann MacEwan, which is now four years old but remains the fullest philosophical statement of sustainable development in the urban context. It describes sustainability as:

> Matching the superficially conflicting goals of development and conservation: development as a means of meeting human needs and improving the quality of life and conservation as the use of resources, especially living ones, in a sustainable way, safeguarding all their benefits for future generations.

Its justification for creating fully paid permanent jobs in place of reliance on MSC labour rests on recognition of the fact that:

> There is more and more circumstantial evidence that bad environments are associated with urban alienation and violence, that good environment could be a decisive factor in fostering local investment and regeneration.

A survey of the infrastructure of the conservation industry is provided by Dartington Institute's report for the NCC, *Employment and Nature Conservation*. Produced in December 1985, it assesses the number of jobs not only in mainstream conservation organisations but in related fields, as follows:

A	Mainstream nature conservation bodies	1,607
B	General conservation bodies	1,741
C	Landowners/owning bodies	2,735
D	Capital works etc.	1,150
E	Public facilities for nature conservation	3,014
F	Other visitor services	–
G	Media/publishing	1,400
H	Production and retail of appropriate goods	1,860
I	Education and Training	150
J	Research, Development, Monitoring	600
	Totals:	14,257

The researchers conclude that there is now an identifiable conservation industry which overlaps with other sectors, notably agriculture and forestry, recreation and tourism, and education and training. They add that while an EEC survey suggested that the effect of conservation on jobs is broadly neutral, 'in the narrower field of nature and landscape conservation the employment effects are strongly positive.' Although not a main part of their brief they also provide figures for MSC workers, given in more detail in their *Work and the Environment* report. Apart from the observation that a massive increase in MSC places could produce full-time supervisory posts, they do not speculate on the degree to which MSC displaces other permanent jobs.

Government, the political parties, agencies and NGOs cannot duck the issue. If the natural environment needs protection, appropriate resources need to be made available for the task to be carried out effectively. As seen above, not one of the political parties particularises about where, and how much, money should be spent.

It is the task of conservation organisations, both statutory and voluntary, to identify jobs which are essential to the care of the city's natural environment. It will be the responsibility of the politicians, if their manifestos mean anything, to provide resources for those jobs at local as well as national level.

There is a danger that, now the general election is out of the way, the parties will feel no need to pander to those voters influenced by 'green' issues. With no electoral incentive for further action, the parties are likely to rest content. There will be local council and county council elections each year, but unless conservationists make protection of the natural environment an issue when candidates are preparing for these hustings, the subject will occupy a lowly place on the politicians' agenda.

There may be many in the conservation movement who naively believe that conservation is an apolitical activity. Yet, as David Tyldesley points out in an open letter to conservationists in the first issue of *Urban Wildlife*, the first journal of urban nature conservation, published in summer 1987:

> I cannot over-emphasise how crucial it is to win the consistent support of elected council members if the urban wildlife programme is to reach its real potential. I believe that the active

involvement of local authorities is the greatest asset that any urban wildlife scheme can acquire. If you need land, resources, money or manpower, professsional skills and a sensitive system of development control and forward planning, then elected members need to be convinced.

In the decade and a half since 1974, urban nature conservation has progressed from being the marginal interest of a handful of professional and amateur enthusiasts. In the late 1980s it is widely seen as an important ingredient of post-industrial urban living. This book has attempted to describe how this came about and to indicate some of the issues that need to be resolved if greening activities are to be sustained. What happens next will determine the character of our towns and cities for the foreseeable future.

References and further reading

green politics: fact and fiction is available from the Green Party, 10 Station Parade, Balham High Road, London SW12 9AZ.
Conservation and Change: Policy for the Environment is available from the SDP, 4 Cowley Street, London SW1.
An Environment for the Future: A Liberal Party Discussion Paper is available from the Liberal Party, 1 Whitehall Place, London SW1.
The Environment is available from the Labour Party, 150 Walworth Road, London SE17 1JT.
A Working Community (LB Southwark, 1986).
Greening the Tories: New Policies on the Environment by Andrew Sullivan (Centre for Policy Studies, 1985).
Conservation and the Conservatives by Tony Patterson (Bow Publications, 1984).
Protecting the Environment, No. 17 in the 'Politics Today' series of leaflets produced by the Conservative Research Department (October 1986) is available from the Conservative Party Central Office, 32 Smith Square, London SWI.
Conservation and Development: The British Approach (DoE, 1986) is an exorbitant £10 for 56 pages.
Nature conservation (HMSO, 1987).
Local Authorities and Wildlife (Wildlife Link, 1986).

Employment and Nature Conservation (Dartington Institute, 1985). *Urban Wildlife* (Packard Publishing), the journal of urban nature conservation, includes in its summer 1987 issue an account by William Waldegrave of his department's funding policies for the voluntary environmental organisations.

Gazetteer

INTRODUCTION

The following guide to urban wildlife sites concentrates on the conurbations that form Greater London and the six metropolitan counties. Two other counties with major built-up areas – Avon and Cleveland – are also included, as are sites in South Wales and Scotland. Leicester is also covered as an example of a city notably adventurous in its concern for wildspace.

The guide, though not comprehensive, is the fullest register of urban sites to be published in collected form. Most attention is given to those which are recognised nature reserves in inner urban areas, but not all sites listed are formal reserves. Parks and public open spaces have been included when there is wildlife interest or if they have nature trails, as are areas such as canals, river valleys and disused railway lines forming green or wildlife corridors. Urban fringe sites are supplemented in some cases by the listing of reserves on former industrial land between towns. Victorian cemeteries, which usually have considerable wildlife value, are mentioned only if they are managed as nature reserves.

Entries for the sites merely sketch the diversity of plant and animal life each supports, fuller information being available from the contact addresses.

Listings of wildlife sites show, where possible, ownership, area (shown in hectares: 1 ha = 10,000 square metres or 2.5 acres) and the organisation managing the land, with relevant addresses given at the end of the section.

Visitors to all sites should observe certain obvious rules, such as keeping to pathways. Sorties into the undergrowth may cause trampling of delicate areas and disturbance of, for instance, nesting birdlife. Taking plants from sites is very bad practice. It is also illegal.

Access to some sites is restricted to prevent damage to habitats and undue disturbance of wildlife, and readers are requested to respect this limitation. They are included in order to give a more complete picture of the inventory of wildlife resources in each area – and also to tempt readers to join the managing organisation, thereby becoming entitled to visit such reserves.

Readers are urged to join local wildlife groups. Without their efforts, many of the sites included would not have been safeguarded, and their continuing maintenance depends on groups having adequate resources. Addresses are given at the end of each section. (Please send an sae if requesting information.) Details may also be obtained from the two leading conservation organisations involved in urban sites:

Royal Society for Nature Conservation (RSNC), The Green, Nettleham, Lincoln LN2 2NR (0522-752326).

British Trust for Conservation Volunteers (BTCV), 36 St Mary's Street, Wallingford, Oxon OX10 0EU (0491-39766).

Readers wishing to provide updating information for future editions should send it to the publisher at the address on the reverse of the title page.

Abbreviations used in the gazetteer:

BR	British Rail
BWB	British Waterways Board
CC	County Council or City Council (The context makes clear which is referred to)
CCT	County Conservation Trust
CEGB	Central Electricity Generating Board
DoE	Department of the Environment
GLC	Greater London Council
GLEU	Greater London Ecology Unit
LB	London Borough of
LEB	London Electricity Board
LNR	Local Nature Reserve (i.e. it is designated as protected and properly managed)
LWT	London Wildlife Trust
MBC	Metropolitan Borough Council
MSC	Manpower Services Commission
NCC	Nature Conservancy Council
NHS	Natural History Society
RSPB	Royal Society for the Protection of Birds
SSSI	Site of Special Scientific Interest
TNC	Trust for Nature Conservation (There is a gradual move towards renaming them all 'Wildlife Trusts')
TRUE	Trust for Urban Ecology

Greater London

Frequent mention is made in this section of the London Wildlife Habitat Survey commissioned by the former Greater London Council and carried out by the London Wildlife Trust in 1984/5. The first report of the survey was published as the GLC's *Ecology Handbook No.4* (available from the Greater London Ecology Unit, address at the end of this section) and covers London's woodlands as well as the range of wildlife sites in Barnet and Lewisham. A number of the sites in these pages are managed by or owe their recognition to the London Wildlife Trust (LWT). Sites are listed by borough.

BARKING

With the Roding, an important river in the London hierarchy, as a western boundary and the small Beam River to the east, the borough has some interesting habitats along its borders. Other wildlife areas are on the Thamesfront where giant industries were built to take advantage of reclaimed marshes and river access for raw materials.

Thameside Community Farm Park
Thames Road.
CEGB. 13 ha. Thameside Association. Wardened (01-594 8449).
In the early 1980s the local community persuaded the Central Electricity Generating Board to release land to the west of the defunct Barking Power Station for the purpose of a nature reserve and city farm. The land consisted mainly of pulverised fuel ash with ditches draining the area and lagoons formed by the unfilled-in lower lying parts. Birch and sallow now provide small coppices for birdlife. The nutrient-poor soil has encouraged the growth of orchids, and despite the acidity the channels support varied plant

and animal life. A hide allows observation of the gulls and waders on the lagoons. The farm is available for school visits by arrangement.

The **Beam River** forms the southern part of the Dagenham Corridor, a green wedge dividing Romford and Hornchurch from the rest of London. The part in Barking is mostly grassland around lakes created by gravel diggings, including:

Eastbrookend
The Chase, Dagenham Road, Romford.
LB Barking. 57 ha. LWT.
This large site is a patchwork of grazed grassland with large lakes and shallow ponds, with the River Beam flowing through it. Scattered throughout are thickets of scrub and small copses of woodland. Together they form an extremely attractive landscape which is also very good for wildlife.

BARNET

The borough covers the catchment of the two streams which join together to form the Brent: Silk Stream to the west and Dollis Brook in the centre. To the east, Pymme's Brook runs into the Lee and in the north Mimshall Brook runs to nowhere, disappearing into the ground at Water's End. The sites described here, some managed by the Hertfordshire and Middlesex Trust for Nature Conservation (HMTNC), are grouped along these four valleys.

Rowley Green
Rowley Lane, Arkley.
LB Barnet. 12 ha. HMTNC and LWT.
The Common, on the north slope of the Arkley ridge, is now mostly covered by oak and birch woodland but is notable for its sphagnum bog which has an unusual (in London terms) range of wetland plants and insect and amphibian species. Remnant acid grassland survives at the centre of the site, which is being managed by the two county wildlife trusts to prevent natural succession further encroaching on the ponds, bog, heath and grassland.

Totteridge Fields
Totteridge Common, N20.
95 ha.
Rising at **Moat Mount Open Space** (87 ha), Dollis Brook forms
a deep valley between Barnet and Totteridge, the fields on either
side having been identified by the GLC survey as a 'Countryside
Conservation Area'. The western part remains as farmland but the
eastern parts are public open space. A riverside walk begins here
and continues to Woodside Park where it is joined by Folly Brook.

Darlands Lake
The Close, Totteridge Village, N20.
LB Barnet. 5 ha. HMTNC.
Folly Brook rises at **Highwood Hill** and runs through
Totteridge Common (5 ha) before reaching the lake, formed
by damming the stream and formerly used as a duck decoy.
Important for overwintering wildfowl, its marshy fringes contain
varied reeds and herbs.

Copthall Railway Walk is on the far side of the golf course
where the abandoned Mill Hill to Edgware tube line crosses
Copthall Playing Fields. The track contines as **Burnt Oak Walk**
across the valley of Dean's Brook.

Coppetts Wood
Woodland Walk, North Circular Road, N12.
LB Barnet. 18 ha.
The Wood, a remnant of the former Finchley Common, includes
ancient woodland – mostly oak with an understorey of hazel,
hornbeam and sweet chestnut which were formerly coppiced –
and grassland which is being invaded by scrub. The nearby
Glebelands (5.5 ha) supports many wetland plant species in the
channels leading from the springs issuing from the gravel capping
of the London clay. The drier areas are also a pleasing mixture
of grassland, scrub and woodland to which there is free public
access.

Barnet is one of the first two boroughs whose sites are described
in the series of *Ecology Handbooks*, mentioned above and available
from GLEU.

BEXLEY

The eastern boundary of the borough (and Greater London) follows not the River Cray but the far side of the valley, thus taking in a chunk of Kentish countryside. Its Thamesfront includes important grazing marshes at Erith and around Dartford Creek. On the hills above the Thames, the woodlands around Lesnes Abbey are among London's finest.

Crayford Marshes
Manor Road and Whitehall Lane, Erith.
80 ha.
At the mouth of the River Darent, the Marshes were in 1983 subject of a council plan to develop a large part for housing and industry. The scheme was investigated in a public inquiry which set important precedents for the protection of wildlife habitats, the inspector describing them in unusually evocative terms for this kind of formal report: 'Much of it is a natural area, left, as it were, to go its own way without regard to the workaday world at its edges. To see a heron land or take off, hear the flight call of a redshank or spot other birds among a network of water-filled ditches (intriguing to the ecologist, amateur or professional), is to appreciate the intrinsic value of the area.'
On the river side of the flood embankment, and showing clearly on the Ordnance Survey map, are the **Anchor Bay Saltings**, London's last remaining salt marsh. The site has been talked of as a possible marina, and the Marshes are once again under threat as the council has renewed its attempts to develop the area.

Lesnes Abbey Wood
Abbey Road, Belvedere.
LB Bexley. 86 ha.
On either side of the small valley in which the Abbey was built in 1176, the Wood is among the 23 identified by the Habitat Survey as being of metropolitan importance. Mostly oak and sweet chestnut, formerly coppiced, it also includes mature hornbeam, wild cherry and field maple in the part overlooking the Abbey ruins. The most spectacular feature of its ground flora is the profusion of wild daffodils each spring.

Greater London 97

On the other side of New Road is West Wood with a stream running through its varied woodland. Woodlands on the east of the Cray include **Joydens Wood** (127 ha, part only in London), **Chalk Wood** (27 ha) and **Gattons Plantation**, formerly owned by the Forestry Commission and being purchased by Bexley Council and the Woodland Trust. Nearby and adjoining the North Cray Road, **Home Wood** is being designated an SSSI.

North Cray Woods
Rectory Lane, Sidcup Hill, Sidcup.
LB Bexley.
An area of ancient oak and ash woodland lies within the grounds of the Foots Cray Meadows. This site is being managed by London Wildlife Trust in conjunction with the North-West Kent Urban Fringe Project.

BRENT

While the River Brent crosses the borough diagonally from north-east to south-west and a long portion of the Paddington Branch of the Grand Union Canal runs through the south from Harlesden to Horsenden Hill, the borough has only a couple of major wildlife sites – but makes the best of them. A recent addition is **The Ducker** (land surrounding Harrow School's former swimming pool, hence its name) where plans for a mosque complex were, in 1987, rejected following a public inquiry.

Brent Reservoir
Birchen Grove, NW9.
LB Brent. 81 ha. Field study centre and ranger service.
Built in 1835 to keep the canal topped up, this large lake (50 ha) manages to combine its use for dinghy sailing with its role as a major bird refuge. Breeding birds include great crested and little grebes, sedge and reed warblers and many others. Winter sees good numbers of wildfowl including tufted ducks, pochard, shoveler, gadwall and teal with snipe, water rail and short-eared owl among other visitors. Rafts have been moored in front of the eastern part of the lake to protect it from disturbance by sailing boats, and also to serve as roosting and nesting places. Popularly

known as Welsh Harp because of the shape created by the two arms where it is fed by Silk Stream and Dollis Brook, the wetland area around the junction with the former illustrates successional vegetation to wet woodland where crack willow predominates.

Barn Hill and Fryent Way Open Spaces
Fryent Way, NW9.
LB Brent. 102 ha. Ranger service.
Barn Hill (20 ha) was formerly part of the Repton-designed Wembley Park which at the turn of the century became a golf course, and was bought by the local council in 1927 – Fryent Way being built across the adjoining fields in 1935. A decorative woodland surrounds the hill, near the top of which, disconcertingly, is a pond – its origin unknown.
Fryent Way (82 ha) was bought by the Middlesex county council in 1938 and leased as farmland until 1957 when it became public open space. Its hedgerows survive with their ditches, some being estimated as 700 years old. Certainly the field pattern hasn't changed much since an estates map of 1597. Fryent has its own eminence, Gotford's Hill, in its centre.

A nature trail plus details of 'Countryside in Brent' happenings is available from the Leisure Services Department, Recreation Division, Brent Council, Brent House, High Road, Wembley HA9 6SX (01-903 1400).

BROMLEY

Largest of London's boroughs by far (15,179 ha compared to Havering's 11,780 ha), its southern part has more in common with Kent than Greater London. The rest of the borough covers the catchment of the Ravensbourne and its tributaries.
As its name suggests, **Spring Park** (12 ha) is one of the sources of the Ravensbourne in the form of The Beck. Giving its name to Beckenham, it runs north through patches of woodland such as **High Broom Wood** (3 ha) adjacent to the Bethlem Royal Hospital, a stretch of woodland and glades alongside a stretch of the river where the bed and banks are happily unimproved. After feeding the lakes of Kelsey Park it is joined by the Pool at Cator Park.
The Pool River rises at Shirley, surfacing briefly at Elmers End before reaching Cator Park, beyond which is **Copers Cope** (1.5

ha), a disused nursery and fragment of ancient woodland on the banks of the stream, recently the subject of a public inquiry into development proposals. The Pool reaches the Lewisham boundary at Lower Sydenham. At Upper Sydenham the borough includes **Crystal Palace Park** (42 ha) below the heights which are a centuries-old divide between dioceses and parishes and are now the meeting point of five boroughs – Lambeth, Southwark, Lewisham, Bromley and Croydon.

The Ravensbourne flows from the ponds at the centre of **Keston Common** (176 ha), a remarkable area containing heather heathland, the ponds and Keston Bog. Notwithstanding its status as an SSSI the ponds and surrounding area are a favourite weekend spot for Londoners chary of the uncharted countryside of deepest Kent.

The Quaggy River rises in Sundridge Park, a southern extension of the green corridor followed by the Green Chain Walk (see **GREENWICH**) and occupied by a couple of golf courses and **Elmstead Wood** (24 ha). A tributary, Kyd Brook, is fed by streams from **Crofton Heath** (68 ha), part of a green wedge separating suburban Orpington from the rest of London. The Heath is a mixture of woodland of 'metropolitan importance' and ground flora described in detail in the *Ecology Handbook*.

Northward the streams meet other feeders from **Petts Wood** (54 ha) and **St Paul's Cray Common** (34 ha). The Wood, owned by the National Trust, is described in the *Ecology Handbook* as 'ancient woodland particularly notable for its rare plants and for the relatively large area of alder-dominated woodland. There are four streams within the woodland and here the flora is richer. The shallow valleys are dominated by alder, often with ash, birch, hazel and alder buckthorn.'

To the north of St Paul's Cray Road is **Hoblingwell Wood** (7 ha) including a valley mosaic of herbs and grassland, scrub and woodland with a pond and swamp feeding a small stream. To the west is:

Scadbury Park
Sidcup By-Pass, Chislehurst.
LB Bromley. 53 ha.
A former hunting park, it was acquired by the council in 1983, having been intended as a housing site. In addition to its variegated

woodland, its farmland with meadows, pool, streams and hedges is continuing in agricultural use but is crossed by public footpaths. Also on the Sidcup By-Pass a short distance to the east are:

Ruxley Gravel Pits
Sidcup By-Pass, St Paul's Cray.
Southern Water Authority. 17 ha. Kent TNC.
A wildlife haven since extraction ended in 1951, it is leased by a local angling association and jointly managed by the society and the Kent Trust as a nature reserve. As well as its areas of open water, marginal swamp vegetation provides a good habitat for invertebrates as well as a range of feeding and nesting birds. The remainder of the area is grassland and scrub with over 500 plants being recorded on the site overall. Access is restricted to Kent TNC members. Access was not, however, denied to a new stretch of the M20 which now zooms across the southern edge of the site.

Beyond the Cray is a large area of countryside with orchards and pick-your-own market gardens, and including two woodlands of interest. Straddling the railway, **Bourne Wood** (24 ha) has streams draining both east and west into the Cray, but there is no public access. A mile or so south is:

The Warren
Crockenhill Road, St Mary Cray.
LB Bromley and private.
A complex of acid grassland and woodland, the eastern and private portion contains a restored lake where amphibians including great crested newt now flourish. Uncontrolled access on the public part of the site by trail riders and air rifle assassins causes problems.

CAMDEN

With Primrose Hill in the south-west and Hampstead Heath in the north, the borough has a generous share of open space, yet the part nearest the City is much less well provided for. The Regent's Canal having been recognised by the council as an important green corridor, planting is in hand to enhance its wildlife interest.

Hampstead Heath
320 ha.
A convenient brief introduction to the history and plantlife of Londoners' favourite common is the *Hampstead Heath Flora* (GLC, 1986). Hunter Davies includes it in his guide to ten London parks, pointing out that if you want the handy map of the Heath with suggested walks, 'You have to barge into the Superintendent's office (just on the left as you enter from Highgate Road) and demand one.'

Highgate Cemetery
Swains Lane, N6.
Private. 14 ha.
The Cemetery remains an illustration of the Victorian idea that burial grounds should be for the recreation and edification of the living as well as cities of the dead. When commercial use and management declined after the war, intruding vegetation added to the decorative planting of Pennethorne's original design. Restricted access. Details of guided tours and a guide to the wildlife as well as the monuments in the cemetery are available from the Friends of Highgate Cemetery, c/o 5 View Road, N6 4DJ. (Please send large sae.)

Camley Street Natural Park
Camley Street, NW1.
LB Camden. 1 ha. LWT. LNR. Study centre (01-833 2311).
Britain's finest example of an urban habitat creation site, it was laid out by the GLC on a former coal wharf by the side of the Regent's Canal in 1983. A bank of woodland shelters a much-dipped pond and wetland. The park became in 1986 only the third statutory Local Nature Reserve in London.

Adelaide Road
Chalk Farm, NW3.
LB Camden. 0.5 ha. Adelaide Road Nature Reserve Association.
Alongside the Euston railway line, the reserve has been established with the familiar mixture of resources deployed in setting up urban community nature gardens. The North London Polytechnic's MSC-funded Urban Spaces Scheme surveyed and mapped the site. A BTCV task force funded by the council constructed paths and

steps, with DoE derelict land grant for fence mending. Local volunteers clear litter and invasive plant species such as Japanese knotweed. A couple of schools study here, and the project is run by a management committee consisting of representatives from the above organisations plus local tenants' associations and the London Wildlife Trust's borough group.

CITY OF LONDON

While the 'Square Mile' contains no major parks there is an unexpected variety of churchyards, squares and private gardens, totalling 15 ha, and wildlife including bats and kestrels. The churchyards, now among the 100 or so open spaces managed by the Corporation of the City of London, comprise half the area's open space – many of them the result of efforts of the Metropolitan Public Gardens Association.

The lawns around The Tower of London, with its famous stock of ravens (imported from Cornwall and the Highlands), and The Temple (consisting of the Middle and Inner Temple), with its former rookery, are among the larger open greenspaces. Largest is Finsbury Circus, tame survivor of what used to be marshy moorland outside the City walls which are recalled in the name Moorgate. Drained, raised and laid out as gardens as early as 1606 they are, suggests the late John Talbot White in his *Country London*, 'effectively London's first [public] park'.

CROYDON

With the largest population of any London borough (317,000) it also has the most public open space (apart from Richmond, which has Richmond Park), a total amounting to the entire area of Islington. The bulk is in the south, a broad strip of downland on a south-west to north-east axis from Coulsdon to Selsdon, where it links with the heaths of the Addington Hills.

In the north, Croydon was once covered by the Great North Wood but today little remains except the names – Norwood, Selhurst, Thornton Heath – apart from patches at Beulah Heights and Convent Wood.

Selsdon Wood
Old Farleigh Road, Selsdon.
National Trust. 81 ha. LB Croydon.
Acquired by subscription in the years following the formation of
a Committee for the Preservation of Selsdon Wood in 1924, the
deeds were handed to the NT in 1936, management being
undertaken by the borough. Oak woodland has been supplemented
by regular planting of other species including beech, larch and
spruce, coppicing being part of the annual programme. Four
pastures provide unimproved grasslands with a good crop of
grasses and herbs. Parts of the woodland are enclosed as bird
sanctuaries.
On the far side of the adjacent golf course on Featherbed Lane is:

Hutchingson's Bank
Featherbed Lane, at junction with Farleigh Dean Crescent,
Addington.
LB Croydon. 20 ha. LWT.
A species-rich chalk downland containing a collection of rare plants
and insects. The site is presently covered by large amounts of scrub
which is shading out the rich plant life.

Bramley Bank
Riesco Drive, Addington.
LB Croydon. 11 ha. LWT.
On a slope overlooking housing this mixed woodland suffers the
effects of heavy use and needs protective management if its
woodland quality is to survive and improve. Its pond has been
restored and now supports five amphibian species. An adjacent
area of acid grassland has been given over to horse pasturage.
To the north of the wood are the handsome grounds of Heathfield
House, rising to:

Addington Hills
Coombe Lane, Addington.
LB Croydon. 52 ha.
An evocative mixture of heather and grassland where management
of the heathland has been put in hand, but there is damaging erosion
of the surface and extent of these areas arising from visitor
pressure. An observation platform offers one of the finest views
across London.

Woodside

Tennison Road, Woodside, SE25.
LB Croydon. 3 ha.
A former claypit of the brickworks has become a lake with good marginal vegetation and invertebrate populations and a popular fishing spot. The lake is safeguarded as a nature reserve and attempts are being made to gain protection for the surrounding grassland.

To the east is **South Norwood Sewage Farm** (Harrington Road, Elmers End, SE25), which is zoned by Croydon council as a country park, its layout to be financed by the building of houses on part of the area.

At its northernmost tip the borough boundary crosses Streatham Common passing just north of **Convent Wood** (5 ha), a privately owned (by the convent) woodland which functions as a wildlife oasis.

EALING

The borough is more or less surrounded by the Grand Union Canal, its northern and western boundary running close to the Paddington Branch and its southern border following the main line. The River Brent meanders through its centre in a C-shape between Hanger Lane and Boston Manor – the river, but not the borough boundary, thereafter continuing to the Thames at Brentford.

Horsenden Hill

Horsenden Lane North, Greenford.
LB Ealing. 100 ha. Ranger service.
Highest point of the borough, the hill survives as a large area of ancient landscape – mostly grassland crossed by hedgerows. **Horsenden Wood** (3.6 ha) in the north-western corner is an oak and hornbeam woodland where the understorey has virtually disappeared as a result of over-zealous park-keeping, but is now being restored as part of the council's more sophisticated approach introduced in 1984. Haymaking has been restarted on 20 ha of meadows where, despite decades of close mowing, a variety of herbs are reappearing including cuckoo flower, ragged robin, pepper saxifrage and sneezewort, with an associated increase in

invertébrates including several butterfly species.

The hedgerows sustain typical woodland plants such as hazel, Midland hawthorn, yellow archangel, dog's mercury, ramsons and bluebell which suggest they originated as strips left over when woodlands were cleared for fields. A few lingering ponds have been cleared and restocked with locally occurring species. A leaflet, *Horsenden Hill Countryside Walk*, (40p inc. p&p) is available from the council: Parks and Amenities Division, 24 Uxbridge Road, Ealing, W5 2BP (01-579 2424).

Perivale Wood
Sunley Gardens, Greenford.
Selborne Society. 11 ha. LNR.
On the other side of the canal the Wood (also known as the Brent Vale Bird Sanctuary) has been managed by the Selborne Society since the beginning of the century. Founded in 1885 and named after the parish of Gilbert White, at one time the Society had several branches around the country but is now only concerned with this single ancient woodland. Identified by the Habitat Survey as one of the only seven woods of metropolitan importance in the whole of north London, the Wood is a perfect example of its type – oak on clay with coppiced hazel understorey – its ground cover including a spectacular burst of bluebells in springtime. Until the 1920s it was managed in traditional style for timber and poles, and its 20-plus species of trees and shrubs include exceptionally large examples of ash, field maple and crab apple as well as the wild service tree. Two small meadows display buttercups and lady's smock, and birdlife is prolific. Though one of London's two earliest Local Nature Reserves there is no regular public access, but visits can be arranged through the Society c/o 12 Hall Drive, Hanwell, W7.

Fox Wood
Hillcrest Road, Hanger Lane, W5.
LB Ealing. 2 ha. LWT.
On the other side of Fox Lane from Hanger Hill Park (8 ha) overlooking the Brent valley, a former reservoir is surrounded by secondary woodland now managed as a nature reserve. Mature oaks with an understorey of holly, hawthorn and blackberry supports a good birdlife including chiffchaff, blackcap, nuthatch, woodpeckers and tawny owl.

On the Greenford side of the valley is the **Litten** educational reserve (1.6 ha), its ponds, grove and grassland which can be visited by arrangement with the warden (01-574 2261).

ENFIELD

London's most northern borough covers the rivers draining from Enfield Chase, a former hunting forest, eastwards into the Lee. At its northmost point, Cuffley Brook runs through Whitewebbs Park past Bulls Cross to the Lee at Enfield Lock. Further south Salmon's Brook, fed by its tributaries from Trent Park country park, runs diagonally south-eastwards almost to the Lee at Pickett's Lock where it is canalised southwards to Pymme's Brook at the Lee Valley Viaduct.

The Pymme provides the borough's inner boundary which runs on the southern side of its valley from New Southgate to the Lee. Later passing through Islington and Haringey, the New River flows more or less north/south through the centre of the borough from the Hertfordshire border at Bulls Cross and exiting at Bowes Park.

Fir and Pond Woods
LB Enfield. 27 ha. HMTNC.
Managed by the Hertfordshire and Middlesex TNC, this is part of Enfield Chase Forest, which once covered 8,000 ha, the woodland being a mixture of hornbeam, oak and birch. As its name indicates, Pond Wood includes a small lake, plus a wet meadow, grassland and heath. The lichens are of special interest, and the breeding bird population includes all three British woodpeckers, little grebe, garden warbler and tree pipit. The pond-fed stream joins the Cuffley at **Forty Hill** (105 ha).

Trent Park
Cockfosters Road, Enfield.
LB Enfield. 227 ha.
Enclosed as a park in 1776 and bought by Middlesex county council in 1952, the mansion is now part of Middlesex Polytechnic while the grounds were developed by the GLC as a country park. At the centre is the Fish Pond, formed by damming Leeging Beech Gutter which runs eastwards to form Salmon's Brook. A nature trail describes the surroundings of the lake and a leaflet describing it

is available from the council at the Parks Department, Civic Centre, Silver Street, Enfield (01-366 6565).

To the west of the park is Beech Hill Park on the far side of which, between Sewits Hill and Newmans Hill is **Covert Way Field** (6.5 ha), a former pasture managed by the council as a nature reserve.

GREENWICH

Though an inner London borough – it is covered by the Inner London Education Authority (ILEA) – it has the characteristics of an outer borough with plentiful wildspace including large tracts of ancient woodland. On its long riverfront the new town of Thamesmead has arisen on the Plumstead Marshes that were rifle ranges and ammunition stores for the Woolwich Arsenal until after the last war.

Tump 53
Bentham Road, SE28.
Thamesmead Trust. 2 ha. LWT. Wardened (01-310 1500).
The moated ammunition stores built around 1890 are known as 'tumps', of which three or so survive. This one, adjacent to a school and houses, is managed as an educational reserve. The island at the centre of the encircling water and reed beds is overgrown with trees and a bird haven. Efforts are being made to ensure a second tump retains its island sanctuary while at the same time allowing fishermen's pitches around the outside of the lake.

Green Chain Walk
Access from Oxleas Wood, Shooters Hill, SE18.
An admirable example of co-ordination between boroughs to promote public appreciation of greenspace is the Green Chain Walk. Covering 15 miles, mostly through Greenwich and Lewisham but also touching Bexley and Bromley, it links over 300 public and private open spaces, the major sites being described in four leaflets available from the council address below.
On the top of Shooters Hill is **Oxleas Wood**, an outstanding area of ancient woodland and one of the first to be maintained by the GLC with the aim of protecting and enhancing its ecological diversity. A feature of its range of trees and shrubs are the plentiful wild service trees, which are also present in the adjacent **Shepherdleas** and **Jack Woods** (77 ha in total). As well as being

a favourite spot for birdwatchers, it's a happy hunting ground for fungus forays. The East London River Crossing route was planned to cut through the Wood, and at the time of writing the outcome of the public inquiry into the road scheme is not known.

The walk described in Leaflet 3 crosses **Eltham Park** (49 ha) which includes among its playing fields **LESSA Pond**, licensed by the LEB to the London Wildlife Trust who say of it: 'A large pond containing a variety of aquatic and marginal vegetation consisting of water milfoil, various duckweeds, celery-leaved buttercup, rushes, sedges and hairy willowherb. The pond is home for frogs, toads, newts, a variety of aquatic insects and a pair of moorhens. Native oak, ash, willow and pine trees are scattered around the pond providing an additional habitat for birds such as kestrel, finches and doves.'

An alternative route to the east of the park passes the ILEA Nature Study Centre, crossing the Bexley Road into **Avery Hill Park** (34 ha) around the mansion that is now part of Avery Hill College of Education. The park includes **Pippenhall Meadows** and Conduit Meadow where environmental works have been undertaken under the guidance of the Green Chain Working Party. The walk skirts the **Royal Blackheath Golf Course**, reputedly the oldest in the country, to the south-west of which is **The Tarn**, Court Road, SE9 (3.5 ha), an ornamental park and bird sanctuary. The Greenwich section of the walk, after passing the remains of Eltham Palace and its magnificent medieval hall, finishes at Mottingham, its continuation through Bromley and Lewisham being covered in Leaflet 4.

The Green Chain leaflets are available from the council planning department at John Humphries House, Stockwell Street, Greenwich, SE10 9JN (01-853 0077).

HACKNEY

Despite a share of the Lee Valley, the borough has little wildspace, the prime sites being man-made.

Stoke Newington Reservoirs
Lordship Road, N16.
Thames Water. 36 ha.
The nearest reservoirs to central London, they attract swifts, swallows, martins and pied wagtails hawking for flies as well as

waterfowl and gulls on the water. In colder weather they freeze over later than those in the Lee valley and elsewhere and become a teeming wildfowl refuge. The New River runs through the waterworks and is part of the area whose future is being considered by the water authority after the closure of the plant in 1989. A New River Action Group has been formed, and a Save the Reservoirs Campaign is backed by the local council. Though the filter beds are likely to be redeveloped, the reservoirs appear safe.

Abney Park Cemetery
Stoke Newington High Street, N16.
LB Hackney. 13 ha.
Along from the old municipal centre, the Cemetery was bought by the council in 1979 and, after a campaign by local conservationists, is run as a nature reserve where educational use is encouraged. The tree and ivy cover makes it the most important bird site in the borough. The North London Polytechnic is preparing a comprehensive interpretative guide, but although advised by a management committee including local organisations, the council doesn't allow volunteer work in the grounds.

Above the Coppermill Bridge across the Lee is access to the Walthamstow Marshes (25 ha) at the tidal limit of the Lee at Lea Bridge. The **Middlesex Filter Beds** (2 ha) around the disused waterworks support a wide range of plant, amphibian and bird life and are to be managed, together with the adjacent **Essex Filter Beds**, as a nature area by the Lee Valley Regional Park Authority.

HAMMERSMITH AND FULHAM

Though former village greens survive as names and patches of greenery at Parsons Green, Walham Green, Brook Green and Shepherds Bush Green, the borough has few sizable areas of open space. Its Thamesfront from Chiswick to beyond the defunct Fulham power station up to Chelsea Creek offers public access at the western end of Chiswick Mall, Furnival Gardens in front of the town hall and **Bishop's Park** (10 ha) around Fulham Palace.

Wormwood Scrubs
Scrubs Lane NW10.
LB Hammersmith and Fulham. 86 ha.
The area that was formerly Old Oak Common is now sadly barren.

A few small patches have been fenced off to allow generation of scrub and trees, but much of the new planting has been poorly planned. A strip of former sidings and allotments along the main Paddington line has developed a young woodland and has been dubbed **Scrubs Wood** by local conservationists. The grassland includes plants such as wild strawberry and salad burnet, and supports slow-worms and lizards and many birds. While there have been negotiations with BR with the aim of creating a nature reserve, its future is threatened by the site's possible use as a sidings for Channel Tunnel rolling stock.

On the far side of the tracks is a stretch of the Paddington Arm of the Grand Union Canal where conservation work is to be undertaken in collaboration with BWB.

HARINGEY

The borough was among the earliest to treat ecology seriously. Acquiring Alexandra Palace in 1980 it constructed a nature reserve within Alexandra Park and organised annual wildlife days in the Palace pavilion. It has also had the benefit of a comparative survey of wildlife sites, *The Ecology of Open Spaces in Haringey*, produced by the London Wildlife Trust and North London Polytechnic.

Alexandra Park
Alexandra Park Road, Hornsey, N10.
LB Haringey. 65 ha.
The *Open Spaces* report infers from the heath grass on the north-west slopes of the central hill that the Park was originally grassland within the encircling woodland. 'The ecological wealth rests in the network of corridors of wood, scrub and rough grassland which have regenerated over the last 20 years and which have increased the established areas of woodland.' It adds: 'Of 300+ bird species recorded for London, about 230 occur each year. The relevant figures for this site are 120 and 95. 46 species are known to have bred, 27 are regular breeding.' The introduction of a pond in the nature reserve on the eastern side of the park next to the Wood Green reservoir and filter beds alongside the main King's Cross line has added a further dimension to the habitats of the area.

Monitoring of the pond's effect has already recorded visits by common sandpiper, water rail and kingfisher in addition to commoner species of duck and gull.

Parkland Walk
Stapleton Hall Road, Finsbury Park, N4.
LB Haringey. 13 ha. Information centre.
Running between Alexandra Palace and Finsbury Park along a disused railway line, the Walk supports no less than 230-plus species of flowering plants and is an important green corridor. The first portion runs to the north of Highgate Wood at Cranley Gardens (0.5 m). The trail resumes south of Highgate tube station running east to Finsbury (1.25 m) passing the information centre at the above address. Butterflies prosper in the shelter of the cuttings, the 19 recorded species being a third of the British inventory. Two rare snails have delighted naturalists who have been keeping records of the site since the 1970s.

HARROW

The borough is dominated by Harrow Weald, streams running from this high ground to all points of the compass. From Stanmore Common a brook runs northwards into the Colne upstream of Watford, passing through the canal feeder Aldenham Reservoir en route. From Harrow Weald Common a stream runs west into the Colne downstream of Watford.
South-east from Bentley Priory the Edgware Brook runs to Dean's Brook at Edgware. South, the Yeading Brook becomes the Crane on its curvaceous course to the Thames at Isleworth. South-west, the River Pinn flows from Pinner Hill via Ruislip Lido to the Colne south of Uxbridge.

Harrow Weald
Two commons survive of the commonland that once covered the whole pebble gravel-capped ridge, Harrow Weald Common and Stanmore Common, both reaching a height of over 400 feet. On the south slope of the hillside are the Bentley Priory fields on the underlying Claygate Beds and London clay. To the east is Stanmore Country Park, to the west, Harrow Weald Park. **Harrow Weald**

Common (19 ha) and **Stanmore Common** (48 ha) at one time formed a heather heathland which has given way to birch scrub and woodland on the former, beech and oak on the latter. Clearings on Stanmore Common allow heathland plants such as tormentil, stitchwort and heather to survive. Stanmore was once 'Stanmere', and the sources of the streams mentioned above include ponds and marshland.

Bentley Priory (65 ha) is mostly rough neutral grassland, still grazed by cattle and rich in plant species. There are also areas of scrub and mixed broadleaf woodland, and at the centre is a lake which is the main element of a 3.6 ha reserve established by the council in 1974. Formed by damming the Edgware Brook, it has good marginal vegetation and is surrounded by a mixed woodland.

Harrow Weald Park lies between Brookshill and the Uxbridge Road. **Stanmore Country Park** (31 ha) has been developed north of Stanmore on the former farmland which includes Cloisters Wood and Pears Wood. Along the course of the former railway linking Stanmore and Harrow is a short nature trail at Vernon Drive, Stanmore, managed by London Wildlife Trust. **The Rattler** (0.2 m) is grassland and scrub frequented by numerous birds and butterflies. Sticking up out of the lower part of the borough is Harrow on the Hill (404 feet) with the Harrow School playing fields to the east including Harrow School Farm in the south-east corner.

HAVERING

While named after the ancient settlement of Havering-atte-Bower on London's northern perimeter, the borough is made up of the three overspill suburbs of Romford, Hornchurch and Upminster, separated from the rest of London by the Dagenham Corridor formed by the River Rom in the north and the Beam River in the south. Second largest of London's boroughs, it has plentiful countryside around.

Duck Wood
Sheffield Drive, off Dagnam Park Drive, Colchester Road, Harold Hill.
LB Havering. 8ha. LWT.
An impressive ancient hornbeam coppice woodland with a series of nine ponds all of which are in various stages of colonisation.

Much work has already been carried out on these ponds and more is still required. The wood is open to the public and well used as a local amenity. To help increase the amount of undergrowth for nesting birds LWT will be planting a hedge around part of the perimeter of the site.

On a small stream feeding the Rom from the east is **Cranham Marsh Woods** (6 ha). Managed by the Essex Trust on behalf of the council, they are wet woodlands interspersed with fen.

Rainham Marshes
Ferry Lane, Rainham.
LB Havering. 640 ha.
Where the Ingrebourne meets the Thames, the Marshes are among Britain's most important bird sites. More than 10,000 wildfowl are recorded as wintering on the meadows still grazed by sheep and cattle, which makes the site one of international significance. It also has its complement of nesting wetland and grassland birds, is hunting territory for short-eared owl and hen harrier, and supports nationally rare wetland plants. The area is a proposed SSSI but part has already been developed as The Watermeads industrial estate.

HILLINGDON

London's third largest borough, and the richest in wildlife sites, is bounded on the west by the River Colne cutting through the chalk that surfaces around Harefield, with streams draining into the Colne in both the north and south. The River Pinn runs diagonally across the borough from the north-east, Ruislip Common Brook joining it from the Ruislip Woods, and meets the Colne south of Uxbridge. In the east Yeading Brook curves west around Northolt aerodrome before becoming the Crane at Cranford and sweeping east through Hounslow and Richmond to the The Thames at Isleworth. Several of the numerous sites are managed by the Hertfordshire and Middlesex Trust for Nature Conservation (HMTNC).

Old Park Wood
Hill End Road, Harefield.
LB Hillingdon. 22 ha. Part (7.7 ha) HMTNC.
An oak woodland of many facets, its variety derives from the

mixture of geological deposits revealed by the streams running down the steep hillside. The acidic gravels on the higher surfaces sustain birch and oak with bracken ground cover. The valleys are richer, with oak and ash woodland meeting alder woodland at the spring line, the ground flora being particularly diverse with several London rarities. The south-east section of the wood is owned and managed by the HMTNC who describe it as 'probably the finest remaining woodland in Middlesex'.

On the other side of Park Lane **Coppermill Down** (6 ha) is a rare example of unimproved chalk pasture (and part of the SSSI described below) where grazing continues.

Harefield Moor
Moorfields Road, South Harefield.
Private. 130 ha.
Formerly wet grassland, the site is mostly a large shallow lake after gravel digging. The open water, together with its islands and surrounding grassland, attracts a large winter wildfowl population. Though a major SSSI the area is not managed for its nature conservation interest, but the canal towpath provides a good vantage point – and the Halfway House a useful refreshment stop. Across the Frays River, one of the streams that diverges from the Colne, is **Harefield Place** (4 ha), a small mixed woodland and wet grassland within the Uxbridge Golf Course managed by the Hillingdon Natural History Society and the HMTNC. To the north of the beginning of the Frays River is **Frays Island**, a small alder and willow woodland.

Denham Lock Wood has recently become a London Wildlife Trust site. To the south of Western Avenue is **Alder Glade** (2.5 ha). Owned and managed by the HMTNC, this stretch of disused railway line and adjacent woodland includes interesting aquatic habitats along the Shire Ditch.

Ruislip Woods
Ducks Hill Road, Ruislip.
LB Hillingdon. 355 ha.
Predominantly hornbeam with oak standards, the woodland is made up of Bayhurst, Mad Bess, Copse and Park Woods, on either side

of the Ruislip Common Brook, a Pinn tributary dammed to form the canal feeder reservoir which is now Ruislip Lido. The Woods constitute 294 ha of this major SSSI, the remainder being the grasslands and heathlands of the adjacent golf courses and Poor's Field common.

Bayhurst has been developed as a country park with nature trails available from the park information centre. Immediately to the north is **Tarleton's Lake** (2.8 ha), managed by the HMTNC to preserve the plantlife, particularly orchids, and varied fauna of this lake, marsh and wood. To the north-west is the farmland of the Breakspear estate, bought by the old London County Council as part of the green belt and including two farms which welcome visitors: Knightscote Farm on Breakspear Road North and the Park Lodge Farm Centre at South Harefield.

Ruislip Lido is now given over to water sports but at its northern end is the **Ruislip LNR** (4.8 ha), a marshy area with diverse plant, insect and mollusc populations managed by the Ruislip and District Natural History Society.

Down the Pinn, south of Brunel University on Royal Lane is **The Grove** a mixed woodland including oak, ash, sycamore, horse chestnut and conifers, scrub of elm suckers, hawthorn and elder, and bluebells among the ground flora. A large pond is surrounded by marshland plants and the whole area is expected to become a formal Local Nature Reserve managed by the London Wildlife Trust on behalf of the council.

Yeading Brook wends its course through west London with large areas of open land along its valley, such as **Yeading Meadows**, left unbuilt on because of flood risk. Circling Northolt aerodrome, it passes through a scatter of woodlands including:

Ten Acre Wood
Charleville Lane, Hayes.
LB Hillingdon. 4.5 ha. LWT.
Oak woodland with Midland hawthorn and hazel understorey has suffered from lack of management and the incursion of horses grazing on the adjacent meadows. Yet a useful ground flora survives and will develop, and the wood provides valuable cover for birdlife in the Northolt open space, one of London's largest

chunks of captive countryside. Yeading Brook and drainage ditches alongside the wood offer wetland habitats where insects such as dragonflies prosper.

Gutteridge Wood (9 ha) to the north is of similar composition and is also likely to be managed as a nature reserve in future.

HOUNSLOW

More than in any other outer London borough, Hounslow's open space – apart from the River Crane bankside – is almost entirely man-made. Its Thamesfront runs from Isleworth to Chiswick, but even its string of rural-looking eyots (or aits) are artificial islands. The River Crane runs through Hounslow Heath, but its longest river is the Duke of Northumberland's River, a cut built to link the Colne and Crane. Its main lakes are the Kempton Park Reservoirs and Bedfont Gravel Pits.

Lots Ait
Ferry Lane, Brentford.
Private. 1 ha.
One of the eight or so small eyots on the left bank of the Thames between Richmond and Chiswick, the island was subject in 1984 of a public inquiry into its development for housing and offices. The inspector agreed, however, that its wildlife interest deserved protection, and its owners are supporting its management by the London Wildlife Trust. Like the other islets, it was built to provide a channel for setting fishnets and has developed a range of habitats in a virtually undisturbed location. The tree and scrub cover is a haunt of woodland birds, and the tidal mud banks are a popular feeding ground for gulls and waders. 20 species of snail have been recorded, and bird visitors include snipe, sandpipers, teal, cormorant, heron and grebe – the divers attracted by the nine or more species of fish found here.

The adjacent **Isleworth Ait** is, courtesy of its owners – Speyhawk – also being managed as a nature reserve by LWT.

Hounslow Heath
Staines Road, Feltham.
LB Hounslow. 80 ha.
Part of the west London heathland that once covered some 1,720 ha, the Heath was crossed by the Roman road of Stane Street (now

the A30) past the top of the Thames loop at Brentford to Staines upriver and on to the garrison town of Silchester. A royal hunting forest in Norman times, its status as commonland was confirmed after attempted enclosures in the Tudor epoch. In post-Restoration years it became a regular army encampment area, with a gunpowder industry already having developed here as early as the 14th century. As part of 19th century enclosures the War Office acquired 120 ha as a training ground next to Hounslow Barracks, but what now remains of the Heath used to be mostly market gardens. After the war, a housing estate having been refused on the grounds of excessive noise of planes from Heathrow airport, the council laid out a golf course along the Crane and, in 1979, the GLC bought the remainder as a park.

The Heath today is mostly coarse grassland with encroaching scrub, providing breeding habitats for many birds. Part close to the railway line remains as true heathland, and other features include patches of woodland and good ponds. A nature trail covers the whole area.

Kempton Park Reservoirs
Sunbury Way, Hanworth.
Thames Water.
Grasslands and woodland surround the lakes of the disused waterworks which in 1986 was location of a plan to build a theme park next to the race course. The council rejected this proposal and designated the site as green belt, but management of this large area is at the time of writing undecided. Visits to the Kempton Park (West) reservoir are by permit from the Thames Water address at the end of the section. While it is less attractive to duck than some of the other reservoirs, tufted duck and pochard are among those that can usually be seen, plus many other species at migration times.

The **Bedfont Gravel Pits** are planned for development as a leisure park but conservationists are arguing for the preservation of the most important wildlife areas in any future scheme.

Gunnersbury Triangle
Bollo Lane, Chiswick, W3.
LB Hounslow. 2.4 ha. LWT. Wardened (01-747 3881).
One of London's most notable conservation victories, the site was

saved after a campaign by local residents against British Rail plans to develop the land with factories and warehouses. A public inquiry agreed the site had outstanding educational potential and development was refused. With GLC cash the council was able to buy the land and arrange its management as a nature reserve by the London Wildlife Trust. Formerly agricultural land, it was cut off by the triangle of intersecting railway lines just before the beginning of the century. Used as allotments in the 1930s, since then it has developed into secondary woodland. A damp area, the dominant tree species are birch and sallow, and ground vegetation includes marshland species such as ferns, horsetails and sedges. Blackcaps, chiffchaffs, willow and sedge warblers nest in the undergrowth, and the open grassland areas attract butterflies such as orange tip, small copper and holly blue.

ISLINGTON

The borough has the smallest amount of open space after Kensington and Chelsea and, unlike that borough, no major parks adjoining its boundaries apart from Finsbury Park. Of the total 100 ha, **Highbury Fields** accounts for 12 ha and **Caledonian Park** for a further 8 ha. To compensate, residents have made the most of the tiniest scraps of vacant land, and the council are exploiting the short stretches of the borough's two canals.

Gillespie Park
Gillespie Road, Highbury, N5.
BR. 1 ha. LB Islington. Wardened (01-226 6393).
One of the best examples of an inner-city habitat creation site, it is being studied as part of an NCC project on public usage of urban nature sites, but there is now a threat to its future as BR want to sell adjacent sidings and the park for housing. A former sidings on the main King's Cross line, its clinker substrate is the usual excellent milieu for a variety of herbs, and a pond has been excavated to provide water and wetland habitats. The park is looked after by a couple of 'conservationist gardeners', a leaflet being available on site.

Other natural or community gardens include the **Culpepper Community Garden**, and **Barnsbury Wood** which is leased by the council to the ILEA but providing access to local residents as well as schools. In the same neighbourhood is the second building of the **London Ecology Centre** (90 York Way, N1 9AG). Immediately opposite, the terrace of the Waterside Inn is a comfortable spot for watching the wildfowl and gulls on the Battlebridge Basin of the Regent's Canal.

New River
Canonbury Grove, N1.
Thames Water.
London's most remarkable canal, the New River was built as early as 1613 to bring drinking water from springs in Hertfordshire to the city. Running 27 miles (originally 38 miles) from near Amwell to the New River Head reservoir at Rosebery Avenue, it is underground through the Angel, Islington, but surfaces at Canonbury before diving underground once again and re-emerging at the Stoke Newington reservoirs. Though now redundant as an aqueduct, the canal and its margins are a valuable green corridor which is jeopardised by Thames Water plans to sell off the land for development. At Canonbury the council has maximised the educational and recreational potential of the length up to St Paul's Road by creating a nature reserve.

KENSINGTON AND CHELSEA

The borough has the least open space within its boundaries of any London borough, but abuts Kensington Gardens and Hyde Park which in some measure compensate. Within its boundaries there are two well-timbered cemeteries, Kensal Green and Brompton, the former with the Regent's Canal running alongside. There are in addition many squares and large gardens which collectively are important for wildlife. The major wildlife site is:

Holland Park
Kensington High Street, SW8.
LB Kensington and Chelsea. 20 ha.
The parkland around the original Jacobean mansion, bombed and not fully restored after the last war, includes the largest woodland area (6 ha) in central London. Most of the trees were planted in the 1880s, but the semi-natural beech wood on the higher north-east corner derives from trees brought from Goodwood in 1749 and forms the most interesting habitat. The elms and sycamores

suffered badly from disease but there has been considerable replanting since the 1970s. The enclosed arboretum in front of what remains of the house includes among other exotics a range of evergreens which provide useful winter roosting cover, and the west lawn enclosure has dense shrub thickets for nesting.

The park's grey squirrels are popular, but their egg-raiding activities are destructive of the birdlife, which includes blackcap, chiffchaff and spotted flycatcher among its residents and great spotted woodpecker, goldcrest, long-tailed tit, coal tit, nuthatch, treecreeper, redwing, redpoll and bullfinch among visitors. The fungi are outstanding, including several national rarities. The council, which inherited the park in 1986 from the GLC who acquired it in 1952, are introducing a management regime intended to increase both species diversity and visitor interest.

Kensal Green Cemetery

Harrow Road, W10.
Private. 22 ha.

Though still a working cemetery and crematorium, much of the area of Victorian burials has disappeared under a coarse weave of long grass, thistles and clumps of blackberry. Its paths wind through elder bushes, yews and limes, good bird territory, and its plants include great burnet, hoary ragwort, sneezewort, wood anemone, dog's mercury, yellow bedstraw, field woodrush, primrose and wild bluebell. The site is being managed by an MSC team with the aim of keeping it visitable, with the owners' permission, as an informal nature reserve. A stretch of the Regent's Canal bank south of the cemetery is to be managed by LWT for its wildlife interest.

Brompton Cemetery (16 ha) between Earls Court and Chelsea football ground is unkempt in a similarly appropriate manner, but has suffered from over-management by MSC and the use of herbicide. Its grassland includes wall lettuce, dark mullein and blue fleabane.

KINGSTON UPON THAMES

Despite its name, Kingston upon Thames has a comparatively short Thamesfront. Its eastern boundary is the Beverley Brook, and the Hogsmill River runs through its centre. For reasons described below, they lack the charm of, say, the Yeading Brook on the other side of the river. The borough also has unexpectedly little public open space, being the third most deprived in this respect. Against this, its southern salient is surrounded by Surrey countryside, its northern border abuts both Richmond Park and Wimbledon Common, and its centre faces Hampton Court Park across the Thames.

Beverley Brook rises at Worcester Park and is the borough boundary for the whole of its course to Richmond Park. Titled 'London's dirtiest river' by conservationists who surveyed its water quality, it receives its main flow from the Worcester Park Sewage Works. Classified as Grade 3 in terms of purity, which means it is 'polluted', samples indicate it is frequently Grade 4 or 'grossly polluted'. Since the Brook is a feature of Wimbledon Common, Richmond Park and Barnes Common before debouching into the Thames at Barn Elms, its condition is a matter of serious conservation concern.

The state of the **Hogsmill River** is also alarming. Rising from chalk springs in former mill ponds at Ewell, it there merits the classification of Grade 1A, or top purity. Sadly, it is also the channel for any overflow from Ewell's sewage storm tanks and in heavy rain – some dozen times a year – the stream runs with neat sewage. Entering the borough at Tolworth, it is joined by the Boneseat Stream which rises in the south of the borough, passing Chessington Zoo on its way north. Downstream the Hogsmill passes through open space which is initially captive countryside but subsides into playing fields. At Norbiton it flows through the Hogsmill Valley Sewage Works on the site of the former Norbiton Common of which little remains apart from names such as Lower Marsh Lane.

In the north of the borough, Coombe Hill and Coombe Wood Golf Courses provide a huge area of private open space.

The lack of public wildspace led the council in 1986 to introduce a policy of identifying and protecting pocket-handkerchief sites as reserves, with educational nature trails to accompany them. Details of the scheme from: Directorate of Education and Recreation, Guildhall, Kingston upon Thames (01-546 2121).

LAMBETH

While the borough has plentiful open space in the form of Clapham Common and Brockwell Park, these have limited wildlife interest. It was a fact commendably recognised by the council's parks department who commissioned an LWT *Ecological Survey of Vacant Land in Lambeth* (1984) and followed with funding for an LWT handbook *Encouraging Wildlife in Urban Parks* (1985). Two wasteland sites of exceptional wildlife interest were identified, both former railway sidings. **Eardley Road** in Streatham is planned as a site for council housing. The other provides a dramatic illustration of the importance – and fragility – of such sites.

Shakespeare Road
Brixton, SE24.
Private. 2 ha.
A narrow strip of land not far from Railton Road, Brixton's 'front line', was noted as being exceptionally interesting by the Brixton Permaculture ecological gardening co-operative. During 35 years' disuse, birch and sallow coppices had established themselves together with a varied ground flora. Rarities included bee orchid, musk thistle and eyebright, the seeds probably carried in on trains from Kent. The council declined to buy the land in 1984 and it was sold to a property developer. In June 1986 his application to build houses on the site was rejected on the grounds of its natural history and amenity value. The next weekend he sent in bulldozers which, despite protestors attempting to block their activity, cleared the area of all its greenery. In spring 1987, the seeds remaining in the soil were producing renewed growth and the council was seeking to acquire the land.

Foremost among the parks is **Clapham Common** (82 ha), a rather dreary expanse of greensward whose few areas of wildlife interest are described in a council nature trail leaflet. **Brockwell Park** (50 ha) on a hill overlooking the valley of the River Effra, which now runs underground, is also covered by a trail leaflet which draws attention to, among other features, the ponds on the west side of the park and their numerous wildfowl. **Ruskin Park** (15 ha) on the slopes of Denmark Hill is named after the author who lived here when the area was mostly green fields. **Kennington**

Park (15 ha) was one of the former commons as was **Streatham Common** (25 ha).

Providing a similar amenity in a neighbourhood severely lacking in open space was **Vauxhall Park** (3 ha), created by Octavia Hill from the grounds of two former mansions. To the north is **Archbishop's Park** (4 ha) at the back of Lambeth Palace. At the Palace gate the former church of St Mary at Lambeth has been converted into a Museum of Garden History. In the churchyard where he is buried, the Tradescant Garden is a memorial to John Tradescant, gardener to Charles I.

Nature trail leaflets, such as *Clapham Common Nature Walk* (LWT), are available from Lambeth Amenity Services, 164 Clapham Park Road, SW4 7DQ.

LEWISHAM

The borough covers the valley of the River Ravensbourne and its tributaries, the River Pool to the south and River Quaggy to the east. Its boundary to the west is the Sydenham Hill ridge with various hilltop and hillside open spaces along its length: Sydenham Wells Park, Horniman Gardens at Forest Hill, Blythe Hill Fields and the outlying Hilly Fields at Ladywell.

Hither Green Nature Reserve
Green Chain Walk, off Baring Road, Lewisham SE12.
BR. 2.4 ha. LB Lewisham.
The only publicly accessible site along the three kilometres of what the GLC Handbook describes as, 'railway sidings, cuttings and embankments, horse paddocks and abandoned allotments'. It is managed by the council which is advised by a local management committee. The self-established habitats now support 19 butterfly and 300 moth species; slow-worms, lizards and grass snakes; and an ant rarity – Watson's ant. More information can be obtained from the Nature Conservation Centre in **Beckenham Place Park** (see below).

Devonshire Road Nature Reserve
Devonshire Road, Forest Hill, SE23.
BR. 2.8 ha. LB Lewisham. Field centre (01-690 6695).
Saved from clearance after a public campaign in 1979, the site is

now managed by the council as an educational reserve (with public access Saturdays 2-4pm). Grassland, scrub and woodland are described in a nature trail leaflet.

On the far side of Forest Hill station at **Dacres Road** is a similar reserve in the making. The railway was built along the course of the old Croydon Canal, part of which survives as a damp hollow which is to be excavated to form a pond. A short distance away on the disused railway line that formerly served Crystal Palace is a 2 ha nature trail forming part of **Horniman Gardens** surrounding the Horniman Museum.

Beckenham Place Park
Beckenham Hill Road, SE6.
LB Lewisham. 120 ha. Nature Conservation Centre (01-690 6695).
The Ravensbourne runs through the park which includes a large golf course as well as 40 ha of ancient woodland, pond and swamp. At the centre of the Park is the Nature Conservation Centre, open to the public on weekend afternoons, where information about wildlife in the borough and park trails are available.

MERTON

Surrounding the settlement where the Roman road to Chichester crossed the Wandle, the borough is bounded on the west by Beverley Brook and Wimbledon Common and on the east by London's third largest common after Wimbledon and Hampstead, Mitcham.
The Wandle enters the borough at Mill Green where the channel from the Beddington Sewage Works brought treated effluent to the river, its natural flow diminished by large-scale extraction of water for drinking and industrial purposes. Dubbed 'the hardest-worked river for its size in the world' in 1805 when it had some 90 mills along its banks (Brown 1982), the river's mills produced everything from flour to gunpowder, copper to calico, paper to peppermint.
Octavia Hill fought to create a walkway along the valley, founding the River Wandle Open Spaces Society in 1911, but although there is a chain of playing fields and land owned by the National Trust, nothing survives of the meadows that once supported the abbeys and manor houses of Merton, Morden and Mitcham. The National

Trust's **Watermeads** (5 ha) is a pleasant riverside walk but not much more, and its **Morden Hall Park** (50 ha) though crossed by channels of the Wandle is of little wildlife interest. Below Colliers Wood, the **Wandle Sewage Works**, closed for some years, has been recognised as a valuable wildlife area by conservationists but not the council.

The southern Pyl Brook runs from Sutton past the Sutton Sewage Works joining Beverley Brook above Raynes Park. East Pyl Brook rising at Spring Hill enters the borough south of **Morden Park** (39 ha) joining its sister stream at Battersea New Cemetery. North of the valley is **Cannon Hill Common** (21 ha) where a small area around a pond is managed as a nature reserve. Downstream is:

Wimbledon Common
Conservators. 440 ha.

As in other places, the lord of the manor tried in the 1860s to enclose the land for 'improvement'. An energetic campaign by local people was successful in preserving the area as a common, to be run by elected conservators. Including Putney Heath across the Wandsworth border, the main part of the Common is an SSSI covering 342 ha. On the gravel plateau is rough grassland with gorse and birch scrub and occasional marshy hollows. Streams flowing from this spring line have created two valley bogs with an array of plants infrequently found in London. Herpetologists are enthusiastic about its newts and lizards; its insect population includes about half the British list; and its birdlife is perennially lively.

Mitcham Common
Croydon Road, Mitcham.
Conservators. 176 ha. LB Merton.

In the south-east corner of the borough and managed by the council on behalf of its Conservators, the Common suffered from infilling until recently. Not only was rough grassland being destroyed, but ponds along Cedars Avenue, Watney's Road and Windmill Road were being systematically filled in. When Arthur's Pond was threatened with a similar fate in 1984 a campaign by local residents succeeded in halting the council's programme. Two rare moth species, butterflies, frogs and toads and breeding birds such as stonechat are among the animal life of what, together with the adjacent Beddington, could be an important wildlife reservoir.

NEWHAM

West Ham is bounded by the Lee, East Ham by the Roding, with the Thames to the south. Second poorest of London's boroughs in terms of orthodox public open space, its areas of wildspace include the marshes around the Beckton outfall of London's main northern sewer.

The Lee enters the borough at Temple Mills where infilling of marshland has provided the Lee Valley Regional Park Authority with a site for its Eastway Cycle Circuit. The side along the Lee has been left wild and is managed by the London Wildlife Trust as the **Bully Fen** nature reserve. Habitats include swamp and wet woodland with rank grassland on higher ground. While hardly a picture of delight, the area supports an extensive insect life and a resilient bird population including among less frequent species cuckoo, pheasant, blackcap and kingfisher. A trail leaflet is available from the Cycle Circuit office, Temple Mills, E15.

The web of channels – canal, river and mill cuts with names such as Three Mills Wall River, Waterworks River and Channelsea River – converge at Mill Meads to form Bow Creek. Surely Britain's least glamorous creek, it passes forlorn factories, gasworks and dead power stations before reaching the equally defunct wharves around the final meander before the Thames. Here at Canning Town is **Thames Wharf and Limmo Peninsular** (17 ha), an area of dereliction which the GLC Habitat Survey identifies as one of London's six most important wastelands. The section on the Thames is mostly nutrient-poor grassland with scrub thickets. The central section at the mouth of the creek offers a riverside walk between the rubble-based grassland and the river where saltmarsh plants and waders appear. In the narrow neck of the meander and viewable from a redundant bridge over the creek just off East India Dock Road, the Limmo Peninsular has a large breeding bird population but, together with the rest of the area, faces development by the London Docklands Development Corporation (LDDC).

The River Roding is flanked by recreation grounds through which, or over which, the M11 extension is being built. Between Barking Creek and the now obsolescent Royal Docks are Beckton marshes, fast being built on by the LDDC.

St Michael's Churchyard
High Street South, East Ham, E6
Private. Interpretation centre (01-470 4525).
A restful burial ground, carefully tended but allowed to be pleasantly overgrown, provides a blend of grassland between the graves and woodland round the fringe, with butterflies and birds taking advantage of both. The interpretation centre, built next to the church at Norman Road, can provide information about the borough's other wildlife sites.

REDBRIDGE

Taking its name from the crossing of the River Roding north of Wanstead Flats at the core of the borough, Redbridge is densely built up in the west and south. In the north-west it includes fragments of Epping Forest, and its north-east border runs through the ancient Hainault Forest, part of a huge country park. A large green wedge just south at Fairlop is also being developed as a country park.
At the northern tip of the borough is Whitehall Plain where the River Ching provides the boundary with Waltham Forest southwards through the Woodford Golf Course. To the east, Knighton Wood is an outlying part of Epping Forest, though much impoverished. South down the River Roding valley is:

Wanstead Park
City of London. 56 ha.
The park which surrounded the former 1715 mansion, in what is now Wanstead Golf Course, has an abundance of trees and a large and elaborate lake. The Roding once flowed through this but now by-passes it. Its islands include The Heronry where a few birds still nest, Lincoln Island and Rook Island. Westwards is a further lake with its own Heronry Pond. Beyond is the Shoulder of Mutton Pond and Reservoir Wood.

On the other side of Blake Hall Road is the southern end of Epping Forest (see **WALTHAM FOREST**) through which runs the Centenary Walk, continuing into **Wanstead Flats** (85 ha). This enormous open space is mostly sports pitches but includes three

large ponds and other corners that, with appropriate management,
could be rich wildlife areas.

Skirting the City of London Cemetery, the borough boundary
follows the Roding below Ilford Bridge to the junction with Loxford
Water. Upstream the Loxford runs through South Park (12 ha),
which has a lake and islets, and further north becomes the Seven
Kings Water passing Seven Kings Park (13 ha) on its way from
Fairlop Plain. Flowing from this vast area a short distance to the
north is **Cran Brook**, traversing Valentine's Park (54 ha) on its
way to the Roding. Forming an important green corridor to the
west, the open land around the hill where Claybury Hospital sits
includes **Claybury Wood** which, health authority willing, is to
be managed as a nature reserve.

Fairlop Plain has been much dug for gravel, the resulting lakes
forming an ingredient of the **Fairlop Country Park** (120 ha)
being constructed in the western part of the Plain. To the north is:

Hainault Forest Country Park
Fox Burrow Road, Romford Road, Chigwell.
Essex CC and LB Redbridge. 400ha.

Part of the former royal hunting forest of Essex, the area was
enclosed in 1851 and mostly cleared for farming. London County
Council bought the part around Lambourne Common in 1903 with
an extension in 1934. Some 90 ha in Havering remains in
agricultural use, the golf course accounts for 100 ha and the main
park, opened in 1970, covers 243 ha. Part of the ancient Hainault
Forest survives and is described in detail in the *Ecology Handbook*.
Of the total 130 ha, two thirds are in Essex, the Redbridge section
being dominated by birch woodland. Trees indicative of ancient
woodland – mature hornbeam, wild service tree, aspen and crab
apple – occur throughout the woodland, while the western part
consists of acidic grassland with younger trees. A nature trail leaflet
is available from the park centre.

RICHMOND

While the borough has by a long way the largest percentage of
public open space (36 per cent compared to the 20 per cent of the
next ranking Westminster), Richmond Park, Hampton Court and
Kew Gardens account for some 2,000 ha out of 2,440 ha. The rest

of the borough is a contrast between this royal inheritance and a more workaday pattern of natural open space.

Crane Park Nature Reserve
Ellerman Avenue, Hounslow Road, Twickenham.
LB Richmond. 1.8 ha. LWT.
In the centre of Crane Park (28 ha) is a reserve on an island in the River Crane initiated by the Richmond and Twickenham Friends of the Earth. Built to provide water power for the gunpowder mill that operated as recently as 1926 (see **Hounslow Heath**) it also has a plentiful supply of willows which make the best charcoal, a constituent of gunpowder. The island has developed a small mixed broadleaved woodland of ash, horse chestnut, elder and hawthorn which supports most of the 45 larger fungi recorded here, including a national rarity. On one side of the island is fast-flowing backwater, on the other the deep slow-flowing mainstream. The millpond in the centre of the island has been drained to allow a damp area where nettles provide a feeding ground for butterfly grubs and cover for abundant grass snakes. The shot tower on the opposite bank is being converted into a study centre.
Below the reserve the Crane turns towards the centre of Twickenham where the Duke of Northumberland's River resumes its independent course to the Thames just south of Syon Park, while the main river issues south of Isleworth Ait.

Ham Lands
Riverside Drive, Ham.
LB Richmond. 80 ha.
Saved from housing development by a change of council control in the 1980s, Ham Lands is an area of grassland and mostly hawthorn scrub on infilled gravel diggings. As well as supporting a plantlife including three orchid species it is probably the most important upstream riparian site for birds in Greater London. Spotted flycatcher, various warblers and all three British woodpeckers are among the 40 and more breeding species, with over 100 species recorded in total. An area of original flood meadow survives under the bank of the river which, being just below Teddington Lock, is still tidal – the Richmond weir being overflown at high tide.

Lonsdale Road Reservoir
Lonsdale Road, Barnes, SW13.
LB Richmond. 9 ha. Management committee.
A trail-blazing campaign saved this former reservoir from being built on, the area becoming London's first £1 million nature reserve – and that in 1970s money. Richmond council, having refused a Metropolitan Water Board application for houses on the site in 1968, was forced to comply with a purchase notice for a sum of almost a million pounds. In an attempt to recoup its outlay, it prepared plans for its own housing and educational buildings, but a local campaign in which the Barnes Wildlife and Animal Welfare Group took a leading part resulted in the scheme going to a public inquiry in 1972, when it was rejected.
A further threat in 1975 was a proposal by a section of the local population for a formal park. Though the notion was favoured by the council it was scuppered by local government retrenchment in the 1970s. In 1980 Richmond agreed the nature reserve idea, and the site is now looked after by a management committee. The long and narrow lake favoured by diving duck such as pochard, tufted duck, goldeneye and goosander has been provided with roosting and nesting rafts and a fringe of phragmites reedbed. A young woodland has developed, supplemented by active tree planting. Already a much-used educational site, a study centre is planned on it.

Barnes Common
Rocks Lane, Barnes, SW13.
LB Richmond. 71 ha.
Reminiscent of Jilly Cooper-with-dogs territory, this sandy common has mostly hawthorn scrub surrounded by bramble and bracken which harbours a common but prolific birdlife as well as manic red setters. A 20 ha area north of the railway around the Rocks Lane/Mill Hill Road crossroads is an SSSI and the only London site of the burnet rose. Beverley Brook runs to the north of the Common through the Barn Elms Park, north of which is:

Barn Elms Reservoir
Merthyr Terrace, Castelnau, Barnes, SW13.
Thames Water. 34 ha.
The cliche 'mecca for birdwatchers' justly describes the focal status

of the site in terms of the number and variety of birds to be seen here throughout the year. Oldest of London's reservoirs, the quartet crossed by two central causeways forms the largest area of open water within four miles of Trafalgar Square (Walthamstow Reservoirs being slightly more distant). Gulls sheltering from winter storms flock here in enormous numbers, and are joined by significant numbers of tufted duck, smew and other diving ducks. At the time of writing, however, there are rumours that Thames Water has plans to develop the site.

SOUTHWARK

Sydenham Hill, once covered by the Great North Wood which extended across south London to Croydon, mirrors the Hampstead heights north of the Thames and until the fire of 1936 was crowned by the Crystal Palace. Two of London's secret rivers flow from the springs on the slopes of the ridge, the Effra appearing briefly as Belair Lake before disappearing into a sewer passing underneath the centre of Brixton, and the Peck, visible in Peckham Rye Park before its subterranean journey to the Thames. On the higher ground above the flood plain villages such as Camberwell and Peckham were once famed for their salubrious qualities, the former in particular (as its name suggests) for its medicinal springs. Until the nineteenth century the area north to the Thames was predominantly market gardens, orchards and pasture.

Sydenham Hill Wood
Sydenham Hill, SE26.
LB Southwark. 11 ha. LWT.
This was the subject of a lengthy battle over plans to build housing on the upper edge of the wood, culminating in public inquiries in 1985 and 86, described in Chapter 4. Though much disturbed by the railway cut through it to serve Crystal Palace and the building of Victorian mansions on its upper slopes, the Wood is a remnant of the ancient woodland which remained a wild place, in all senses, until several decades into the 19th century. Adjacent to it is **Dulwich Wood** (20 ha), commercially managed by the Dulwich College Estates Governors until after the war. Beyond is the former Dulwich Common where a few hedgerows survive between golf course and playing fields.

Dulwich Upper Wood
Farquhar Road, SE19.
LB Southwark. 3 ha. TRUE. Wardened (01-761 6230).
The back gardens of villas demolished after the war have become an educational reserve which includes some good examples of woodland regeneration.

Nunhead Cemetery
Linden Grove, SE15.
LB Southwark. 20 ha.
One of the finest of the Victorian cemeteries, it has become a rich wilderness, the northern half being formally recognised as a nature reserve. Management is being undertaken in part of this area by the Friends of Nunhead Cemetery, the work involving the removal of sycamore and the encouragement of a more diverse flora. The Friends can be contacted c/o 144 Erlanger Road, Telegraph Hill, SE14 5TJ.

Benhill Road Nature Garden
Bantry Road, Camberwell, SE5.
LB Southwark. 0.5 ha. Management association.
A reserve has been developed on the site of post-war prefabs, a couple of which remain. The grassland attracts birds and butterflies, the planting of trees will eventually create a tree belt, and a small but successful pond has frogs and dragonflies.

Other good examples of natural parks in neighbourhoods otherwise lacking wildspace include **Goldsmith Road Nature Garden** and **McDermott Road Nature Garden**, both in Peckham, and **Marlborough Grove Nature Park** north of the Old Kent Road. A short distance away, the **Bricklayers Arms** sidings, though identified in the GLC Habitat Survey as one of the half-dozen most important wildlife sites in Greater London, is to be redeveloped.

Lavender Pond
Rotherhithe Street, SE16.
LB Southwark. 0.5 ha. TRUE. Wardened (01-232 0498).
An ambitious example of habitat creation, the Pond was re-excavated from the filled-in Lavender Dock, part of the complex of mostly timber docks that closed in 1970. Popular with fishermen, not part of the original management plan, the Pond is fringed with marshland and a bank generously planted with trees. A short

distance away on the other side of Salter Road is the **Rotherhithe Ecological Park**, also managed by TRUE. At 2 ha it is the largest wholly-created nature site in the country, and presents a range of habitats including a shallow pond and heath. Also just off Salter Road is the **Surrey Docks Urban Farm**.

A booklet, *Brightening Up Your Neighbourhood – The Story of the Southwark Environment Programme*, is available from the Planning Department, Angel Court, Borough High Street, SE1. *The Sydenham Hill Wood File* (170pp, looseleaf) and *The Great North Wood* by Lucy Neville are both available from the Southwark Wildlife Group c/o Kingswood House, Seeley Drive, SE21.

SUTTON

An outer London borough with virtually no countryside (Epsom and Ewell kept it), and whose main area of open space is a sewage works, needs to think carefully about how it makes the most of its natural environment. For some years the council has sponsored a large MSC project tidying up, in an ecologically beneficial sense, the banks of the River Wandle and surrounding areas and is beginning to pay attention to the possibilities of a more varied management of its formal parks.

Beddington Park
Church Road, Croydon Road, Wallington.
LB Sutton. 56 ha.
The River Wandle, rising at Wandle Ponds just over the Croydon boundary, flows through the Park, a stately parkland surrounding the former seat of the Carew family. To the north is the Beddington Sewage Works and the fields where sludge from the filter beds was deposited. This large area of opportunity (in planners' terminology) is to be dug for gravel, the resulting lakes to be landscaped for active water sports. The corner nearest the Park is intended as a nature reserve.

St Philomena's Lake
Shorts Road, Carshalton.
Private. 1 ha. LWT.
In the grounds of the convent that now occupies Carshalton House is a spring-fed pond which has been cleaned out and restocked with

appropriate plants. It supports a varied invertebrate and amphibian population and, in addition to educational trips, can be visited on open days.

A short distance along the High Street are Carshalton Ponds into which runs the Carshalton branch of the Wandle. Rising in the picturesquely named Frying Pan and Hogpit Ponds of Carshalton Park (9 ha), the river runs through The Grove recreation ground and along Mill Lane to:

Wilderness Island
River Gardens, Carshalton.
LB Sutton. 2 ha. LWT.
A peninsular formed by the junction of the two branches of the Wandle and the railway crossing contains two large ponds and a damp willow carr wood.

An information leaflet about sites in the borough with excellent location maps is available from the council Planning Department, 24 Denmark Road, Carshalton, Surrey SMF 2JG (01-661 5619).

TOWER HAMLETS

Just as the Victorians early recognised the lack of open space in the East End and built Victoria Park to redress the balance, so the council in recent times was one of the first to support the creation of community gardens and urban farms. To supplement its efforts, the GLC built the second-largest of its new inner city parks, Mile End Park, along the Regent's Canal which runs through the heart of the borough.

Tower Hamlets Cemetery
Southern Grove, E3.
LB Tower Hamlets. 11 ha.
One of London's finest specimens of an overgrown Victorian garden of rest, it supports over 120 tree and plant species. The ivy-clad trees are particularly favoured by birds such as tawny owls, and there are proposals to manage the area as a formal nature reserve.

St Jude's Nature Park

St Jude's Road, E2.

LB Tower Hamlets. 0.5 ha. East End Wildlife Group. Wardened (01-403 2078).

Laid out in 1980, St Jude's is one of the earliest nature gardens. As described in the model leaflet *Parks and Farms in Tower Hamlets*, produced by the Tower Hamlets Environment Trust for the council's Tourism Working Party in 1985, it provides a mixture of 'trees, shrubs and wild flowers, which attract a rich wildlife to the area. Not only butterflies and other "minibeasts" but also frogs, hedgehogs, goldfinch and kestrels. The park is used for nature study by school groups but any interested groups or individuals are welcome.'

Mudchute Farm

Pier Street, E14.

LB Tower Hamlets. 12 ha. Mudchute management association (01-515 5901).

A pioneering city farm, it opened in 1977 and has a full complement of farm animals including a large stock of horses. Around it is the Mudchute built up from dredgings from the docks, now grassland where the horses graze. On its southern edge a drainage ditch has a useful range of aquatic plant and animal life.

Inspired by Mudchute's success, Stepneyites launched the **Stepping Stones Farm**, Stepney Way, E1 (01-790 8204) in 1979. As the *Parks and Farms* leaflet accurately describes, 'this four-acre farm has been described as "the jewel of Stepney". The whole site is easily accessible yet has lots of little private corners.'

The *Parks and Farms* leaflet is available from the Tower Hamlets Environment Trust at 192/6 Hanbury Street, E1 5HU (01-377 0481).

WALTHAM FOREST

Named after the southernmost part of Epping Forest in which Waltham Abbey was established by Henry II as part of his penance for the murder of Thomas Becket, the borough surrounds the long wedge of surviving woodland between the Lee and Roding rivers.

Epping Forest
Bury Road, Chingford, E4.
City of London. 2,430 ha.
The Greater London boundary includes Pole Hill with its vista over
the Lee valley and Hawk and Bury Woods above Chingford Plain.
Overlooking the valley of the River Ching, which here forms the
borough boundary, is Queen Elizabeth's Hunting Lodge, the start
of the Centenary Way – established to celebrate the saving of
Epping Forest. Southwards, the way passes Warren Pond,
following the Ching across Woodford Golf Course and Highams
Park (9 ha) to:

Walthamstow Forest
Oak Hill, Woodford Green.
City of London. 52 ha.
Like the rest of Epping Forest the woodland is predominantly
pollarded or coppiced hornbeam, and is one of the seven north
London woods identified by the Habitat Survey as of metropolitan
importance. As the *Ecology Handbook* reports: 'Although it is not
particularly rich in species, it has a very varied structure and is
valuable for its border with large areas of unimproved acidic
grassland'.

Walthamstow Reservoirs
Ferry Lane, Tottenham, N17.
Thames Water. 133 ha.
Among the earliest of London's reservoirs, their islands provide
nesting sites for a variety of birds including Britain's fifth-largest
heronry. Large numbers of wintering duck congregate here and,
the Lee Valley being a migration route for waders, 30 species of
these have been recorded. Sandpiper, greenshank and redshank
are regular visitors in spring and autumn, and snipe, dunlin and
green sandpiper are also frequent.

Walthamstow Marshes
Spring Hill, Clapton, E5.
Lee Valley Regional Park Authority. 35 ha.
A major conservation battle was fought around this last area of
flood meadows in the lower Lee valley in the late 1970s and early
1980s. The Park Authority had hoped to boost its coffers through

gravel extraction with the lakes subsequently landscaped for water sports. A Save the Marshes Campaign was opposed not only by the Park planners but by Hackney and Waltham Forest councils, and was backed by the GLC who refused permission for extraction – a ruling upheld after a public inquiry in 1981. The Park's Countryside Service now includes guided tours of the Marsh among its active programme of events. A leaflet, *Walthamstow Marsh – A Guide to the History of the Area*, is available from them at Myddleton House, Bulls Cross, Enfield, EN2 9HG (0992-717711).

Ainslie Wood
Ainslie Wood Road, E4.
LB Waltham Forest. 1.75 ha. LWT.
Included in the NCC's 'inventory of ancient woodlands', this mixed oak woodland was formerly part of Epping Forest. In addition to common species of woodland birds, tawny owls, treecreepers and spotted flycatchers have been observed. The area's plant and animal life is under pressure from the heavy and inappropriate use to be expected on such a small site surrounded by housing, such as rubbish dumping and BMX-ing.

WANDSWORTH

Centred around the crossing of the River Wandle just above its junction with the Thames, the borough has remnants of wildspace at Putney Heath and Wandsworth Common and London's finest non-royal park in Battersea Park.

Wandsworth Common
SW18.
LB Wandsworth. 70 ha.
The wildest part in the south includes heathland and scrub as well as the satisfyingly unkempt Central Pond. The area is described in a detailed nature trail available from the Nature Study Centre at Neals Farm in the north-western segment of the Common.

Putney Heath
SW15.
Wimbledon Common Conservators. 137 ha.
The southern part of the Heath is to all intents and purposes part

of Wimbledon Common. The northern area, separated by the Kingston Road and adjoining Roehampton High Street, is also managed by the Conservators and, though much built on, is in places pleasantly rough-hewn.

Battersea Park
SW11.
LB Wandsworth. 80 ha.
Built on the former Battersea Fields using excavations from the Royal Docks during the 1850s, the park is a cornucopia of delights. Within a formal design its ingredients include a riverfront promenade, a well-sculpted lake, deer enclosure and, most recently, a nature reserve in addition to the sports pitches and running track. The author W. H. Hudson lauded its birdlife which is varied and prolific. The lake (6 ha) supports tufted duck, pochard, shelduck, great crested grebe and herons as well as resident mallards and Canada and greylag geese, with many other species visiting. To supplement the park's trees and shrubberies, a former leaf dump has become a nature reserve known as **Mist's Pitch** after the naturalist who for many years has chronicled its 20 species of trees, 100 flowering plants, 21 butterflies and 65 bird species.

WESTMINSTER

Enshrined in its name is Westminster's origin as the western rival of the original City of London. The minster was the foundation of the Thamesfront development which made Whitehall the monarchy's main court and the heart of Parliament and Government. But even while the West End expanded, the western half of today's borough remained open land. Henry VIII formed a hunting forest stretching from Westminster northwards to Hampstead, and successive monarchs preserved large parts of it as royal parks. From Charles I's time these were progressively opened to the public.
Two streams ran through the area. The Tyburn flowed from Regent's Park past what is now Marble Arch and formerly supplied St James's Lake. To the west, as its name suggests, the Westbourne ran from Hampstead, and was dammed to form the Serpentine, before running into the Thames at Ranelagh. Apart

from the parks and the Paddington Recreation Ground in the now heavily built-up Maida Vale, many churchyards and Georgian squares are smaller enclaves of greenery.

Hyde Park and Kensington Gardens
DoE. 144 ha and 110 ha.
Despite the sparcity of enclosures the two parks are rich in birdlife which is assiduously recorded each year in the leaflet *Birdlife of the Royal Parks* (HMSO). Over 90 species are seen here, with more than 30 species nesting – many, of course, water fowl attracted by the Serpentine and its banks. Just to the east of West Carriage Drive, the boundary between the two parks, is Epstein's statue of Rima, the spirit of the forest in W. H. Hudson's *Green Mansions*, a tribute to the author's writings on London's wildlife. Convenient maps of these and other royal parks are features of Hunter Davies' *A Walk Round London's Parks*. Also under the management of the Hyde Park staff is Buckingham Palace Gardens, undisturbed apart from summer garden parties and corgis, and thus a prized location for long-term surveys of city fauna and flora by naturalists of all species.

Green Park and St James's Park
DoE. 21 ha and 37 ha.
While the former is just a little dull, the latter has the lake which is a permanent happening, such is the throng of wildfowl and humans congregating there. Because of the difficulty of keeping the water in a self-purifying state, the lake is periodically drained for desilting. Similar problems have been afflicting The Serpentine, closed to bathers in 1986.

Regent's Park and Primrose Hill
DoE. 188 ha.
Last of the royal parks to be laid out in formal fashion, Regent's Park was designed by Nash on the site of what was called Marylebone Park. This was leased out as agricultural small holdings until Nash's client, the future George IV, decided to indulge in some speculative building on a grandiose scale. Many of the later Victorian parks were also intended as the focus for desirable residential neighbourhoods, Nash having pioneered the

concept. The lake is especially fine, with a famous – but now somewhat diminished – heronry on one of its islands and a bird sanctuary at its northern tip. Between the park and its extension at Primrose Hill runs the Regent's Canal, passing the London Zoo established here in 1828. Shamed by their much-publicised initial refusal to allow the London Wildlife Trust to plant a symbolic primrose to mark the Trust's launch in 1981, the staff have since established a primrose bank on a secluded side of the hill.

Contacts
London Wildlife Trust (LWT), 80 York Way, N1 9AG (01-278 6612/3)
British Trust for Conservation Volunteers (BTCV), 80 York Way, N1 9AG (01-278 4293)
Trust for Urban Ecology (TRUE), South Bank House, Black Prince Road, London SE1 7FJ (01-587 1562)
London Natural History Society, c/o British Museum (Natural History), Cromwell Road, SW7 5BD
London Ecology Centre, 45 Shelton Street, WC2H 9HJ (01-379 4324)
London Borough Joint Ecology Committee (LBJEC), c/o Camden Town Hall, Euston Road, NW1 2RU
Greater London Ecology Unit (GLEU), County Hall, SE1 7PB (01-633 5000)
Thames Water, New River Head, Rosebery Avenue, EC1R 4TP. An excellent leaflet, *Wildlife of the Tidal Thames*, is available free from this address, as is the leaflet *Birdwatching at reservoirs in the London area.*
Essex Naturalists' Trust, Fingringhoe Wick Nature Reserve, South Green Road, Fingringhoe, Colchester CO5 7DN (0206-28678)
Hertfordshire and Middlesex Trust for Nature Conservation, Grebe House, St Michael's House, St Alban's, Herts AL3 4SN (0727-58901)
Kent Trust for Nature Conservation, 125 High Street, Rainham, Kent ME8 8AN (0634-362561)
Surrey Wildlife Trust, Hatchlands, East Clandon, Guildford, Surrey GU4 7RT (0483-223526).

References

A-Z London Street Atlas has in its de luxe coloured edition a useful superimposition of the national grid reference system lines, enabling sites to be identified with great accuracy.

The Royal Parks of London by Richard Church (HMSO, 1965) has not been adequately replaced by new HMSO park guides.

A Walk Round London's Parks by Hunter Davies (Hamish Hamilton, 1983; Zenith paperback, 1984) includes useful maps.

The Thames Transformed by Jeffery Harrison and Peter Grant (Andre Deutsch, 1976).

The Tidal Thames by Alwyne Wheeler (Routledge and Kegan Paul, 1979) is a delightful 'History of a river and its fishes'.

Ecology and nature conservation in London (GLC, 1984): Ecology Handbook No. 1.

A guide to habitat creation by Chris Baines and Jane Smart (GLC, 1984): Ecology Handbook No. 2.

Nature conservation guidelines for London (GLC, 1985): Ecology Handbook No. 3.

A Nature Conservation Strategy for London (GLC, 1986): Ecology Handbook No. 4.

Hampstead Heath Flora by Joyce Bellamy and others (GLC, 1986): Habitat Handbook No. 1.

Open Space in London by Stuart Carruthers, Jane Smart, Tom Langton and Joyce Bellamy (GLC, 1986): Habitat Handbook No. 2.

Nature conservation strategies for the following boroughs are to be published in the Ecology Handbook series, now produced by GLEU (see above): Brent; Southwark and Greenwich; Hounslow and Hillingdon; Hackney and Waltham Forest; Sutton and Croydon; Ealing and Richmond; Barking and Dagenham.

Bristol and South Wales

BRISTOL

Upstream of Bristol city, the eastern limit of the built-up area of Kingswood – a separate area in local government terms but here treated as part of Bristol – is Siston Brook which joins the Avon near Willsbridge. Its valley was followed by the Bath to Bristol Suburban Railway which is now a cycle and walk way looping northwards and westwards to the city centre. The River Frome provides a green wedge almost to the centre. At the Avon gorge, above Brunel's high level suspension bridge, Clifton and Durdham Downs look across to the Leigh Woods. As its name suggests, Westbury forms the western part of Bristol on the River Trym, the stream – supplemented by Hazel Brook on which is Blaise Castle – flowing into the Avon at Salt Mills.

South Bristol has developed patchily around and between the streams flowing from the Dundry Hill ridge. The Malago runs to the city centre, creating the valley followed by the road (A38) and railway to the south-west. To the east a stream runs from between Stockwood and Hengrove to the Avon at St Anne's. To the west is Colliter's Brook flowing through Ashton Vale to the Avon where it turns north through the Gorge. The Avon Wildlife Trust (AWT) is the local county trust and is very active in the area.

Willsbridge Valley
Long Beach Road, Willsbridge, BS15.
Kingswood DC. 1.5 miles. AWT. Visitor centre (0272-326885).
Willsbridge Mill has become the Avon Wildlife Trust's wildlife visitor centre and field study unit, conveniently situated at the centre of Avon county between Bristol and Bath. Pedestrian access is possible from Willsbridge Hill but car parking is as above. A

nature trail extends up the valley, and trail booklets are available. A footpath southwards leads to the Avon, which can be followed thereafter by the towpath on the north bank.

Dundridge Farm Woodland and Tips
Conham Road, Conham BS15.
Private.
An ancient acidic woodland with sessile and English oak canopy which includes old hazel coppice.

Crew's Hole Woodland
Crew's Hole Road, BS5.
Bristol CC.
A small area of mature acidic woodland supports several plant species rare in Bristol, including sessile oak and sheeps sorrel. Also part of the St Anne's Valley complex is:

Trooper's Hill
Trooper's Hill, BS5.
Bristol CC.
Part of the Crew's Hole open space, this is the best example of acidic grassland in the conurbation and supports a variety of grasses and herbs, and butterflies such as graylings.

Frome Valley
North of Crew's Hole a series of open spaces, such as St George's Park and Rose Green, link with the valley of the Frome at Eastville Park, which from here until the M4 is fringed with woodlands and fields including grassland at Oldbury Court estate. At Ridgeway the 'Suburban' trail offers a view across the city near where it passes the Alcove pond, continuing on to Rodway Hill at the edge of the built-up area. On the far side of the valley, **Stoke Park Hospital** is surrounded by pasture where rough grassland survives on the steeper slopes. Woodland stretches westwards up the hill but suffers from the incursion of grazing cows and horses. A nature trail leaflet describing the river walk, produced by the Bristol Naturalists' Society, is available from the council, whose address is below. Towards the centre at **Narroways Junction**, a small area of partially enclosed herb-rich unimproved grassland owned by British Rail is leased by St Werbergh's City Farm.

Brandon Hill Nature Park
Jacobs Wells Road, BS8.
Bristol CC. 2 ha. AWT.
At the heart of the city Brandon Hill includes on its western side a nature park managed by the Avon Trust. Two small ponds by the side of the footpath crossing the hill support a variety of marshland plants and insects. Scrub has been left to develop lower down as a shelter for birds, and amidst the grassland is a butterfly garden planted out with native herbs. At the west gate of the park is the Avon Trust's HQ and a shop where a trail booklet is available. An urban wildlife centre is to be opened here in 1988.

Avon Gorge
Bridge Valley Road, BS8.
Bristol CC.
Facing the Leigh Woods – which are a National Nature Reserve owned and managed by the NCC – the slopes and ledges of the Gorge support limestone grassland species including national rarities.

Clifton and Durdham Downs
Circular Road, BS8.
Bristol CC.
Once famous for their variety of plants, the botanical interest of the Downs has been mostly destroyed. Some areas of interesting vegetation have survived, notably on the thinner soils near the Gorge and in the shallow quarries near Upper Belgrave Road. Plants found include rock rose and spring sedge by the Gorge and wild thyme and spring whitlow grass. A variety of birds are found here including lesser whitethroat which breeds in the area of scrub.

Badock's Wood
Bowness Gardens, BS10.
Bristol CC. Management association.
In the valley of the River Trym where it is joined by another stream, this small open wood is dominated by ash, sycamore, oak and horse chestnut with good ground flora. A nature trail circles both sides of the river. The reserve is managed by the city council, assisted by local people, and a trail leaflet is available from the Badock's Wood Community Society c/o the city council.

Kingsweston Down
Grove Road, BS9.
Bristol CC. 8 ha. AWT.
The area round Blaise Castle is mostly woodland, including stands of pure beech as well as oak, sycamore and ash-dominated mixed woodland. The reserve is a herb-rich grassland on the limestone ridge. The southern part of the estate supports the richest woodland flora and fauna in Bristol.

Other woodlands in the vicinity include: **Greenhill Plantation**, a small wood dominated by mature English oak, ash and sycamore with an interesting ground flora; **Thirty Acre Wood**, varying in quality but with abundant bluebell and red campion in places; **Penpole Wood**, where many trees and shrubs have been planted but where the ground flora is poor as a result of much past disturbance; **Moorgrove Wood**, managed by Henbury Comprehensive School.

Lawrence Weston Moor
Lawrence Weston Road, BS11.
Bristol CC. 12 ha. AWT.
Habitats range from hay meadows through to reed beds divided by rhynes (drainage ditches) and hedgerows.

Avonmouth Sewage Works
Kings Weston Lane, BS11.
Wessex Water. 11 ha. AWT.
A series of freshwater lagoons and ditches attracts an impressive variety of water birds and dragonflies. The reserve is only part of the 52 ha Katherine Farm site owned by the water authority. Around the sewage treatment works remain several of the original meadows but their botanical interest has declined through a lack of recent grazing. A trail booklet is available from AWT, but access is by permit only to avoid too much disturbance to the birds.

Crabtree Slipwood
Sylvan Way, BS11.
National Trust.
On the banks of the Avon south of Shirehampton Park is a diverse area of calcareous grassland with several scarce plants including

rock rose and milk vetch, where large numbers of butterflies can be seen.

Adjoining is **Horseshoe Bend**, a small area of woodland and calcareous grassland with plants such as marjoram, centaury, primrose and violet which attract large numbers of common butterflies. Downstream is **Lamplighters' Marsh**, a narrow strip of land between the river and the railway which has an interesting community of fresh and brackish water plants.

A footpath on the south bank of the Avon returns to the docks at the centre of Bristol through **Leigh Woods** and passing:

Ashton Court
Kennel Lodge Road, BS3.
Bristol CC. 350 ha.
The estate includes diverse habitats including woodland, grassland and various ponds, a small area being managed by the Avon Wildlife Trust.

Crox Bottom
Durville Road, BS13.
Bristol CC.
The valley of Pigeonhouse Stream includes two pools with exceptionally rich flora attracting a large variety of birds and dragonflies. Surrounding grassland includes unimproved areas on both calcareous and neutral soils. The stream rises at **Dundry Hill**, the slopes of which stretch across the south of Bristol. A rich wildlife habitat consisting largely of unimproved grassland with good hedgerows, part is an Avon Wildlife Trust reserve.

Stockwood Open Space
Stockwood Road, BS4.
Bristol CC. 18 ha. AWT.
Relict farmland includes hay meadows, woodland, hedgerows, ponds and an old tip which are described in an AWT nature trail booklet.

A walk down the road through Keynsham or on the path, crossing the Avon by ferry at Hanham Court, returns to Willsbridge Mill.

Contacts

Thanks are due to Ralph Gaines and Rupert Higgins of the Avon

Wildlife Trust for providing information on which the above gazetteer is based.

Avon Wildlife Trust, The Old Police Station, 32 Jacobs Well Road, Bristol BS8 1DR (0272-28018/25490).
Parks Manager, Bristol City Council, Colston House, Colston Street, Bristol, BS1 5AQ (0272-266031) offers trail guides to Ashton Park and Blaise Castle, as well as the Oldbury Court estate on the banks of the Frome.
BTCV South West, Old Estate Yard, Newton St Loe, Bath BA2 9BR (02217-2856).

SOUTH WALES

Cardiff and Swansea are the two major cities in, respectively, South Glamorgan and West Glamorgan. The selected sites included here are in the three Glamorgan counties and Gwent.

SOUTH GLAMORGAN

CARDIFF

A Cardiff Wildlife Group was established in 1979 and includes representatives of local councils, the NCC, Glamorgan Wildlife Trust and University College Cardiff. Under the auspices of this group, an MSC project produced a Cardiff Wildlife Survey in June 1984.
The River Taff runs through the centre of the city, its estuary including an important bird site at **Penarth Flats**. Inland is:

Glamorgan Canal
Forest Farm Road, CF4.
Cardiff CC. 23 ha. LNR.
The area surrounding the short stretch of the disused canal is managed by the council as a Local Nature Reserve. In addition to the canal and adjoining areas of marsh, access to the latter being by permit only, the LNR also incorporates **Long Wood**, an ancient semi-natural deciduous woodland, a length of former railway cutting and some old hay meadows. The canal and woodland form the Glamorgan Canal/Long Wood SSSI.

Radyr Woods Community Nature Area
Heol Isaf, Radyr, CF4.
S. Glam CC, Cardiff CC and Radyr Community Council.
On the other side of the valley an area of deciduous woodland and grassland with wetland includes the Hermit Wood Local Nature Reserve.

Bute Park
North Road, CF1.
Cardiff CC. 2 miles.
A nature trail follows the side of the Taff upstream from the castle. A trail leaflet is available from the council.

Contacts

Leisure and Amenities Department, Cardiff City Council, Heaton Park, Cardiff.

PENARTH

Cosmeston Lakes Country Park
Mile Road, Penarth.
Vale of Glamorgan BC and S. Glam CC.
Surrounding flooded limestone quarries, the park encompasses the 4.6 ha Cosmeston Park SSSI which includes open water, fen, woodland and limestone grassland habitats. The site supports a regionally important dragonfly population and provides breeding sites for over 40 different bird species. Around 300 species of flowering plants have also been recorded.

BARRY

Porthkerry Country Park
Barry.
Vale of Glamorgan BC.
On the town's western fringe, the park includes the 4.9 ha Cliff Wood Local Nature Reserve (which is also the Cliff Wood/Golden Stairs SSSI), a good example of mixed deciduous woodland. The ground flora includes purple gromwell, a locally rare species.

WEST GLAMORGAN

SWANSEA

Blackpill
Mumbles Road, SA3.
Easily overlooked from the Swansea to Mumbles bike path parallel to the A4067, Swansea Bay provides an overwintering and passage site for a large number of waders. Although forming part of a complex which includes the Gwendraeth, Burry and Severn Estuaries, it supports a significant number of species in its own right. Counts for ringed plover and sanderling here alone exceed 1 per cent of British and Western European populations. Other species such as oystercatcher, grey plover, bartailed godwit, knot and dunlin are locally important. Gull-watching can be rewarding for 'twitchers' with some notable vagrants having been recorded in recent years.
Inland from Blackpill Bridge is the River Clyne and the Clyne Valley country park. Adjacent are **Hen Parc Woods**, privately owned but with a network of paths created by local residents. Extensive oak and birch woodland has a ground flora including hard fern and common cow-wheat. There are also small areas of ash, wych elm and alder woodland.

Mumbles Hill
Mumbles Road, SA3.
Accessible from the coastguard lookout at Mumbles Head, the hill's loess-covered lower slopes support heathland dominated by gorse and bell heather. The exposed limestone of the upper slopes bears limestone grassland with such attractive species as autumn lady's tresses and autumn gentian.

Bishops Wood
Caswell Road, Caswell, SA3.
Swansea CC. LNR.
A relatively recent ash and wych elm woodland has a typical understorey of spindle, field maple and hazel. Oak and birch woodland occupies the north-eastern end of the site on more acidic soils. A surrounding area of limestone grassland supports a wide variety of species including thyme and rockrose, which attract

many sorts of butterflies such as the silver-washed fritillary and silver-studded blue. More information on this site can be obtained from the City Conservator at Swansea City Council, The Guildhall, Swansea.

Cwm Llwyd Wood

Waunarlwydd Road, SA5.
West Glamorgan CC. LNR.
A typical coalfield oak woodland includes occasional ash and birch, with an understorey of rowan, hazel and holly. Alder, sallow and alder buckthorn cover the wetter areas, where there are occasional clumps of royal fern.
Several interesting marsh areas can be found below the woodland. Species-rich areas with yellow flag and yellow loosestrife can be contrasted with acidic drainage flushes and pastures supporting such species as bog asphodel, devilsbit scabious and heath spotted orchid. Further information can be obtained from the County Ecologist, West Glamorgan County Council, County Hall, Swansea.

Rosehill Quarry

Rosehill, Mount Pleasant, SA1.
Swansea CC.
A local environmental project, supported by Swansea City Council, is developing an abandoned sandstone quarry as an educational and recreational resource. Notable species include royal fern and the regionally uncommon blue-tailed damselfly.

Swansea Canal

West Glamorgan CC.
A disused waterway featuring marginal marsh and alder and willow woodland, its adjacent meadows support a flora typical of the unimproved areas of the coalfield. It is currently under consideration for designation as an LNR.

Crymlyn Bog Nature Reserve

Dinam Road, SA1.
NCC. 40 ha.
This is part of the Crymlyn Bog (234 ha) – to the majority of which there is no access – which is the most extensive area of lowland

fen in Wales, with some of the species and communities being more characteristic of East Anglia. Much of the bog is covered by a wide variety of fenland communities which range from sphagnum moss-dominated poor fen through to others with bottle sedge, bog bean and marsh cinquefoil. Taller and more eutrophic (nutrient-rich) areas support both greater and lesser reedmace, sawsedge and common reed. Purple moor grass dominates in the drier areas while the eastern margin bears tussock sedge and scrub woodland.

A marginal marsh around pools on the edge of a former pulverised fuel ash tip supports an interesting flora including lesser water-plantain, bladderwort, false fox, sedge and sea club-rush.

The denser areas of reed host a sizeable population of reed and sedge warblers during summer while notable winter visitors include marsh harrier. This is also an extremely good site for dragonflies, with a total of 13 species recorded to date. Further information can be obtained from The Warden, 31 Bryn-y-Mor Road, Swansea.

Crymlyn Burrows
Elba Crescent, Fabian Way, SA1.
Private.
Crymlyn Burrows are a series of beach, dunes and saltmarshes on the western side of the River Neath Estuary to which there is *de facto* access. Part of Swansea Bay, it is the only remaining stretch of coast within the Bay which has not been modified by coastal developments.

Formerly the site was part of a larger area in which freshwater peats accumulated, followed by the deposition of sand in the Middle Ages. Sea water flows into the low-lying areas between the dune ridges where saltmarshes have developed and which in turn grade into freshwater marsh at the head of the creeks to the west. Here the successional stages in the development of dune plant communities can be seen and there is a rich flora.

Pant-y-Sais
Ashleigh New Road, SA10.
Neath BC. 18 ha. LNR.
A strip of fenland supports a rich range of wetland plants as well as insects and their predators.

Drummau Road Quarry
Drummau Road, Neath Abbey, SA10.
Private.
A varied dragonfly fauna has been recorded at the ponds in the floor of this abandoned sandstone quarry. Notable species sighted here include the ruddy darter and the keeled skimmer.

Eglwys Nunydd
Glamorgan TNC. 100 ha.
South of Port Talbot between Margam steel works and the M4 is a reservoir which is the most important site in the county for overwintering waterfowl particularly coot, pochard and tufted duck. Great crested grebe breed annually. Access by permit only. On the other side of the railway are **Margam Moors**, privately owned with no access, representing the last remaining example of the once extensive coastal levels in West Glamorgan. Marsh, meadow and ditch communities support species such as flowering rush, frogbit, arrowhead and Cyperus sedge at the edge of their range. Others such as lesser water-plantain, tubular water dropwort and marsh helleborine are of more local interest. The uncommon dragonfly *sympetrum sanguineum* has been found in the ditches along with other nationally rare invertebrates.

MID GLAMORGAN

PORTHCAWL

Kenfig Pool and Burrows
Kenfig, CF33.
Mid Glamorgan CC. 810 ha. LNR. Visitor centre (0656-743386). The pool, fringed by marshland and wet woodland, abounds in plants and insects, and in addition to its breeding population attracts many passage and overwintering bird species. The sea shell composition of the dunes has produced a lime-rich substrate, with over 500 flowering plants being recorded here. Leaflets are available from the reserve centre.

TONDU

Cwm Risca
Fountain Road.
British Coal. 1.6 ha. Glamorgan TNC.
A pond, scrub and grassland on coal tip land lies a short distance away from the Glamorgan Trust's headquarters in a former National Coal Board site office.

Tondu Iron Works
Private.
A former iron works, much of the site is wooded, with abundant bird life. The bulldozing of trees on part of the site was halted by concerted action by local residents.

TONYPANDY

Craig Pont Rhondda
Llwynypia.
Rhondda BC.
A coppiced sessile oakwood with an acid ground flora is an SSSI adjacent to the Glyn Cornel Environmental Studies and Activities Centre.

ABERDARE

Dare Valley Country Park
Cynon Valley BC. 320 ha. Visitor centre.
In a valley formerly mined for coal, the park includes three nature trails showing examples of plants typical of the coalfield. Leaflets are available from the park centre.

MERTHYR TYDFIL

Taf Fechan
Merthyr BC. 41 ha.
The river runs through a steep valley, producing a variety of habitats from wetland through woodland to the grassland on the upper slopes.

GWENT

NEWPORT

Allt-yr-Yn
Newport BC.
North of the town on the banks of the Brecon Canal, this area, based on an old estate, is now considered by Newport Borough Council and the Gwent Trust for Nature Conservation to be a nature reserve. It offers a range of habitats including woodland, open water, unimproved grassland and scrub.

There are a number of other areas in Newport which have been identified as being important for wildlife in the Gwent Trust's report for Newport Borough Council, the Newport Habitat Survey being available from the Trust address below.

PONTYPOOL

Llandegfedd Reservoir
Pontypool.
Welsh Water.
An SSSI with a diverse range of overwintering water birds between October and March. Welsh Water are presently looking at improving the bird watching facilities at this site. More information from Welsh Water, Nelson, Treharris, Mid Glamorgan.

Monmouthshire and Brecon Canal
Newport to Pontypool.
BWB.
Although cruising is permitted, care is taken to retain wildlife features. Part forms the **Five Locks** nature reserve managed by the Gwent TNC.

Contacts

Grateful acknowledgements are due to the NCC South Wales regional office for providing the bulk of the above gazetteer.

NCC, 43 The Parade, Roath, Cardiff CF2 3UH (0222-485111).
Glamorgan Trust for Nature Conservation, Glamorgan Nature Centre, Fountain Road, Tondu, Bridgend, Mid Glamorgan CF32 0EH (0656-724100).

Gwent Trust for Nature Conservation, Shire Hall, Monmouth, Gwent NP5 3DY (0600-5501). The Trust's wildlife group in Newport is c/o 16 White Swan Court, Monmouth, Gwent NP5 3NY (0600-5501).

Birmingham and
the Midlands

Entries cover firstly Birmingham and the four westerly districts of the county, followed by Coventry and Leicester to the east.

Birmingham and the Black Country still bear the scars of the mining and manufacturing that made it the heartland of Britain's industry during the 19th century and after. The old quarries and spoil heaps remain unbuilt-on among the modern housing. Redundant mills and factories, victims of changing patterns of trade, stand desolate alongside new motorways and superstores. The survival of these open spaces has meant that despite post-war development the region is rich in areas recolonised by the natural world, many of which are now safeguarded as parks and nature reserves.

During the mid-1970s a pioneering survey of Birmingham and the four districts of Wolverhampton, Walsall, Sandwell and Dudley revealed, as described in the resulting report *The Endless Village*, that the 'average British municipal park is barren compared with many of the so-called derelict areas of the Black Country'. Thanks to a mixture of municipal enlightenment and public pressure, some – such as Beacon Hill, Rough Wood, and Hay Head – were adopted as public open space with minimal disturbance of their habitats. Others such as Merry Hill Farm have been bulldozed for warehouse sites or, as in the Sandwell Valley, have been badly mauled during their conversion into more orthodox recreational areas.

The threats to sites of even outstanding importance continue. The bog and fen surrounding the pool next to a colliery tip at Stubbers Green Road was of such rarity in the region that it was designated as an SSSI. Despite this the owners proposed to construct a factory on it and, only a month before a public inquiry into the plans, sent in mechanical diggers to drain the land, thus damaging its unique value.

BIRMINGHAM

The area is fortunate in being served by the Urban Wildlife Group (UWG) which, despite its title, is a fully-fledged county trust whose involvement in many West Midlands sites is described below.

River Cole

The Cole, one of the two River Tame tributaries running through south-east Birmingham, is the focus of 'Project Kingfisher' – a scheme, sponsored by the local council in conjunction with the Urban Wildlife Group, through which a wider variety of habitats is being created along the river banks: woodland, wet meadow and scrub. Kingfishers can already be found nesting and feeding here following the reduced pollution of the stream in recent years. The River Cole and Chinn Brook Conservation Group are working to encourage sensitive management of the southern section of the river. Places where newly created sites can be visited include: **Haybarn Recreation Ground**, Coventry Road, Small Heath; **Batchelor's Farm Recreation Ground**, Bordesley Green; **Newbridge Farm**, Hob Moor Road; and **Brook Meadows**, Shard End.

The Ackers

Armory Road, Tyseley, B11.
Birmingham CC.
Formerly a derelict site, it has been transformed by local voluntary groups assisted by the Urban Wildlife Group into a nature park, although it is primarily used as a recreation ground. It is managed by the Ackers Trust, the name 'Ackers' derived from the Birmingham slang for the aqueduct that runs nearby.

Edgbaston Park and Pool

Edgbaston Park Road, Edgbaston, B15.
Private. 15.6 ha. Birmingham NHS.
The lake, fed by Chad Brook which runs into the River Rea, is fringed by reedmace and willow carr which gives way to alder woodland and beech wood in drier areas. The pool and its surroundings, one of only ten SSSI's in the West Midlands, is surprisingly only one mile from the city centre. It is a haven for many aquatic species, small mammals and breeding wildfowl, including great crested grebe, and no less than 233 species of higher

plants have been recorded here. The pool and its adjoining woodland forms part of a former park created around 1730. It is leased by Birmingham Natural History Society who issue visitors' permits.

Harborne Walkway Nature Trail
Access from Nursery Road, Harborne, B15.
Birmingham CC. 1 mile.
The Harborne Walkway follows the abandoned line of the Birmingham-Harborne railway which was closed in 1963. The trail has been allowed to become wild and passes through a mixture of naturalised garden and natural woodland vegetation, past a pool area and alongside Chad Brook. Just a few examples of birdlife along the Harborne walkway include redwings from September to April, swifts from April to August, wrens and house martins. Butterflies include large and small white, meadow brown, wall brown and small skipper. A nature trail leaflet is available from City Planning Department, 120 Edmund Street, Birmingham B3 2RO.

Moseley Bog
Yardley Wood Road, Wake Green, B14.
Birmingham CC. 4 ha.
A beautiful woodland and bog area supporting a wide variety of wildlife including many rare plants, butterflies and birds. It was saved from development after a campaign by the local community who formed the Friends of Moseley Bog group which has been working alongside the Urban Wildlife Group, pressing for the site to be declared an LNR. The mixed deciduous woodland here has developed around an old mill pond and on adjoining land. Moseley Bog is a remnant of the wetlands which provided inspiration for many of the magical places described by Tolkien in *Lord of the Rings*. **The Dell**, a small woodland owned by the City Housing Department, borders this site.

Plants Brook Reservoirs
Kendrick Road, off Eachelhurst Road, Sutton Coldfield.
Birmingham CC. 11.4 ha. Birmingham CC and UWG.
At one time the reservoirs were scheduled to be filled in and developed into an equestrian centre, but after pressure from the

community supported by the Urban Wildlife Group, and with help from the city council they are now preserved for amenity use. An area to the west of the reservoirs has become an official nature park, where a timber walkway leads through alder- and willow-fringed wetland with its population of frogs, toads and newts. Surrounding the lake are wildflower meadows which attract many butterfly species. A permanent interpretation centre is planned. The community nature park is managed by Urban Wildlife Group and the local community, the remainder being managed by Birmingham City Council through a steering committee consisting of residents, conservation groups and other interested parties.

Queslett Quarry
Queslett Road, Queslett, B42.
Private and Birmingham CC. 14 ha.
A former gravel pit, it includes a small pool, marsh (with marsh orchids), willow scrub and grassland which supports a diversity of plants. The Urban Wildlife Group and local schools have carried out a tree planting programme. There are plans to secure LNR status for this site.

River Rea
The River Rea, which runs within half a mile of the city centre, is a major wildlife corridor linking important sites such as the Mill Lane Community Nature Park and Wychall Reservoir. The Urban Wildlife Group is working with the city council advising on minimising detrimental effects which could be caused by insensitive river engineering. Places along the river where wildlife areas can be visited include: **Mill Lane Community Nature Park**, Mill Lane, Longbridge, B31; **Wychall Reservoir**; **Lifford Reservoir**; and **Kings Norton Playing Fields**.

Sutton Park
Town Gate, Park Road, Sutton Coldfield.
Birmingham CC. 1,000 ha. Visitor centre.
An extensive and historic site, this complex of dry and wet heath, deciduous woodland, marsh, bog, pools and streams forms a diverse habitat for a great variety of fauna and flora, including many uncommon species. An SSSI, the park is a popular amenity for the whole of the West Midlands. The visitor centre in the park

distributes guides and maps and provides biological and historical information.

The park was preserved for hunting from Saxon times to the reign of Henry VIII with the status of Royal Forest being conferred for much of this period. In 1528 Henry VIII presented the park to the people of Sutton Coldfield. It was later very much affected by the Industrial Revolution. Powell's Pool was formed by the construction of a dam in 1730 and a mill was built, first for cotton spinning, later for rolling sheet metal and finally for manufacturing agricultural implements. Blackroot and Longmoor Pools were also designed to provide water power.

This century the park has been through many changes. Temporary roles include its use for growing corn during World War Two and in August 1957 it was occupied for 14 days by 35,000 scouts for their World Jamboree. Sadly, other transformations have been of a more permanent and detrimental nature. Much of the park was drained in the first half of this century and drainage work in the 1950s seriously diminished the size of and variation of marsh plants by Little Bracebridge Pool. Clearance work and use of insecticides to combat mosquitos was responsible for the loss of the nightjar as a breeding species. However, despite these obstacles, the park remains an extremely valuable site for many common and uncommon species.

Woodgate Valley Country Park

Clapgate Lane, Woodgate, B32.
Birmingham CC. 80 ha.
Within the boundaries of the country park at Woodgate Valley is a fascinating array of habitats, both natural and reclaimed. A mill pond, a drained reservoir and an old clay pit have now become valuable wildlife areas complementing the natural habitats in the park. These include wetland, grassland, scrub, brooks (including a stretch of the Bourn Brook, which runs east towards the Rea), ditches and mature trees. Hedgerows containing ash, alder, hazel, hawthorn and holly criss-cross the valley and mark old field boundaries. These hedgerows and fields provide a valuable habitat for woodland and open meadow creatures and plants. The occurrence of bluebells, dog's mercury and wood anemone together with varied tree and shrub layers suggests that the hedges are very old and could be associated with ancient woodland.

Woodgate Valley was threatened with future building development until 1984. The city council responded to a massive public campaign, supported by the Urban Wildlife Group, and its designation as a country park now secures its preservation for future generations.

Yorks Wood
Ford Bridge Road, Tile Cross, B37.
Solihull BC. 9.5 ha.
This ancient woodland, in the valley of the Cole on the fringe of the city, dating back to the 1400s, is now surrounded by housing. It contains oak, ash, rowan and hazel trees and in spring is carpeted with bluebells. There is one small pond, and breeding birds in the woodland include great tits, wrens and willow warblers. The local conservation body, the Yorks Wood Preservation Group, was initiated by the Urban Wildlife Group and has carried out a variety of work including pond, litter and ditch clearance. Fences with stiles now reduce access by motorbikes and also cut down vandalism.

Aston Nature Garden
Aston Park, B6.
Next to Aston Park is a small nature garden created at the request of the local community on the site of a former house and garden. The area was designed by landscape architects at the Urban Wildlife Group.

Birmingham Settlement Urban Ecology Project
318 Summer Lane, B19.
A demonstration site illustrates techniques of planting on small areas for the purpose of encouraging wildlife and increasing public awareness of the value of such nature gardens as part of the urban environment.

Richmond Nature Garden
Soho Hill, Handsworth.
An inner city site has been developed by the Urban Wildlife Group for the local community and schools on the site of a demolished terraced house.

DUDLEY

Beaconhill Quarry
Wolverhampton Road, Sedgley.
25 ha.
This disused quarry has been colonised by calcareous grassland and thorn bushes which provide a valuable habitat for insects and birds. It is the largest area of calcareous grassland in the West Midlands, and species which can be found here include quaking grass, greater knapweed and upright brome. Originally a geological SSSI it has now been renotified as much for its botanical importance as for its geological value.

Dudley Castle Hill
Gervase Drive.
Dudley MBC. 17 ha.
Ash and beech are dominant in this mixed broadleaved woodland, with luxuriant herb and shrub layers, including dog's mercury and wood anemone, all sustaining a wealth of insect and bird species. Willow warblers, chiff-chaffs, great tits, blue tits and blackcaps may all be spotted here. Dudley Council are presently developing a nature trail through the woodland and it provides a natural attraction between Dudley Castle and the Black Country Museum, only half a mile from the town centre.

Fens Pools
Pensnett Road, Brierley Hill.
BWB, Dudley MBC and private. 45 ha.
The area was saved from insensitive river engineering through intervention by the Urban Wildlife Group. Fens Pools provides great recreational opportunities for the local community from sailing to bird watching. There is now an active conservation group, the Pensnett Wildlife Group, who are highlighting the value of the site by organising nature strolls and talking to the local schools. Acting as balancing lakes for the Stourbridge Canal system, the three pools, which together comprise Fens Pools, and the surrounding scrub and grassland form a rich and diverse habitat supporting a wide range of wildlife. Great crested newt, grass snake, adder's tongue fern and a colony of over 900 southern marsh

orchids are just four of the resident species. Unusual visitors to the pools have included great northern diver and hoopoe.

The Fens Pools green wedge forms part of a larger network of green sites including the Buckpool Gully and Barrow Hill area. They combine to form a lifeline which stretches into the Staffordshire countryside.

Ham Dingle
Oakfield Road, Pedmore, Stourbridge.
Dudley MBC. 5.8 ha.
This attractive deciduous woodland with steep valley slopes and small streams running north to the River Stour contains a variety of habitats and associated plants. There are indications that the wood could be of ancient origin.

Saltwells Wood
Saltwells Lane, Brierley Hill.
Dudley MBC. 37 ha. LNR. Interpretation centre (0384-261572).
An extensive area of woodland, scrub grassland surrounds **Doulton's Clay Pit**, a geological SSSI. The wood supports a wide range of rare plants, amphibians and invertebrates and has a large bird population. It is itself designated an LNR and lies at the heart of the Blackbrook Valley running south to the Stour. The interpretation centre is situated at the centre of the reserve with access from Pedmore Road.

River Stour
Running from the Dudley boundary at Halesowen some eight miles through urban Cradley Heath and Lye to Stourbridge, the river is flanked by housing and industry yet contains extensive stretches of natural beauty and contrasting character. It is identified as a wildlife link in the county nature conservation strategy, but presently suffers from a lack of comprehensive planning and management. Dudley council is currently undertaking a study with a view to the development of a linear walkway.

Particular places to visit include: **Haden Hill Park**, near Old Hill; **Stour Vale Pond**, a recently created habitat off Bagley Street, Stourbridge; and **The Earls**, near Halesowen, an area of grassland, marsh and woodland.

Cotwall End Valley

Cotwall End Road, Sedgley.

Dudley MBC. 39 ha. Wardened.

A mosaic of grassland, disturbed ground, open water and hillside woodland, this is recognised as important green wedge land supporting a wide range of plants and animals. It includes **The Dingle** which, as its name suggests, is a dell or hollow, from which a stream runs down towards the Stour. It is notable for its small sphagnum bog. The Cotwall End Valley is managed by a warden and team based at the Nature Centre at the western end of Catholic Lane.

Wren's Nest

Wren's Hill Road.

Dudley MBC. 48 ha. Visitor centre.

Primarily this area is of immense geological importance. It is a National Nature Reserve which is internationally famous for its abundant marine invertebrate fossils, over 300 species having been recorded. The occurrence of limestone makes the area of biological interest too, as it is favourable to lime-loving plants which may be found in only a few sites throughout the county. Other features include calcareous grassland, hawthorn and hazel scrub and broadleaved woodland, the presence of which is partly due to planting which took place in the early 18th century – compensation for the damage caused by limestone quarrying. Another consequence of quarrying work are the caves which although now closed to the public are of particular importance as potential bat-roosts. The presence of limestone makes Wren's Nest attractive to invertebrates, especially snails, and the pill millipede may also be found. It is quite possible to find many invertebrates side by side with their prehistoric counterparts.

The location of Wren's Nest in a densely built-up and industrial area makes it especially valuable as a refuge for wildlife and people. A full description of the reserve was published in 1974 by the NCC.

SANDWELL

Galton Valley Canal Park

Smethwick.

BWB and Sandwell MBC. 2 miles.

The park runs from close to the M5, near Oldbury, along the

Birmingham Canal to within two miles of Birmingham city centre. The canal embankments are relict heathland and support a good variety of plants, notably mountain fern and shield fern. Its situation, running through what is otherwise a densely urban environment, makes it a valuable wildlife corridor. **Smethwick Summit**, in Roebuck Lane, one of the area's few woodlands, straddles an island on the highest stretch of the canal, which runs in two tracks at this point.

Holly Wood
Queslett Road, Great Barr, B22.
Sandwell MBC. 54 ha. Staffs TNC.
An attractive broadleaved bluebell woodland adjacent to a small wet grassland area, this is a community nature park well used by local residents and schools. A community management committee, Friends of Holly Wood, was established with help from the Urban Wildlife Group to tidy the woodland and improve the quality of the habitats here. Holly Wood was formerly part of the grounds of St Margaret's Hospital, severed by the M6. These grounds are now managed as a private reserve by the Walsall Group of the Staffordshire Nature Conservation Trust.

Sandwell Valley
Forge Lane.
Sandwell MBC, RSPB etc. 100 ha.
A large area of open land in the heart of the West Midlands conurbation surrounds streams running into the Tame. Containing a variety of wildlife habitats, the valley extends into the city of Birmingham and is crossed north/south by the M5. It includes birch wood and mixed woodland containing oak and sweet chestnut, and many of the open areas are bordered by hedgerows. There is a rural studies centre at Sandwell Park Farm in Dartmouth Park in the west. The RSPB nature reserve, with its reserve centre in Tanhouse Avenue in the north, includes educational facilities.
Other places of interest to visit in the Sandwell Valley include: **Swan Pool**, to the west of Park Lane, which is valuable for migratory birds. There is a nature trail behind Park Farm, off Park Lane to the east, which contains several pools where wildfowl, pochards, gadwall, ruddy duck and kingfishers may be seen. **Sotts**

Hole in Dagger Lane, north of Dartmouth Park, is a sunken woodland with a bog area, which was landscaped by the Urban Wildlife Group and is a proposed LNR.

Sheepwash Lane
Sheepwash Lane, Great Bridge.
BWB. 14 ha.
Balancing lakes for the River Tame, the pools and unimproved pasture on this site are of particular value for birds, including little ringed plover, wintering stonechat and passage waders. There is also a stream which runs northward to the Tame.

West Bromwich Parkway
Access from Lying Lane, West Bromwich, or Downing Street, Handsworth.
BR and Sandwell MBC. 4 miles.
A cycle/walkway follows the course of this disused railway from West Bromwich to Handsworth. An impressive red sandstone outcrop is a feature of the route which also includes an area of relict heathland. It is of botanical interest, dark mullein and Mediterranean thistle being of note, and black redstarts have also been spotted here.

WALSALL

Barr Beacon
Beacon Road.
Barr Beacon Trust. 17.2 ha.
The Beacon (227m) dominates a rural landscape which has been protected for agriculture, recreation and wildlife. It commands a magnificent view of the West Midlands and lies at the centre of the Beacon Regional Park, a 12-mile-long area of countryside reaching from Handsworth in Birmingham to Chasewater on the Staffordshire border. The park is a patchwork of fields, hedgerows, woods, streams and canals – including most of the length of the Rushall Canal, and there are many areas of country park picnic sites and nature reserves linked by a network of paths and canals.

Chasewater
Brownhills
Staffs CC, Walsall MBC and BR. 300 ha.
This vast expanse of water with surrounding bog, fen and

heathland habitats is one of the borough's most important wildlife sites. Both a wildlife haven and recreation facility, the lake is of particular value for wildfowl. Its overwintering birds number 10-15,000 and include glaucous gulls and Iceland gulls. The adjacent wetlands boast colourful and unusual plants such as the insect-trapping round-leaved sundew and several species of orchid. It also has important heathland, both wet and dry.

Clayhanger
Pelsall Road, near Brownhills.
Private. 6.5 ha.
A diverse area of former mineral workings, on the bank of the Rushall Canal, between Pelsall Road and Clayhanger Village, incorporates pools, marsh, grassland and acid spoil heaps. It is a proposed LNR supporting a wide variety of wildlife notably meadow thistle and snipe and is about to be notified as an SSSI. The Urban Wildlife Group has consistently campaigned to protect the site from development, the latest proposal being for opencast mining.

Cuckoo's Nook
Barr Common Road, Aldridge.
8.5 ha.
The site, which includes **The Dingle**, is a mixed acidic broadleaved woodland with diverse ground flora, bisected by streams. Immediately south is **Birch Wood**, an acidic oak wood with abundant birch and holly. A pond with rare moss species adds considerable value to this site.

Hay Head
Longwood Lane.
Walsall MBC and private. 7.6 ha.
The variety of habitats which have developed around this disused limeworks and canal support a variety of plants uncommon in the district, including wood anemone and greater spearwort. Local naturalists cherish Hay Head for its birds, mammals and insects and the disused canal is a well-known frog and toad breeding site. A nature trail guide is available from: Libraries & Museums Service, Central Library, Litchfield Street, Walsall (021-526 4530).

Leckie Road Wildlife Park
Stafford Street.
Walsall MBC. 0.5 ha. Wardened.
This community nature park was established by the Urban Wildlife Group on derelict housing land in 1982. The local community and schools have helped with tree planting and meadow establishment. Today the park with its meadow, developing woodland and small pool, fringed with yellow flag and reed-mace, provides an informal, natural site with great amenity both for residents and wildlife. It is managed by two part-time wardens.

Park Lime Pits
Park Road.
Walsall MBC. 30 ha.
Disused lime quarries, part of which have flooded to form two large pools since being abandoned over 100 years ago, have developed an impressive variety of trees, plants and other wildlife. Many birds feed and nest in the dense hawthorn and blackthorn and in the summer there are large numbers of moths and butterflies. Park Lime Pits are currently being developed as a country park, with new tree and shrub plantings and a continuous hard track running the length of the site. They form part of a proposed LNR which will also include Lady Pool (to which there is no access at present).

Stubbers Green Road Bog
Stubbers Green Road, Aldridge.
Private. 3.2 ha.
This wetland site includes an acid bog area, a habitat extremely rare in the region, which has developed on land affected by past mining activities. The bog supports a rare and fascinating plant community, with sphagnum moss, southern marsh orchid and cotton grass just three of the unusual occurrences. Thriving amphibian and insect populations add further interest (though there is no public access at present). An SSSI, the site is gradually being encroached upon and destroyed by its owners who are attempting to drain the land with a view to future warehouse development. The Urban Wildlife Group continues to fight to save the bog.
A quarter-mile to the north-west, also on Stubbers Green Road, is **Swan Pool** (1.7 ha), a nationally important swallow roost.

Walsall Arboretum and Extension
Broadway North.
Walsall MBC. 40 ha.
Only a stone's throw from the centre of Walsall, this extensive park contains a variety of habitats which are valuable for wildlife. The park extension contains a stream, rough grassland and scrub, ditches and wet hollows as well as overgrown hedgerows which are extremely valuable due to their increasing scarcity in the countryside. Its large size and the variety of trees and shrubs, streams and lakes, make the arboretum of considerably greater value than the average town park.

WOLVERHAMPTON

Ladymoor Pool
Coseley.
Wolverhampton MBC and Dudley MBC. 7.8 ha.
A small wetland area developed on disturbed ground, the site was reclaimed by the former county council whose upgrading of the reserve included the planting of 10,000 trees, the creation of a conservation area and the excavation of a pond which is now host to a pair of mute swans. The site also supports uncommon plants and a community of birds.

Northycote Farm Park
Northycote Lane, Moseley.
Wolverhampton MBC. 5 ha.
Part of an agricultural area on the northern fringe of Wolverhampton, it lies adjacent to the Waterhead Brook along whose course mill pools and fish ponds still survive. Within the Bushbury green wedge, it is being developed by Wolverhampton council as a recreational and wildlife resource.

Peascroft Wood
Peascroft Lane, Bilston.
4.7 ha. Bilston Conservation Society.
In a heavily built-up district, this is both a valuable wildlife habitat and public amenity.

Valley Park
Compton Road, Compton.
Wolverhampton MBC, BR and BWB. 2.5 miles.
A linear park which follows the Smestow Brook and Stafford and Worcester Canal from Wolverhampton Stadium near Aldesley, out to the Staffordshire countryside at Wightwick. A walkway developed on the bed of the former Oxford, Worcester and Wolverhampton Railway runs along embankments and through cuttings, grassland and woodland where a variety of wildlife abounds. Over 180 plant species have been recorded in this delightful wildlife corridor. Further information is available from the Urban Wildlife Group.

Contacts

Grateful thanks are due to Richard Hadley, Kate Green and Tom Slater of the Urban Wildlife Group for the compilation of the Birmingham-Wolverhampton gazetteer.

Urban Wildlife Group, 11 Albert Street, Birmingham B4 7UA (021-236 3626).
Birmingham Nature Centre, Pershore Road, Edgbaston, B4 7RL (021-643 9261).
Centre for Urban Ecology, Birmingham Settlement, 318 Summer Lane, B19 3RL (021-359 3562). It shares the running of a Resource Centre with the Midlands 'think green' network at the same address.
BTCV West Midlands, Conservation Centre, Firsby Road, Quinton, Birmingham B32 2QT (021-426 5588).
Staffordshire Trust for Nature Conservation, Coutts House, Sandon, Staffs ST18 0DN (08897-534)

COVENTRY

A number of sites are managed by the Warwickshire Nature Conservation Trust (WARNACT), which also manages two nature gardens within the city at **Bell Green** and **Wellington Street**.

Stoke Floods
Stoke Hill Estate.
Coventry CC. 7.6 ha. WARNACT.
Stoke Floods reserve consists of wet grassland and reeds

surrounding a lake fed by the River Sowe. The flora includes many wetland species, especially around the lake, including yellow flag, hemlock, reed canary-grass and great hairy willowherb. The grassland supports many attractive plants such as greater burnet and meadow cranesbill. A wide variety of water birds are recorded here, but mallard, tufted duck, coot and moorhen are the most characteristic. Mute swan and great crested grebe also breed regularly. The reserve has many interesting visitors on migration including common and black terns, greenshank, grey and yellow wagtails and shoveler. Seven species of warbler are found on the reserve in summer and of these willow warbler, blackcap and whitethroat are known to breed.

Wyken Slough
Alderman's Green Road.
Coventry CC. 1.2 ha. WARNACT. Wardened.
On what was originally farmland, coal mining from the 17th to 19th centuries was probably the cause of subsidence in which the Slough (or marsh) was formed. With the end of mining the area became derelict and, when the construction of the M6 in the 1960s isolated the fields from the surrounding farmland, much of the area fell into disuse. The reserve consists of a small reedbed adjacent to Wyken Pool. Adjoining rough pasture contains traditional meadow species such as great burnet and pepper saxifrage. Eight species of dragonfly and damselfly have been recorded on the site. It is an important winter haunt of reed bunting, meadow pipit and snipe and occasional jacksnipe, and among the more uncommon visitors are shoveler, greenshank, black and common terns and bearded tit. Management work and wardening is carried out in collaboration with the Friends of Wyken Slough.

Contacts

Further information on wildlife sites, in Solihull as well as Coventry, from WARNACT, Montague Road, Warwick, CV34 5LW (0926-496848).

LEICESTER

The River Soar runs through the middle of the city north towards the Trent, its course accompanied by the Grand Union Canal and a now disused railway line. There are a number of notable sites in Leicester, due in part to the activity of the local group, the City Wildlife Project (CWP).

Riverside Park
Leicester CC. 8 miles.
The Riverside Park developed by Leicester City Council runs the full eight-mile length of the city following the course of the River Soar and Grand Union Canal. It incorporates all the open space adjoining these waterways, including Abbey Park, Castle Gardens and grazed washlands, and supports a rich and varied flora and fauna. Interpretative boards and leaflets describe the history and ecology of the Riverside Park, the latter available from the council address given below.

Aylestone Meadows
Canal Street, LE2.
Leicester CC. 100 ha. Nature trail managed by CWP.
A large and important green wedge which penetrates the south of the city following the washlands of the River Soar and River Biam. The area contains a mosaic of habitats including marsh, herb-rich grassland, scrub, still and flowing water. The large population of breeding birds includes yellow wagtail and kingfisher and overwintering birds include snipe and water rail. New ponds and a wetland complex have recently been created, and a nature trail has been established by the City Wildlife Project with board walks to enable access through wet areas.

Great Central Way
Access from Evesham Road, Middleton Street, Briton Street, etc.
Leicester CC. 2.8 miles.
A pedestrian/cycle route has been developed by the council along the route of the disused Great Central railway. Dense scrub-covered embankments support a variety of birds, and the tracksides and cuttings support a rich flora and a variety of breeding butterflies including grizzled skipper. Recently landscaped sections include wildflower verges created from seed.

Rally Nature Garden
Tudor Road and Richard III Road, LE2.
Leicester CC.
Created from wasteland on the site of one of Britain's earliest railways by the City Wildlife Project and the local community, the garden forms part of a larger community park designed and won by local residents when the land was threatened by a road proposal. This inner-city nature garden contains a great variety of habitats including a rockery and buddleia scrub which regularly attract 20 species of butterfly. Over 200 species of native and ornamental plants can be found on the site.

Watermead Ecological Park
Oakland Avenue, LE4.
Leicester CC. 1.5 ha. CWP.
The park was developed by the City Wildlife Project on disused grazing land by the River Soar. The central feature is a small lake of 2,000 square metres which supports a rich variety of flora and fauna including breeding dragonflies. Hedgerows, grassland (under various management regimes), woodland planting and a marsh area complete the range of habitats. The adjoining small ash woodland is being managed as part of the park.

Freeman's Common Nature Park
Islington Street, LE2.
Leicester CC. CWP.
The last remnant of this once extensive common has been safeguarded from development so far because the BBC has erected a transmitting mast on the site. CWP hopes that it will soon be managing the site as a nature park. This inner-city site adjoins a wide railway cutting which increases the variety of wildlife visitors. The flora includes a large colony of primroses.

Knighton Spinney
Knighton Park, LE2.
Leicester CC. 3 ha. CWP.
A mature plantation woodland located within Knighton Park is managed by the City Wildlife Project as a nature reserve. The rich

flora includes wood anemone, dog violet and yellow archangel and birdlife includes breeding woodpeckers, nuthatches and treecreepers. Contact City Wildlife Project prior to visit.

Beaumont Leys
Bennion Road, Krefield Way, LE4.
Leicester CC.
The recent Beaumont Leys housing and industrial development retains within it a number of semi-natural features including derelict ash coppices which the City Wildlife Project is regenerating and bringing into amenity use. The area contains 25 per cent of Leicester's remaining woodlands, several of which are very rich in species such as bluebells, violets, orchids, woodpeckers and small mammals.
On the edge of Beaumont Leys **Castle Hill Country Park** (140 ha) is being developed by Leicester City Council in the valley of Anstey Brook. Other sites to visit include **Keeper's Lodge Spinney** and **Beaumont Wood** adjacent to Beaumont Leys Shopping Centre.

Anstey Lane Verges
Anstey Lane, Beaumont Leys, LE4.
Leicester CC. 0.5 mile. CWP.
Anstey Lane was an ancient drovers' track and is thought to have been a major medieval thoroughfare into Leicester. The City Wildlife Project is managing a half-mile stretch of scrub and grazing land adjoining the road. It is the best remaining example of calcareous grassland in Leicester and is bounded by an ancient hedgerow. The flora includes betony, agrimony and pepper saxifrage and supports large breeding colonies of butterflies.

Old Tilton Line Nature Reserve
Humberstone Park, Ambassador Road, LE5.
Leicester CC. O.5 mile. CWP.
This section of disused rail line was acquired by Leicester City Council and is managed by the City Wildlife Project as a nature reserve. The embankments are covered by dense scrub and mature conifers and broadleaved trees, which provide homes for a variety of birds such as gold crest and coal tit. Contact City Wildlife Project prior to visit.

Piper Way Nature Area
Piper Way, LE3.
Leicester CC. 0.7 ha. CWP.
Developed by the City Wildlife Project with the help of local people on the site of a former spinney ravaged by Dutch elm disease, it includes a lined pond and marsh, wildflower meadows, scrub and woodland block planting. An impressive feature is the carefully managed annual wildflower meadow packed with corncockle and corn marigold.

The Orchards Nature Park
Groby Road, LE3.
Leicester CC. 2.7 ha.
Disused allotments and orchard are largely covered by scrub and young woodland with grassy clearings. An old carter's pond is also contained within the nature park which supports a wide variety of flora and fauna and is particularly rich in insects.

Contacts

For providing the gazetteer, thanks are due to David Nicholls and Phil Lomax, Project Director and Senior Supervisor of the City Wildlife Project.

City Wildlife Project, 215 Charles Street, Leicester LE1 1LA (0532-552550).
Leicester City Parks Department, 1 The Square, Leicester LE1 2NB (0532-29656).
Leicester Wildlife Group, Leicestershire and Rutland Trust for Nature Conservation, 1 West Street, Leicester (0532-553904).

Other urban wildlife groups in the Midlands are:
Nottingham City Group, Nottinghamshire Trust for Nature Conservation, 310 Sneinton Dale, Nottingham NG3 7DN (0602-588242).
Northampton City Group, Northamptonshire Trust for Nature Conservation, Lings House, Billing Lings, NN3 4BE (0604-405285).

and in Shropshire:
The Telford branch of the Shropshire TNC is c/o Stirchley Grange, Stirchley, Telford, Shropshire TF8 7PW.

and in East Anglia:
Norwich Wildlife Group, c/o 48 Wellington Road, Norwich (0603-663889).

Manchester and the North-West

The conurbations of Manchester and Liverpool are covered in that order, the Merseyside areas of Warrington, Widnes and Runcorn being sandwiched between them.

GREATER MANCHESTER

The region surrounds the web of rivers flowing into the River Mersey, primarily the Irwell in the north and west, the Tame in the east and the Goyt in the south east. While the city of Manchester centres on the meander of the Irwell at its confluence with the River Irk, Greater Manchester remains a cluster of towns focused on such river valleys in the hilly terrain north and east, with low-lying land in the Mersey plain to the south and west. After coverage of **MANCHESTER** city, the districts are treated in the following sequence.

From the north-east the River Roch runs from the Pennines through **ROCHDALE** and meets the Irwell south of **BURY**. The Croal joins south of **BOLTON**, where the Irwell begins its wide sweep eastwards.

The River Irk, rising in Rochdale, flows through the north of Manchester before debouching into the Irwell at Victoria Bridge. The upper valley of the River Medlock forms the boundary between Oldham and Tameside, and bisects Manchester on its course to the Irwell just to the south of the city centre. The Mersey crosses south Manchester forming a wide valley on either side of its embanked meanders. To its north, Platt Brook – later Chorlton Brook – joins it at the Trafford border. To its south two north-flowing streams form its eastern and western boundary. Gatley

Brook divides Manchester and Stockport, while Fairywell Brook divides Manchester and Trafford, converging with the Baguley Brook at Brooklands. South of Manchester Airport the River Bollin becomes the county boundary with Cheshire.

The region's eastern limit lies well into the Pennines, the River Tame forming the effective edge of **OLDHAM**'s built-up area before continuing through **TAMESIDE** and into **STOCKPORT**. The latter's south-east/north-west axis is the River Goyt, fed from the north by the River Etherow. Lady Brook, later Micker Brook, flows through its south western territory.

TRAFFORD lies in the triangle whose southern edge is the River Bollin, the north-western margin being the Mersey and, above Flixton, the Irwell. **SALFORD** is largely encompassed by the Irwell loop opposite Manchester. West is **WIGAN**, with its river, the Douglas, draining into the estuary of the Ribble.

There is a network of warden services which cover most of this area.

MANCHESTER

Blackley Forest and Heaton Vale Reservoirs
Blackley New Road, M9.
15 ha.
On the valleyside of the River Irk, woodland on the side of Blackley Cemetery and reservoirs offer a wide range of wildlife habitats.

Boggart Hole Clough
Rochdale Road, Blackley, M10.
Manchester CC. 33 ha.
On the sides of Boggart Brook before it joins the River Irk is a remnant clough woodland which accommodates a flourishing bird population.

Moston Sidings
Williams Road, Moston, M10.
2 ha.
An unusual marsh on an exposed clay area supports cotton-grasses and orchids among other plants. The Lancashire Trust for Nature Conservation is seeking to manage the area as a nature reserve.

Fletcher Moss
Millgate Lane, Didsbury, M20.
5 ha.
This attractive wildlife area within a bend of the Mersey is important for its ponds, marsh and wet woodland which has a rich insect and bird population.

Sunbank Wood
Sunbank Lane, Thorns Green, Altringham.
15 ha.
An oak and sycamore woodland near Manchester Airport, this site is noted for its rich woodland floor plant communities and birdlife. A short distance south is **Cotteril Clough**, a very old and natural clough woodland with mature oak, ash and alder. An SSSI, it is important for its ground flora, insect life and birds.

Ashton Canal
Ducie Street, M1.
BWB. 6.5 miles.
One of Manchester's many canals, this remains navigable but also supports many unusual aquatic plants. The Rochdale Canal also terminates at the basin.

Contacts

The assistance of the Greater Manchester Countryside Unit in providing the information on which the gazetteer for the Greater Manchester districts is based is gratefully acknowledged.

The Unit, which provides a countryside advisory service to and on behalf of the ten district councils, and is funded by them with additional support from the Countryside Commission, is based at Tameside MBC, the address being: Council Offices, Wellington Road, Ashton-under-Lyne (061-344 3104).

Medlock Valley warden service (061-330 8355).

The Lancashire Trust for Nature Conservation, whose head office is at Preston, has a Manchester office c/o The Environmental Institute, Greaves School, Bolton Road, M27 2UX (061-736 5843).

The Cheshire Conservation Trust is at Marbury Country Park, Northwich, CW9 6AT (0606-781868).

The Manchester Wildlife Group is c/o 31 Stanley Road, Whalley Range, M16 (061-226 2029).

The Colour Atlas edition of the Geographia guide to Manchester offers convenient identification of open space and a useful section on local contact addresses.

ROCHDALE

Hollingworth Lake
Smithy Bridge Road, Littleborough.
Rochdale MBC. 48 ha. Wardened (0706-73421).
Part of the Hollingworth Lake Country park, the reservoir is among the best waterfowl areas in the region, featuring wintering wildfowl, migratory birds and shore waders which can be seen from a lakeside trail. A sanctuary area protects breeding birds in summer.
Passing near the lake is the **Rochdale Canal**, now disused and an important aquatic system for plant and animal life.

Healey Dell
Shawclough Road.
62 ha. Wardened (0706-350459).
One of the best remnant clough woodlands in the region, it lies on the valley of the River Spodden. Its habitat diversity is increased by colonisation of industrial areas such as mill ponds and railway tracks.

Ashworth Valley and Naden Brook
Ashworth Road, Heywood.
77 ha.
Extensive oak and birchwood clough woodland with associated acidic grasslands and heath, it is particularly good for birdlife.

Alkrington Woods and Rhodes Lodges
Alkrington Hall Drive, Manchester New Road, M24.
37 ha.
Noted for its mill ponds and deciduous woodlands, it offers a wide spread of natural history interests.

BURY

South-east of Ramsbottom and on the Irwell as it flows south from the west Pennine moors is **Gollinrod Wood** (27 ha), an area of oak wood and willow scrub with a general wildlife value. South-west is **Broad Hey Wood** and **Woodhey** (15 ha), part of which is ancient or long-established woodland, which has an attractive understorey and rich ground flora locally.

Kirklees Brook
Garside Hey Road, BL8.
29 ha.
Noted for its wide and interesting range of industrial and semi-natural habitats, it includes numerous mill ponds which support a very rich flora and fauna.

Elton Reservoir
Buckingham Drive, Daisyfield, M7.
22 ha.
A canal feeder reservoir, it attracts many waterfowl including ducks, geese and swans, and is also good for passage migrants and wading birds which use the sandy margins and shallows.

Mere Clough
Clifton Road, Prestwich, M25.
A large area of long established mature woodland on Bradley Brook has a good range of other wildlife habitats and an excellent natural history interest.

Manchester, Bolton and Bury Canal
Wellington Street, Bury, BL5 to Nob End.
5 miles.
Following the Irwell to its junction with the Croal, the now disused channel is noted for its aquatic flora containing several uncommon plants. Marginal marsh communities are also of interest.

Contacts
Croal-Irwell Valley Warden Service (0204-71561).

BOLTON

Bradshaw Brook runs down from the moors parallel to the Croal, which it joins near the town centre. The valley contains several sites of high wildlife interest including woodlands and old mill ponds. Good deciduous woodlands, scrub, water areas and associated reedbeds and marsh occur. Kingfisher, grey wagtail and dipper are regularly seen along the stream. **Jumbles Reservoir** near the head of the valley is famous for its breeding and wintering wildfowl. There is a Jumbles warden service (0204-853360).

Doffcocker Lodge
Moss Bank Way, Doffcocker, BL1.
Bolton MBC. 10 ha.
Among the best sites in the region for wintering wildfowl, it has large numbers of ducks including rare visitors. Recently drained for repair work and the creation of an island, it is to be managed as a nature reserve.

Rumworth Lodge
New Tempest Road, Lostock, BL6.
Bolton MBC. 7 ha.
Whooper swans are among the winter visiting waterfowl which are a feature at this reservoir. The surrounding grasslands attract winter thrushes and in summer the reedbeds and marsh provide cover for breeding reed and sedge warblers among others.

Bull Hill
Hall Lane, Farnworth, BL4.
Bolton MBC. 20 ha.
One of three adjacent industrial sites on the banks of the River Croal, it has, like the others, a range of habitats resulting from its former uses. Acidic plant communities occur on the hill itself with species-rich flushes locally. An important lime flora is found on the alkali waste and wetlands in the old gravel workings and filter beds in the valley floor.

Moses Gate
Hall Lane, Farnworth, BL4.
Bolton MBC. 14 ha.
This country park features old mill ponds and developing woodlands, the ponds and reedbeds being excellent for water birds including swans, geese, ducks, grebes and visiting kingfishers. The reedbeds, scrub and young woodland attract many warblers.

Nob End
Prestolee Road, Radcliffe, M26.
11 ha.
Most of the site consists of alkali waste tipped around the turn of the century and naturally colonised. The lime flora is very attractive and species-rich, with many uncommon plants and huge colonies of fragrant orchids and several species of marsh orchid. The best industrial site in the county, it has great scientific and educational value and its plant ecology has been described in several scientific papers and books.

Contacts
Croal-Irwell Valley warden service (0204-71561).

OLDHAM

Daisy Nook
Stannybrook Road, Failsworth, M35.
Oldham MBC. 19 ha.
A country park at the heart of the Medlock Valley, the area is important for its oak and ash woodlands and other attractive wildlife features. Crime Lake, which is noted for its wildfowl, is nearby.

Huddersfield Narrow Canal
Uppermill to Stalybridge.
8 miles.
This disused canal in the Tame Valley has developed a surprisingly rich and varied aquatic flora and fauna including many unusual species and rarities.

Contacts
Medlock Valley warden service (061-330 8355).
Tame Valley warden service (061-344 3306).

TAMESIDE

Holden Clough
Oldham Road, Bardsley, Ashton-under-Lyne.
24 ha.
The best and most extensive example of a natural clough woodland in the county, it consists mostly of oak woodland with a high general

wildlife interest.

East and slightly south is **Greenhurst Clough** (10 ha), Greenhurst Road, another clough woodland with a variety of habitats for plants, insects and birds.

Hollinwood Branch Canal
Broadbent Street, Ashton New Road, M11.
0.5 miles.
The best site in the county for aquatic plants, it is an SSSI.

Eastwood and Acre Clough
Hough Hill Road, Stalybridge.
RSPB. 22 ha.
Important for its oak woodland birds, it has a diversity of habitats including scrub, grassland and marshland.

Hulme's and Hardy Wood (10 ha), at Hulme's Lane, Stockport Road in Denton, is a mature woodland with many plant species, and **Gee Cross Clay Workings** (1 ha) at Joel Lane in Hyde, has an abundance of wild flowers which have colonised these old clay workings near the Werneth Low country park (warden service 061-368 0667).

Contacts

Etherow-Goyt Valley warden service (061-427 6937).
Medlock Valley warden service (061-330 8355).
Tame Valley warden service (061-344 3306).

STOCKPORT

Marple and Torkington Woods
Stockport Road, Marple.
53 ha.
A very large woodland rich in plants and birds lies on either side of Torkington Brook.

Kirk and River Wood
Chadkirk Road, Romiley, SK6.
21 ha.
Between the Goyt and the Peak Forest Canal are attractive mature

woodlands. The canal, running to Dukinfield in Tameside, is rich in aquatic flora and fauna in some stretches.

Poise Brook and Goyt Valley
Marple Road, Offerton, SK2.
25 ha.
Where the brook joins the Goyt is a mature deciduous woodland with good birdlife and woodland flowers.

Gatley Carrs
Brookside Road, Gatley, SK8.
3 ha.
An area of reedbed and marsh alongside Gatley Brook offers an attractive variety of plants amid the M63/M56 spaghetti junction.

Contacts

Mersey Valley warden service (061-905 1100).
Etherow-Goyt warden service (061-427 6937).

TRAFFORD

Trafford Ecological Park
Mosley Road North, Trafford Park, Stretford, M17.
Trafford MBC. 4 ha.
A former tip in an area of heavy industry which was formerly part of the grounds of a country house has been developed as the first ecological park in the North-West. Four types of woodland, meadow, wetland and lake are being created. The old lake is a wildlife reserve used by many water birds, and the surrounding area has a fine show of orchids in June. Access by arrangement with Trafford Leisure Services (061-872 2101).

Brookheys Covert
Sinderland Road, Altringham.
2 ha.
A mature oak woodland alongside Sinderland Brook has an exceptionally rich fauna and flora. An SSSI, in addition to its woodland habitats it has interesting wetland areas in former marl pits.
Adjacent is **Hogswood Covert**, recently denotified as an SSSI.

Contacts

Bollin Valley warden service (0625-52940).
Mersey Valley warden service (061-905 1100).

SALFORD

Worsley Woods
Greenleach Lane, Worsley, M28.
36 ha.
An interesting complex of mature plantations surrounds a stream feeding the Bridgewater Canal. Today the modern version of the pioneering example of a bulk transport route, the M62, runs overhead.

Oakwood
Manchester Road, Clifton, M27.
32 ha.
Attractive woodland and lake areas on the side of the River Irwell are part of a recent landscaping scheme.

Chat Moss
Astley Road, Irlam.
An extensive area in the Mersey plain between Manchester and Wigan includes several important wildlife sites. Remnant mossland derived from lowland peat bog habitats survives in a few places, known as mosses. The dried-out peat supports birch scrub, acidic grassland, bracken and heath. Much of the area is being converted to agricultural use. The western boundary of the area is formed by Glaze Brook.

Contacts

Croal-Irwell Valley warden service (0204-71561).

WIGAN

Astley Moss
Rindle Road, off East Lancashire Road, Tyldesley.
British Coal. 25 ha.
Remnant peat mossland, a footpath crosses the site – which is being acquired as a nature reserve by the Lancashire Trust for Nature Conservation.

Pennington Flash
St Helens Road, Leigh.
Wigan MBC. 104 ha. Wardened (0942-605253).
A large mining subsidence lake is the centre of a country park (263 ha) and has major ornithological importance for wintering wildfowl and breeding ducks. A nature trail and small reserve add to the wildlife interest.

Hey Brook Valley
The valley, which runs between Leigh and Wigan, contains a series of wetlands resulting from mining subsidence, the ponds and reedbeds attracting many waterfowl and small wetland birds with a large number breeding. Immediately east of Wigan, **Borsdane Wood** (31 ha) covers both sides of the valley, being an old oak woodland good for birds and plants.

Wigan Flashes
Ince-in-Makerfield.
One of the best wildlife areas in the region has been created as a result of coal-mining subsidence, tipping, ash extraction and flooding. The subsidence lakes, known locally as flashes, include Scotsman's Flash and Pearson's Flash, and are a haven for waterfowl and small wetland birds which find cover and nesting sites in the reedbeds. The lake nearest to the Ince-in-Makerfield power station was however threatened by a plan to demolish its cooling towers, the rubble to be used to infill the pool. There are currently plans for the borough to acquire the site as a nature reserve. Several rare plant species have been found and there are large colonies of wild orchids in the marshy areas and on industrial waste.

Douglas Valley
Wardened (0942-833043).
Wigan is situated where the River Douglas turns in a hairpin bend from its initial southwards course north-west towards the Ribble estuary. North-east of the town the river supplies the **Worthington Lakes Reservoirs** (25 ha), the northern part of which is the **Arley Nature Reserve**, managed by the RSPB. The Leeds and Liverpool canal follows the valley, and between it and the river, only a mile or so north of the town centre, are

the **Haigh Plantations** (84 ha), now part of the Haigh Hall country park.

On the other side of town, the **John Pit Woods** (34 ha), a woodland good for fungi, clothe the sides of a stream running into the river from Shevington. On the south bank **Dean Wood** (35 ha), a long established oak woodland, follows the valley of a stream marking Greater Manchester's western boundary.

Contacts

Wigan wildlife warden (0942-827071).

WARRINGTON

A model of how to transform a place that was a by-word for ugliness into a 'green town', Warrington has benefited from the efforts of a new town development corporation, now merged with its Runcorn equivalent. The borough lies athwart the lower Mersey between Manchester and Liverpool with few dramatic geographical features to its advantage. It was formerly a location for massive industrial plants, many of which have now been demolished and redeveloped. The pioneering approach of the Warrington New Town Development Corporation to the landscaping of new housing areas has been described in Chapter 3, and the borough has followed the Corporation in setting up its own ranger service. The interpretative material describing the area's wildspace is excellently produced and is available from the address given at the end of the section. Sites here described follow the course of the Mersey from the east to Widnes and Runcorn in the west, which together form the Halton district of this northern extension of Cheshire.

Birchwood Forest Park

Off Moss Gate, Birchwood, WA3.
Warrington BC. Ranger centre (0925-824239).
On the 1,000 acres that were formerly an ordnance factory, Britain's greenest suburb has been built. After only ten years or so, thanks to extensive woodland planting including fast growing species which will later be thinned out, the area already has a well-established appearance. Trees and shrubs grow not only along the roadsides and between the groups of houses but in the street frontages as well.
At the south-east corner of the district is:

Risley Moss
Ordnance Avenue, Birchwood, WA3.
Cheshire CC. 81 ha. Visitor centre (0925-824339).
One of the few remaining mosses in the North-West, it was restored to form a nature reserve after decades of peat digging and the dumping of waste from the Risley ordnance depot. Birch and willow scrub were removed from the open mossland and drainage reversed to raise the water table and encourage the regeneration of the sphagnum peat bog. A dense birch woodland in the west was thinned and underplanted to increase the variety of ground cover, and interspersed with glades for picnicking and play. A mature mixed woodland in the north, a former Victorian game covert, has been cleared of the bulk of its rhododendron and the undergrowth replanted. An observation tower looks out over the moss, which includes scrapes to encourage the diversity of birds feeding and breeding here.

Woolston Park
Somerset Way, WA.
Warrington BC. 20 ha. Ranger cabin (0925-824398).
Surrounding Spittle Brook just north of the Mersey, the park incorporates a complex of wetland areas fringed by reedbeds and newly planted woodland.

Appleton Dingle
Lyons Lane, Stockton Heath, WA4.
Warrington BC. Ranger cabin (0925-68787).
South of the Mersey, the steep valley of Dingle Brook offers woodland walks which can be extended down the Lumb Brook Valley to the Bridgewater Canal. Westward along the canal is **Walton Hall and Gardens**, headquarters of the Warrington council ranger service, address below.

Sankey Valley Park
Bewsey Old Hall, Bewsey Bridge, WA5.
Warrington BC. Ranger centre (0925-571836).
An ambitious linear park extending up the valley towards St Helens on either side of the St Helens Canal, its varied points of interest are described in a generous folder of leaflets covering everything

from butterflies to the history of the canal. The hall and environs include a Wild Flower Centre which offers advice, materials and assistance for those wishing to establish wild flower gardens within the borough.

The canal, which has a ranger cabin at Waterways carpark, Cromwell Avenue, has claims to be Britain's oldest, having received Parliamentary approval in 1755 and being opened in 1757. Though the canal closed to through traffic in 1963, the length between Warrington and Widnes includes a marina which locks into the Mersey at Fiddler's Ferry, a spot offering a pub with a splendid vista over the tidal mudbanks. At the Widnes end of the canal between it and the river is **Spike Island**, a good birdwatching spot as well as active recreation area with a ranger service organised by the Mersey Valley Partnership – ranger cabin at Upper Mersey Road, West Bank, Widnes (051-420 3707).

WIDNES

Pickering's Pastures
Mersey View Road, Hale Bank, Widnes.
Halton BC. 12 ha.
Public open space overlooking the Mersey adjoins Hale Marshes, an important wetland bird site which can be viewed from the **Mersey Way** which continues towards Liverpool. The *Walk the Mersey Way* leaflet is available from the Mersey Valley Partnership, address below.

RUNCORN

Runcorn Town Park
Norton Priory Walled Garden, Warrington Road.
Halton BC. 400 ha. Ranger centre (0928-65029).
Extending the whole eastern flank of the town, with new housing to its east, the park includes everything from a dry ski slope in the south to the walled garden of the former priory nestling in a small valley above the Mersey in the north. As well as playing fields the area has mature woodland, a lake, the Runcorn branch of the Bridgewater Canal, which at one time terminated here, and a short length of the Manchester Ship Canal.

Runcorn Hill

Highlands Road.

Halton BC. Ranger cabin (0925-60793).

On the other side of town, the hill overlooks the estuary after it has squeezed between the Runcorn bluffs and the West Bank promontory. A former quarry area, its red sandstone has developed some scrub among the more formal grassland.

Contacts

Mersey Valley Partnership, Camden House, York Place, Runcorn (0928-73346).

Warrington BC, Head Ranger, Walton Hall, Walton, Warrington (0925-601617).

The leaflet *Going Places in Open Spaces* which provides an admirable at-a-glance guide to the sites described above is available from both of these.

MERSEYSIDE

After Liverpool city and Knowsley, the region's other three districts are covered from east to west, which also happens to be alphabetically.

LIVERPOOL

The city developed around the port at the mouth of the Mersey in the late 17th and early 18th centuries handling, like Bristol, the sugar and slave trade with the West Indies. In the 19th century it became a major export as well as import centre, its low-lying waterfront lending itself to the excavation of docks adjoining the deep water of the Mersey channel. A ridge of high ground extends along the banks of the Mersey a short distance inland, pushing the Leeds and Liverpool Canal in a northwards loop. Patches of countryside survive along its north-east boundary, but otherwise the area is heavily built up, with parks such as Sefton Park providing the main open space. One of the leading local wildlife groups in the area is Landlife.

Clay Banks, Speke to Hale
Dungeon Lane, Speke.
Liverpool CC. 1.5 miles. 10 ha.
Part of the Mersey Way path running to the Merseyside boundary at Hale and then on to Warrington and beyond, the cliffs here are of calcareous boulder clay which support many uncommon plants including bristly ox-tongue and teasel, and a particularly interesting spider fauna.

To the north, on Alderfield Drive and straddling the Knowsley and Cheshire boundary, is **Mill Wood**, one of the few woodlands in the city with a balance of oaks and native shrubs. The mixed environments of woodland, field, watercourses and ponds are used for educational purposes, a reserve guide being available from Landlife, at the address below.

Croxteth Park
Croxteth Hall Lane, Croxteth.
209 ha. Includes LNR.
Parkland containing a complex of habitats including deciduous and coniferous woodland, pasture, marl pits and formal gardens with over 100 bird species recorded here, 57 of them breeding. **Mull Wood** is managed as a Local Nature Reserve, being a 20 ha pheasant shooting wood planted on rough pasture c1800, with an adjoining field and wetland.

Priory Wood
Southwood Road, St Michael's.
An example of one of the nature areas created or improved by Landlife is this small woodland in an overgrown garden at the entrance to the former International Garden Festival site. A nature trail begins at the spot where the Lane runs into **Sefton Park**, the trail guide being a Landlife production and available from them.

School nature gardens created by Landlife in the district include those at St Cleopas, St Saviour's, St Hilda's, St Clare's and Belvedere schools.

Contacts

Lancashire Trust for Nature Conservation, Croxteth Group, c/o Croxteth Hall, Liverpool L12 0HB (051-228 5311).

Landlife, The Old Police Station, Lark Lane, Liverpool L17 8UU (051-728 7011).

Other useful contact addresses can be found in the information section of the Colour Atlas edition of the Geographia guide to Liverpool, which also conveniently highlights open space.

KNOWSLEY

Halewood Triangle
Abberley Road, Hunt's Cross.
Knowsley MBC. 28 ha.
A diverse site on former railway land with a mature oak woodland, willow and birch scrub, grassland, heathland and ponds. 72 bird species have been recorded, 39 of which have bred. The site is at the beginning of the **Loopline**, a path and cycle track which follows the railway track almost ten miles north to Aintree. The council plans a ranger service and visitor centre.

Contacts

Joint Countryside Advisory Service, Bryant House, Maghull, Merseyside L31 2PA (051-520 1606) covers the boroughs of Knowsley, St Helens and Sefton.
Country Parks Manager, Leisure Services, Knowsley MBC, Municipal Buildings, Archway Road, Huyton, Merseyside L36 9UX.

ST HELENS

Burgy Banks
Island's Brow.
Private. 34.5 ha.
A diverse mixture of scrub and grassland habitats has developed on waste materials, mainly sand from the plate glass industry – the detritus being locally known as 'burgy'. Several coastal dune species of plant are present, including lyme grass and rest harrow. The area was the subject of a planning inquiry into development plans in 1984, the council and others opposing housing plans on the strength of its wildlife interest. Its future remains uncertain. At the south-west corner of the site the Rainford Brook becomes the canalised upper section of the St Helens Canal, now disused.

Southwards, derelict sections of the canal lead to the town centre. A short distance east lies the **Sankey Valley Park** which stretches to the centre of Warrington. From the north the canal is fed by the Black Brook via:

Carr Mill Dam
Carr Mill Road.
A mill dam extended as a feeder reservoir for the St Helens Canal via the Black Brook. Like many other stream-fed lakes, the shallower areas around the influx of the two streams in the north – the Black Brook and the Goyt – provide good marginal vegetation which is cover for nesting birds such as great crested grebe. The large expanse of open water is also surrounded by grassland and woodland.

Glass House Close Wood
Old Nook Lane.
St Helens MBC. 3.5 ha.
Despite considerable recreational pressure and vandalism, this oak wood, with wetter areas dominated by alder and willow, retains considerable interest.
Downstream are **Tootal Fields**, also known as **Stanley Bank Meadow**, a fine example of unimproved herb-rich lowland grass lands supporting a diverse meadow flora, and **Stanley Bank Wood** (7.5 ha), both privately owned.

Sankey Valley Park
Blackbrook Road.
St Helens MBC. 4 miles. Visitor centre (0744-39252).
The Carr Mill Dam to Newton Brook section of the park, created by the borough and former county council, follows the canal, occasionally extending to take in larger sites such as Colver House Wood. The stretch of canal between the wood and the visitor centre is becoming silted up and there are extensive stands of marginal vegetation, particularly great reedmace. A rich invertebrate fauna has been recorded, including water spiders.

Sutton Mosses
Sutton Moss Road.
A remnant of the formerly extensive moss system, now mostly

covered by the Bold colliery tip, Sutton Moss supports a range of wetland habitats. These include a large reed swamp dominated by great reedmace, drier areas of heather and purple moor grass, wet meadow and willow scrub. There is also a small area of a relict raised bog community containing sphagnum mosses and bog cotton grass.

A short distance away at St Helens Junction station is the St Helens branch of Landlife which, in **Herbert Street**, has created a model example of the landscaping of an end-of-terrace vacant site. Its pretty and unvandalised appearance contrasts with the nearby **Peckers Hill Road** 'temporary landscaping' on the other side of Station Road. The latter, carried out by a Countryside Landscape Unit of half a dozen or so MSC workers, is desolate and untended.

Contacts

Groundwork Trust, St Helens and Knowsley, 32-34 Claughton Street, St Helens, WA10 1SN (0744-39396).
Landlife St Helens, 531 Herbert Street, St Helens (0744-814762).
A Policy for Nature (draft, 1986) is available from: Land Manager, Community Leisure Department, Century House, Hardshaw Street, St Helens (0744-20656).

SEFTON

Leeds to Liverpool Canal
Running from the heart of the city, northwards just inland of the docks, the canal loops eastwards at Crosby following the Rimrose Brook. **Rimrose Valley Marsh** (9 ha), on either side of the stream below Rimrose Valley Road, is an extensive wetland with outstanding botanical interest, including four species of marsh orchids, and an important population of breeding sedge warblers. As well as linking such sites, the canal is important for its canalside and aquatic habitats.

Seaforth Nature Reserve
Pumping Station Compound, NW Royal Seaforth Dock.
Mersey Docks and Harbour Company. 40 ha. Lancashire TNC.
Two large pools were reclaimed in 1961 from beach and derelict

sand dune habitats, with rubble still being dumped in the south-east corner in the 1980s. The result is a mixture of habitats from the salt water of the outer pool, which tops up the whole docks system, to the fresh water of the inner lake with marshland and dry sandy areas. Over 190 species of bird have been recorded, the site being on the migratory route along the west coast, the spring passage of little gulls being the reserve's ornithological speciality. Access, by foot, is through the Freeport entrance off Crosby Road South and leaflets are available in the public hide overlooking the ponds.

WIRRAL

Eastham Woods
Ferry Road, Bromborough.
Wirral MBC. 27 ha.
Now a country park, the woodland interest is mainly ornithological, with a wide range of breeding species including all three woodpeckers, nuthatch, redpoll and kestrel. The site also includes the rocky foreshore and sandstone and clay cliffs just north of the entrance to the Manchester Ship Canal.

Brotherton Park and Dibbinsdale
Spital Road, Bromborough.
Wirral MBC. 47 ha. LNR. Ranger service (051-334 9851).
The parkland on either side of the Dibbin Brook includes the largest remnant of semi-natural ancient woodland in Merseyside. Declared an SSSI mainly for this reason, it also encompasses other interesting habitats such as the stream itself and bordering marsh and meadow. A nature trail follows paths along the brook, a trail leaflet being available from the ranger office in the Woodlees Cottages at the park entrance or from the address below.

New Ferry
Dock Road North, New Ferry.
A coastal site of ornithological interest consists of the muddy beach stretching a mile or so north to Rock Ferry, which is an important autumn roost for terns, and the reclaimed land north of Bromborough Dock. Ponds, scrub and a sewage works attract large numbers of passage and wintering birds including waders and finches.

Bidston Marsh

Bidston Link Road, Wallasey.

19 ha.

Alongside the M53 motorway as it loops towards the Mersey tunnel is an area of poorly drained grazing and waste land which supports a number of less common plants and attracts passage and wintering birds. **Bidston Hill** rises to the south, forming a sandstone ridge with fairly extensive lowland heath and woodlands. A good range of breeding birds is supplemented by migrant passerines, particularly roosting finches and thrushes. The Bidston marine observatory and lighthouse are prominent hilltop features.

Contacts

Thanks are due to Mick Brummage of the Joint Countryside Advisory Service (address under **KNOWSLEY**) for assistance in preparing the Merseyside Gazetteer.

Head Ranger, Wirral MBC, Wirral Country Park, Station Road, Thurstaton (051-648 4371).

Department of Leisure Services and Tourism, Wirral MBC, Westminster House, Hamilton Street, Birkenhead L41 5SN (051-647 2366).

Lancashire Trust for Nature Conservation, Cuerden Valley Park, Cuerden Pavilion, Bamber Bridge, Preston PR5 6AX (0772-324129).

Yorkshire and the North-East

The counties of South and West Yorkshire, Cleveland and Tyne and Wear are covered in that sequence.

SOUTH YORKSHIRE

Coverage of Sheffield, the largest city of the region, is followed by brief mention of sites in the other three districts of Rotherham, Barnsley and Doncaster.

SHEFFIELD

The city centres on the junction of the north-flowing River Sheaf and the River Don where the latter loops north-east towards Rotherham and Doncaster. Its valley is also followed by the Sheffield and South Yorkshire Navigation.

Endcliffe Park
Hunters Bar, Ecclesall Road, S11.
Sheffield CC. 15 ha.
On the banks of the River Porter, this is one of the valleys running down from the Pennines that provided the water power for the mills producing Sheffield's traditional steelware. The only surviving mill is the Shepherd Wheel higher up the valley, but within the park are two of the many dams which stored the water supply for the mill wheels. Holme Wheel Dam was used until recently for boating and is now a well-known bat study site, famous for its diversity and huge populations of bat species flocking in summer. The island in Nether Spur Gear Wheel Dam is now a waterfowl habitat. The park is the starting point for a walk described in the leaflet

Sheffield's Round Walk (45p), which is available – along with ones describing other walks – from the Recreation Department address below. The ten-mile route covers green spaces in the south-west of the city and includes **Bingham Park** (6.5 ha) which continues into **Whiteley Woods** (39 ha) where three mill dams include Shepherd Wheel, a working mill till 1930. Higher up, Forge Dam is location of a planned arboretum.

Sorby Plantation
Quiet Lane, Fulwood, S10.
Sheffield CC. 5 ha. Sorby NHS.
Partly planted by the Sorby Natural History Society in 1973, it is a botanically rich area of grassland and marsh which is managed by the Society in conjunction with the council as a nature reserve, a booklet being available from the Society's address given below.

Beyond the Mayfield Valley where many of the farms are council-owned, **Porter Clough** (7 ha) offers wooded slopes where Scots pine and beech predominate.

Limb Valley
Whirlow Bridge, Ecclesall Road, S11.
Sheffield CC. 50 ha.
The valley of the Limb Brook includes mixed deciduous and coniferous woodland – parts being Pennine oak woodland – and areas of upland heath and bog. The valley with its botanical, zoological and ornithological interest, has been an ecology site for the Sorby Society since 1976. A nature trail guide and booklet is available from the Society.

Ecclesall Woods
Abbey Lane, S7.
Sheffield CC. 123 ha.
The city's largest suburban woodland is a mainly mixed deciduous woodland with a rich ground flora, and is well known for its insect and bird life. The Ecclesall Wood bird sanctuary (13.5), established by the Sorby Society in 1928, is the city's oldest nature reserve.

On the other side of the valley are **Ladies Spring Wood** (14 ha), a natural Pennine oak wood designated an SSSI, **Parkbank**

Wood (8 ha) and **Chancet Wood** (7 ha). Beyond the
Meadowhead quarries is **Graves Park** (83 ha), Sheffield's largest.
A short nature trail in the southern part of the park is described
in a free leaflet.

Rivelin Valley
Rivelin Mill Bridge, S6.
2 miles.
A nature trail down the River Rivelin to its junction with the River
Loxley at Malin Bridge is described in an enjoyable leaflet (45p
from the Recreation Department) which, as well as outlining the
natural history, gives an account of the many mills which formerly
operated on the riverbank. None of the mills survive but the
millponds do, some silted up and marshy, others dredged and
popular with fishermen.

Loxley Valley
Rowel Lane, Loxley, S6.
Sheffield CC and private. 26 ha.
Scene of the great Sheffield Flood caused by the bursting of the
Dale Dyke Dam in 1864, the valley, with its industrial archaeology,
river and woodlands, is managed as a countryside management
project by the city's Recreation Department. The woodland is
mostly ancient deciduous, with oak dominant. There are also
grasslands and a series of millponds where successive colonisation
can be seen.

Sunny Bank Wildlife Park
William Street, S10.
Sheffield CC. 1 ha. Sheffield CWG.
A new project being developed by Sheffield City Wildlife Group
in partnership with the city council and the local community and
funded by the DoE Urban Programme, the park has experimental
maintenance schemes and is a valuable educational habitat.

Sheffield Canal
Maltravers Street, S4.
BWB. 4 miles.
This runs from the canal basin, now being restored, to Tinsley
Locks. The canal is now free of pollution and shows a wide range

of habitats. A leaflet is available from Sheffield City Museum. The canal leads the walker into the Lower Don Valley which has a number of interesting features, including the large **Tinsley Sewage Farm** which is a superb habitat (contact Yorkshire Water Authority for permit). A report, *Lower Don Valley: Wildlife and Geology*, has been produced by the Natural Sciences Section of the city's Museums Department.

Wincobank Hill
Jenkin Avenue, S9.
Sheffield CC.
Standing above the Lower Don Valley it is the site of a Celtic hill fort of the Brigantes. The woods are mainly oak/birch and are regenerating and being planted up to provide an attractive habitat.

Ecological Park
Brightside Lane, S9.
British Rail. TRUE.
An area of railway land has been taken on by the Trust for Urban Ecology and is being developed for urban ecology studies. Details from Oliver Gilbert of Sheffield University's Landscape Architecture department.

Don Valley
The industrial section of the River Don is botanically rich, and has been well surveyed by the Sorby Society since 1972. A booklet is available, and the aforementioned Oliver Gilbert is carrying out an up-to-date survey of the area as an NCC project.

Contacts
Thanks for assistance in compiling the above list of sites are due to Mike Wild and Dennis Patton of the Sheffield City Wildlife Group, and to Derek Whiteley of the Sorby Society.
Sheffield City Wildlife Group can be contacted c/o 2 Trafalgar Road, Sheffield 6 (0742-312414).
Sorby Natural History Society can be contacted c/o 730 Ecclesall Road, Sheffield S11 8TB.
Information about the city's many wildlife sites can be obtained from:
Recreation Department, Sheffield City Council, PO Box 151,

Meersbrook Park, Sheffield 8 9FL (0742-500500).
Ecology Unit, Natural Sciences Section, City Museum, Weston Park, Sheffield S10 2TP (0742-27226).
Countryside Unit, Department of Land and Planning, Town Hall, Sheffield 1 (0742-734211).
Department of Recreation and Environmental Studies, Sheffield City Polytechnic, Totley Hall Lane, Sheffield S17 4AB (0742-369941).
Department of Landscape Architecture, Sheffield University, Northumberland Road, Sheffield 10 (0742-768555).

ROTHERHAM

Droppingwell Valley
Droppingwell Road, S61
Rotherham MBC.
Around a stream forming the boundary between Sheffield and Rotherham, the valley has been restored to its former rural character under a county council scheme which involved local people in tree planting and other landscaping works.

Littleworth Open Space
Rowmarsh.
Rotherham MBC.
A colliery spoil tip has been turned into a new woodland with local schoolchildren planting whips (saplings) on the reclaimed site.

Contacts

Information about open space in the district is available from: Countryside Management Service, Rotherham MBC, Recreation Offices, Grove Road, Rotherham S60 (0709-382121).

BARNSLEY

The valley of the River Dearne between Barnsley and its junction with the River Don at Mexborough formerly contained extensive marsh land and meadows known as 'ings'. Though drained to provide agricultural land, subsequent subsidence caused by extensive coalmining in the region has resulted in the re-creation of wetlands, many of which have become interesting birdlife sites. Several are now managed by the Yorkshire Wildlife Trust (YWT).

Carlton Marsh
Carlton-Shefton road.
Barnsley MBC. 14 ha.
In the early 1980s the Yorkshire Wildlife Trust succeeded in persuading the South Yorkshire county council to create a nature reserve on land which was liable to uncontrolled flooding. Ponds having been dug by BTCV and Trust volunteers and planted with reeds and other wetland species, the reserve offers a range of habitats from acid grassland, willow scrub, marshland and pools.

Wath Ings
Brampton-Darfield road, Broomhill, Wombwell.
Yorkshire Water Authority. 24 ha. YWT.
Somewhat difficult to get to, with no car park and a poorly signed track across the desolate colliery tip wasteland, the reserve consists of two main lakes which attract an abundance of waterfowl and waders. With the co-operation of the Water Authority the character of the area was protected from the effects of wholesale drainage, becoming a formal reserve in 1976. Migrating species in autumn and spring include snipe, redshank, golden plover and dunlin and rarer birds such as the occasional osprey. Ducks and swans are among overwintering visitors, some staying to breed. Kingfishers can be seen feeding here, and little ringed plovers nest on the coal spoil heaps from the mine away to the east. A description of the site is contained in a leaflet describing the Yorkshire Trust's four reserves in the district, available from the Trust address below.

Contacts

Information on open space in the borough from: Leisure Services Department, Enviromental Services, Barnsley MBC, 27/29 Western Street, Barnsley S70 2BT (0226-203951).

DONCASTER

Denaby Ings
Dearne Bridge, Mexborough.
British Coal. 20 ha. YWT.
Alongside the River Dearne just above its junction with the Don, the lakes and marshland lie between the former course of the river and a colliery railway embankment now disused. Two hides are

reachable from the carpark next to the Dearne Bridge, and a further hide overlooks the Cadeby Flash on the Cadeby road. As well as a wealth of wildfowl, the reserve – established in 1967 – supports more than 300 wild flower species and over 40 grasses. Insects are prolific and varied and the wetlands are haven for plentiful amphibians. A site plan is included in the Yorkshire Trust leaflet mentioned above.

Sprotbrough Flash
Sprotbrough.
British Coal. 14 ha. YWT.
Beside the River Don, the flash consists of a long and large lake caused by mining subsidence. The lakeside vegetation provides cover for waterbirds which can be observed from the public footpath along the riverbank.

Potteric Carr
Carr Hill Industrial Estate, Balby Carr.
British Rail. 104 ha. YWT.
A large area just outside the town has regained its reedfen and marsh quality due to subsidence in the 1960s and protection against disturbance provided by the criss-crossing of railway embankments. Managed by the Yorkshire Trust since an initial agreement with BR in 1968, there is free access to the Low Ellers hide and Bessacarr Nature Walk from the entrance via Burnham Close off Stoops Lane, but direction signs are few and the starting point takes some finding. Permits for the Balby Carr Nature Trail are available in return for an sae sent to: R. Heppenstall, 8 Littleworth Close, Old Rossington, Doncaster.

Sandall Beat Wood
Doncaster MBC. 76 ha.
On the far side of Doncaster race course this large mixed plantation originates from the early 19th century. A leaflet describing the woodland is available from the Doncaster Museum, address below.

Thorpe Marsh
Marsh Lane, Bentley-Barnby Dun Road.
CEGB. 60 ha. CEGB/YWT.
Next to the Don as it heads north across the Yorkshire plain, this

area of farmland was intended by the Central Electricity Generating Board for the tipping of ash from the adjacent power station. Pressure from the Wildlife Trust backed by the county council produced an alternative layout which now includes the Thorpemere lake and a field centre on a disused railway embankment. The main interest is the unimproved grassland covering most of the reserve, providing a variety of traditional countryside plants and territory for winter visiting birdlife such as fieldfares. Abundant hedges plus dense scrub on the embankments produces cover for nesting birds. Permits and leaflets describing the site are available in return for an sae sent to: A. Mitchell, 79 Jossey Lane, Scawthorpe, Doncaster.

Contacts

Information about wildlife sites in the district can be obtained from: Doncaster Museum, Chequer Road, Doncaster DN1 2AE (0302-62095).

WEST YORKSHIRE

LEEDS

Situated on the River Aire where it emerges from the Pennines into the Yorkshire plain, the city was centre of the woollen industry, its factories powered by water and later coal. At the head of a major canal, the Aire and Calder Navigation, it is also linked to Liverpool on the west coast by the Leeds and Liverpool Canal.
From the city centre a canalside walk described in *The Museum of Leeds Trail* (70p from the Tourist Office address given below) leads six miles to Kirkstall Abbey.
A short distance upstream is the junction with Oil Mill Beck in the valley of which is:

Clayton Wood
Low Lane, Horsforth, LS18.
Leeds CC.
Although much reduced by quarrying and housing the wood still provides a habitat for a number of woodland bird species, with all three woodpecker species thought to breed here. Some ponds to the south have a variety of interest.

Bramley Fall Wood
Leeds and Bradford Road, Moorside, LS13.
Leeds CC.
Reachable from the canal towpath, this mainly oak woodland has a good fungus flora and breeding population of woodland birds.

Meanwood Valley
Rising in the countryside to the north and joining the Rive Aire just to the east of the city centre, Meanwood Beck provides an important green wedge along its valley. Outside the built-up area, **Adel Dam** is a Yorkshire Wildlife Trust reserve with observation hides overlooking the lake and a woodland fringe harbouring species such as warblers, woodpeckers and tawny owl. To the north, **Golden Acre Park** comprises 54 ha of mature woodland as well as formal gardens, and beyond is **Breary Marsh**. Across the watershed, a mile or so to the east, is **Eccup Reservoir**, a major bird site, its outlet stream running north to the River Wharfe. Issuing from the Dam, Adel Beck is accompanied by a Mill Stream, the two running past **Adel Moor** and through the **Adel Woods**, notably **Scotland Wood**. Passing under the Meanwood Ring Road the river becomes Meanwood Beck, with **Weetwood** on the west of the valley and the **Meanwood Woods** on the east.

Lower down the valley, just above its junction with Stain Beck, **Grove Lane Pond** is a former millpond, half of which was infilled as part of a council landscaping scheme. The remainder now supports a huge population of frogs and some smooth newts, together with freshwater plants that are becoming less common in the Leeds area. The water supply and management of the pond is organised by the Leeds Urban Wildlife Group.

On the west of the valley **Woodhouse Ridge** is a public park, mostly wooded but with areas of hawthorn scrub. Spotted flycatchers breed here as do great spotted woodpeckers and occasionally nuthatches. The common resident woodland birds are joined by other species in the autumn and winter. On the facing slope is **Sugarwell Hill**, where breeding birds include species associated with open country such as skylark, meadow pipit, partridge and grey wagtail. The valley is a migration route for wheatears, whinchats and various warblers, and there is a good butterfly population. Kingfishers are often seen here. The Beck disappears into a culvert during most of the rest of its course to the Aire.

Roundhay Park

Princes Avenue, LS8.

Leeds CC. 270 ha.

One of the largest natural parks in Britain, it includes various more formal features added in the last century such as the Waterloo Lake and Canal Gardens. Its relatively undisturbed woodland supports woodpeckers, nuthatch, treecreeper and spotted flycatcher. The Great Heads Beck which feeds the lake thereafter becomes Wyke Beck, running through the east of Leeds and joining the Aire by the Thorpe Hall power station.

Contacts

Grateful thanks are due to Peter Larner of the Leeds Urban Wildlife Group for the information on which much of the above sites list is based.

The Leeds Urban Wildlife Group is c/o 91 Clarendon Road, LS2 9LY (0532-444289).

Information about the city's parks is available from the Tourist Information Centre, Central Library, Calverley Street, LS1 3AB (0532-462453/4).

Leisure Services Department, Leeds City Council, 19 Wellington Street, Leeds LS1 1DG (0532-463165).

Yorkshire Wildlife Trust is at 10 Toft Green, off Micklegate, York (0904-59570).

Information on wildlife sites in Bradford, Calderdale, Kirklees and Wakefield is available from West Yorkshire Ecological Advisory and Information Service, Cliffe Castle, Keighley (0535-64184).

CLEVELAND

The county covers the industrial areas north and south of the Tees: Stockton-on-Tees in the centre, Hartlepool to the north, and Langbaurgh to the east.

STOCKTON-ON-TEES

Gravel Hole Quarry

Shearwater Lane, Norton, TS20.

ICI. 1.5 ha. Cleveland NCT.

A disused sand and gravel quarry, colonised by a rich variety of lime-loving plants. Access is by permit only.

Adjacent on Billingham Beck is **Billingham Bottoms**, one of the urban fringe recreational sites managed by the county council and one of the few remaining natural flood plains in the county. The site is of botanical and ornithological interest and is wardened.

Cowpen Marsh
Port Clarence-Hartlepool Road.
ICI. 65 ha. Cleveland NCT.

The main part of the reserve consists of freshwater marsh, largely used for grazing, and several 'fleets' popular with waterfowl and waders. A smaller but valuable part is an area of inter-tidal salt marsh. From the public hides overlooking the Tidal Pool and Seal Sands most of the British list of resident and regular waders can be seen at suitable times of the year. Regular winter visitors include merlin and short-eared owl. There are remnants of medieval saltworkings. The site is used for educational visits by the nearby Teesmouth Field Centre, but apart from usage of the public hides, access is by permit only.

Bassleton Wood
Bassleton Lane, Thornaby.
Cleveland CC. 12 ha.

On the banks of the Tees, the mixed deciduous woodland has a good ground flora. Adjacent, in a meander of the river, is the low-lying area of **The Holmes**. In addition to the public footpath to the east of the wood there are a number of footpaths both through the wood and round the grass banks of The Holmes.

LANGBAURGH

Normanby Brickworks
Flatts Lane, Normanby.
Cleveland CC. 24 ha.

The northern half of the former brickworks has been developed as public open space, the southern half being left as an area for wildlife. Formerly fields, they are reverting to woodland. Half a mile to the west along the Normanby Branch Walkway is **Ormesby Brickwoods** where woodland is being encouraged to develop. To the east of Flatts Lane is **Ten Acre Bank** (20 ha), woodland on the side of the Eston Hills now managed by the county council. North-east along the hillside is:

Lackenby Bank
Lazenby.
ICI. 100 ha. Cleveland CC.
A mainly secondary woodland, there are plans here for a field centre and warden service.

Coatham Marsh
Tod Point Road, Redcar.
British Steel Corporation. 54 ha. Cleveland NCT.
A spectacular example of how wildlife can flourish in even the most unpromising surroundings, the site is between Redcar immediately to the east, the ICI Wilton chemical works half a mile away to the south and the British Steel Redcar plant to the west. Previously saltmarsh stretching to the Tees and used as saltings, its previous 120 ha have been reduced in more recent times by industrial development, drainage and infilling. There is also some 30 ha of newly moulded land with two interesting lakes constructed about ten years ago on what was formerly a refuse tip. The site survives through its zoning as a buffer between industry and the residential area.
The marsh, ponds and grassland attract a very large number of bird species, some 200 having been recorded. 34 species have bred here, and thousands of birds visit on passage or during the winter, including 31 species of wader, seven of geese, all three British swans and 19 duck species. The flora is also diverse and interesting, over 170 species being recorded. Two hides are available for permit holders, and although there is no general public access there are vantage points from the lane.

Contacts

Cleveland County Council, which has one of the most impressive urban fringe schemes anywhere in the country, produces a model series of site leaflets available from: County Planning Officer, Gurney House, Gurney Street, Middlesbrough, Cleveland (0642-248155).
The Cleveland Nature Conservation Trust is at The Old Town Hall,

Mandale Road, Thornaby, Stockton-on-Tees, Cleveland ST17 6AW (0642-608405).
A Cleveland Conservation Forum is c/o CLEAR (Cleveland Environmental Advice and Resource Centre), Zetland Buildings, 4 Marton Road, Middlesbrough, Cleveland TS1 1DE (0642-240860).

TYNE AND WEAR

The region includes the districts of City and North Tyneside on the north bank, Gateshead and South Tyneside on the south bank, and Sunderland on the similarly gorge-like estuary of the River Wear.

NEWCASTLE-UPON-TYNE

The city centres around a crossing of the River Tyne overlooked by a former Roman fort and a Norman castle from which the town derives its name. The built-up area stretches on both sides of the river, its valley almost as deep as a gorge, on its course to the North Sea at Tynemouth.

Throckley Ponds
Church Road, Hexham Road, Throckley, NE15.
Newcastle CC. 7 ha. NWT. Wardened.
The Northumberland Wildlife Trust (NWT) manage this reserve on the banks of the Tyne within Newburn country park, the site lying among the derelict land of former industries along the valley bottom. The opposite bank a short distance downstream is the location for the 1990 National Garden Festival, planned as part of the reclamation of the riverside area. The reserve consists of a pond among colliery spoil tips which have developed pine and birch woodland cover. The long and narrow pond has surrounding grassland which attracts snipe, fieldfare, redwing and brambling in winter.
At **Grange Farm**, through a partnership between the farmer, city council and Benwell Nature Club, management is being undertaken of an oak woodland dene, two streams, a couple of ponds and neutral grassland with wet flushes.

Throckley/Walbottle Dene

Woodside Avenue, Hexham Road, Throckley, NE15.
Newcastle CC.
Possibly ancient oak woodland, the Dene has received minimal management over the last few hundred years. The ground flora is especially diverse, but has suffered from vandalism, and there is a varied bird population. Management measures are now being implemented, and an added attraction is the industrial archeology of the site – old coalmines and wagonways.

Sugley Dene

Dene Avenue, Newburn, NE15.
Newcastle CC.
Perhaps the steepest of the denes, it is predominantly oak and ash woodland with characteristic ground flora. Surrounded by housing estates, it is an important wildlife corridor linking with the Tyne.

Denton Dene

Copperas Lane, Denton, NE15.
Newcastle CC.
Another of the oak wooded valleys descending to the Tyne from the north, it retains sections of what are possibly ancient woodland. An important local wildlife corridor, it is receiving considerable landscaping improvements.

Benwell Nature Park

Atkinson Road, Benwell, NE4.
Newcastle CC. 2 ha. Study centre (091-273 2983).
On land once occupied by terraced housing above the Scotswood Road, the council initiated the construction of a nature park modelled on London's William Curtis Ecological Park. The work, carried out by the BTCV since 1982, includes the building and stocking of a pond, the planting of over 16,000 native trees and the creation of features such as an area of turf from a limestone quarry replanted over artificial outcrops of limestone. The vegetation is establishing itself, and although the site has not yet achieved a mature appearance, it is very well used by local schools.

Jesmond Dene
Jesmond Dene Road, NE2.
Newcastle CC. Interpretation centre.
Flowing from the north of the city, the Ouse Burn forms a deep valley from Gosforth to its junction with the Tyne. Predominantly oak woodland redesigned by Lord Armstrong, its habitats include steep damp gorge sections and open semi-natural grasslands. It is particularly diverse in breeding bird species.
To the south of Benton Bank are Armstrong Park and Heaton Park which, although without outstanding wildlife features, continue this important green corridor through the centre of the city. A short distance to the west are All Saints Cemetery and Newcastle General Cemetery.

Walkergate Wildlife Garden
Coutts Road, Walker Gate, NE6.
Newcastle CC. Walkergate Infant and Junior Schools.
Built on a derelict site adjacent to a primary school, the garden was laid out by children, parents, teachers and local people under the guidance of the BTCV in 1981, with a further planting of 2,000 trees in the spring of 1982. Habitats include mixed woodland, hazel coppice, conifer woodland, hedgerow, limestone rockery, butterfly garden, alder woodland, wetland and pond. During school hours there is public access through the school gates.

Big Waters
Six Mile Bridge, Seaton Burn.
Newcastle CC. 15 ha. NWT.
A subsidence pond caused by mining, it lies in the valley of Seaton Burn which runs eastward to the North Sea at Seaton Sluice (see **Holywell Dene** in **GATESHEAD**). The area also includes fen and carr with an old ridge and furrow grassland, and is important for overwintering wildfowl. Breeding bird species include great crested grebe, mute swan, sedge warbler and reed bunting. The nature reserve, run by the Northumberland Wildlife Trust, is part of a larger recreational area.

Contacts
Information on open space within the city is available from:
City Environmental Services Department, Saville Place, NE1.

Urban Fringe Area Management Scheme (UFAMS), c/o City Planning Department, Civic Centre, St Mary's Place, NE1.

The Northumberland Wildlife Trust is c/o Hancock Museum, Barras Bridge, NE2 4PT (091-232 2359).

BTCV North East is at Springwell Conservation Centre, Springwell Road, Wrekenton, Gateshead, Tyne and Wear (091-482 0111).

North East Environmental Network (NEEN) is at: Newcastle Architecture Workshop Ltd, 6 Higham Place, NE1 8AF (091-232 8183).

NORTH TYNESIDE

WALLSEND

Rising Sun Country Park
Kings Road North.

North Tyneside MBC. 162 ha.

On the site of the former Rising Sun Colliery, the country park includes agricultural land, forest and public open space surrounded by housing and industry. Within the area lies the **Swallow Ponds Nature Reserve** (14 ha), a subsidence pond managed by the Northumberland Wildlife Trust. The reserve supports breeding birds such as little grebe and attracts passage waders and winter visitors such as whooper swan. The pond may be viewed from the public right of way along the former Killingworth Waggonway where a hide allowing wheelchair access is to be constructed.

Near the head of the Wallsend Burn which runs through the park is **Hadrian Park Pond** off Addington Drive. Part of a relict fen system, it retains a rich invertebrate and amphibian fauna. A privately owned site close to a new housing estate, it is hoped to protect and develop it as a nature reserve.

Willington Gut
Church Bank.

Private.

Where Wallsend Dene meets the Tyne, the tidal stream has formed a small but important saltmarsh. Adjacent areas of neutral and acidic grasslands and base-rich flushes add to the site's importance and potential for ecological teaching.

WHITLEY BAY

Marden Quarry
Broadway.
North Tyneside MBC. 6.6 ha.
Surrounded by housing, this nature park was created in 1976 by infilling a deep water-filled quarry to make a shallow lake with islands for breeding waterfowl. The site also has areas of calcareous grassland supporting cowslips, quaking grass and burnet saxifrage. Extensive old elder scrub supports a good lichen flora.

Brierdene
The Links.
North Tyneside MBC. 5 ha. Warden (091-258 5085).
The walkway crosses Brierdene Burn, at the mouth of which is a natural park overlooking the sea. Appropriate management has allowed a variety of scrub and grassland vegetation to develop, providing food for flocks of goldfinches in autumn. Its coastal position has also attracted rarer birds such as bluethroat, and areas of boulder clay encourage plants such as lady's mantle, glaucous sedge and pepper saxifrage.

St Mary's Island
The Links.
North Tyneside MBC. Warden (091-258 5085).
The island, which is surmounted by a lighthouse, and has an extensive rocky foreshore with a tract of coastal clifftop grassland, is one of the most important and popular wildlife sites in the borough. The foreshore supports large flocks of wintering waders, including purple sandpipers attracted by the rich marine invertebrate fauna. The grasslands support a diverse flora including thrift, scurvy grass and sand sedge. The area is wardened and the lighthouse has recently been bought by the council to provide a visitor centre.

Avenue Branch Line
Hartley Avenue, Monkseaton.
North Tyneside MBC. 1.25 miles.
A stretch of former railway from Monkseaton towards Blyth is now a bridleway whose wayside flora includes locally rare species such as dyer's greenweed, common twayblade and false fox sedge.

Holywell Dene
Hartley Lane, Old Hartley.
Private.
The wooded valley of Seaton Burn forms part of the borough and county boundary and contains a rich woodland ground flora. An extensive network of footpaths follows the wooded valley inland, and the area is being used increasingly by local schools for environmental education.

Earsdon Nature Trail
Front Street, Earsdon.
2 miles.
The village churchyard is starting point for a trail which takes in a disused pit heap colonised by acid grassland, and Backworth Pond which has an unusual colony of sea aster around its margin. Guided walks are available in summer (contact 091-258 5085).

Annitsford Pond and Wildlife Garden
Harrison Court, Annitsford.
North Tyneside MBC. 1.4 ha. NWT. Wardened (091-258 5085).
A bridge and boardwalk allow wheelchair access to this mining subsidence pond which has extensive bullrush beds. An adjacent wildlife garden (0.3 ha) has been laid out by the local primary school, educational visits to which can be arranged through the headteacher on 091-250 0325.

Contacts

Further information on sites in the district from Chief Recreation and Amenities Officer, North Tyneside Borough Council, George Street, North Shields, NE30 1EL (091-258 5085), to whom thanks are due for providing site details.

GATESHEAD

Derwent Walk
Hexham Road, Swalwell, NE16.
Gateshead MBC. 11 ha.
A disused railway line in what is now a country park, the

embankments of the line show secondary colonisation by birch and willow scrub which run into the adjacent woodlands of the Derwent valley. Many flushed areas occur along the line which support such species as pendulous sedge, meadowsweet, valerian, wood woundwort and Dutch rush. Several bat colonies occur in the Nine Arches Bridge.
South along the Walk is:

Paddock Hill
Lockhaugh Road, Blaydon.
Gateshead MBC. 16 ha.
Paddock Hill wood is managed by Gateshead Council as part of the Thornley Wood interpretative centre. A mixed deciduous woodland on a steeply sloping bank running down to river Derwent is dominated by sessile oak on the upper slopes with birch, ash and alder on the lower slopes. The understorey includes hazel, rowan, ash saplings, cherry and spindle, the latter being very restricted in its distribution and is rare in Tyne and Wear. The ground flora is very rich, especially in the flushes on the lower slopes. Notable species are pendulous sedge, buckler fern, scaly male fern, hard fern, giant horsetail, marsh woundwort, goldilocks, toothwort and wood pimpernel. On drier slopes the ground flora includes wood anemone, bluebell, wood sage, stitchwort and bramble. Breeding birds include sparrowhawk, wood warbler, great spotted woodpecker and nuthatch. Red squirrels, roe deer and noctule bats also occur in the woodland.

Shibdon Pond
Shibdon Road, Blaydon.
Gateshead MBC. 13 ha. Durham CCT.
A subsidence pond surrounded by marshland and grassland forms a major reserve at the mouth of the Derwent Valley. The pond supports a variety of fish and amphibians, with water voles abundant among the reeds. The wetland merges with acid heathland with sphagnum mosses and heather. Breeding birds include yellow wagtail, lesser whitethroat, grasshopper warbler and sedge warbler and water rail. Numerous waterfowl plus heron, kingfisher and other species visit the site, which can be viewed from the footpath running alongside the reserve.

Windy Nook

Howard Street, Albion Street, High Felling, NE20.
Gateshead MBC. 4 ha.
This small area of grassland with a pond has considerable local value to wildlife and is a good educational resource. The main area of grassland has many wayside herbs such as birdsfoot trefoil, knapweed, red bartsia, yellow toadflax and tansy together with the shrubs hawthorn, elder and rose. Small mammals are common in the rough grassland which in turn support predators such as fox and kestrel. The pond is a spawning site for frogs and many sticklebacks occur.

Contacts

Grateful acknowledgement for the above site information is due to Robert Strachan, who carried out an impressively detailed and readable survey of Gateshead and the other two south Tyne districts on behalf of Durham CCT in 1985.

Durham County Conservation Trust is at 52 Old Elvet, Durham DH1 3HN. Its local Gateshead group is c/o 54 Lyndhurst Grove, Low Fell, Gateshead NE9 6AX (091-482 1158).
Information on sites in the district can also be obtained from UFAMS, Temporary Building, Swinburne Street, Gateshead, NE8.

SOUTH TYNESIDE

JARROW

River Don

Church Bank, NE32.
South Tyneside MBC.
By the remains of the Jarrow Priory the River Don meets the Tyne. During most of its course the river is within a heavily built-up area, but retains its wildlife importance. The lower reaches are tidal and retain saltmarsh communities which are rare in urban areas. The river corridor is being improved as a wildlife routeway with extensive tree planting, new ponds and riverside features. A footpath link for walkers is part of the plan.

SOUTH SHIELDS

Harton Down
Chatton Avenue, NE34.
South Tyneside MBC. 3 ha.
A magnesian limestone hill in the middle of extensive housing estates is rich in a variety of wild flowers, and is for this reason an SSSI.

Across the Leas to the cliffs is **Marsden Bay**, one of the North-East's main bird watching spots. The cliffs support over 4,000 breeding pairs of kittiwakes plus colonies of fulmars, gulls and cormorants. Outside of the breeding season, the spring and autumn migrations of birds crossing the North Sea bring large numbers of common birds here, with regular sightings of rarities. **Marsden Old Quarry**, some 400m inland, has a reputation as one of the best landfall sites for rare birds on migration.

BOLDON

Mount Pleasant
Newcastle Road, West Boldon.
CEGB. 3 ha. Durham CCT.
A small pond and extensive reedbeds on the River Don with grassland, scrub and tree-planted areas have been developed as a nature reserve – access by arrangement only. To the north the council has created a 3 ha lake which has adjacent herb-rich meadows attractive to wildlife, to which there is free public access.

Boldon Flats
Moor Lane, NE36.
Church Commissioners. 24 ha. South Tyneside MBC.
In an area of low-lying fields, some of which are extremely rich in plants associated with old meadows. In winter the fields are flooded to create a refuge for wintering wildfowl and wading birds. The proximity of the coast enables waders to feed and roost at the flooded flats at high tide. Ditches and pools are kept full of water throughout the spring and summer for the benefit of the aquatic invertebrates and large populations of amphibians. The Flats are best visited from October to April when they can be viewed from Moor Lane.

Contacts

Thanks for the above site entries are due to John Durkin of the South Tyneside Planning Department, Central Library, Catherine Street, South Shields, NE33 (0632-567531).

SUNDERLAND

Timber Beach
Wessington Way, SR5.
Sunderland MBC. 5.5 ha. Durham CCT.
On the north bank of the River Wear is the largest remaining area of saltmarsh along the coast between Teesmouth to Lindisfarne. Its plant communities show classic patterns of colonisation from intertidal mud and rock through saltmarsh grass with herbs to upper saltmarsh. Steep slopes back the marsh, their dense hawthorn scrub supporting a wide range of breeding birds. To the east of Hylton Dene, tipped ballast supports calcaraeous grassland. Adjacent wasteland covers an extensive area of reclaimed land from former works which supports a vast array of plants.

Mowbury Park
Park Road, SR2.
Sunderland MBC. 6 ha.
Right in the centre of town, Sunderland's oldest public park incorporates a disused quarry of geological and botanical interest. The quarry face supports plants such as wall rue, and the damp areas in the grassland beside the north-facing slopes show yellow loosestrife and Duke of Argyll's tea plant. The pond has emergent vegetation of interest, and visiting water birds include heron, common sandpiper and tufted duck.

Contacts

The Sunderland Group of the Durham CCT is c/o 7 Hovingham Gardens, Sunderland SR3 (0783-226246).

Scotland

As mentioned in Chapter 6, little attention has so far been given to wildlife sites within the two major cities, and site listings are consequently sparse.

GLASGOW

The city, whose original celtic name of Gleschow means 'beloved green place', spreads across the Clyde valley, the River Kelvin flowing through its west end and White Carr Water traversing south Glasgow. Surrounding the city are half a dozen districts based on the other industrial towns of Strathclyde South. Glasgow sites are listed firstly on the north bank westwards, then on the south.

Bishop Loch
Lockend Road, Easterhouse, E4
Private.
An SSSI, the site is described in one of the College of Technology's surveys (see below) as 'one of a series of small base-rich lochs lying on the northern fringe of Glasgow; others in the series include Possil, Hogganfield, Woodend and Lochend. The loch has a well-developed marginal flora, and prolific and diverse freshwater invertebrate fauna, and is attractive to a wide range of breeding, roosting and transitory bird species.' Because of multiple private ownership no management is being undertaken and its acquisition by the city council as a country park is under discussion.

Auchenshuggle Wood
London Road, Auchenshuggle.
Private.
The wood was the site of the city's first community nature park having been established by the BTCV (now Scottish Conservation

219

Projects) in 1981. The only area of semi-natural woodland in the east end it includes a population of northern marsh and common spotted orchids in June and early July, together with a number of hybrids. Conservationists successfully argued in favour of safeguarding the wood from housing development at a public inquiry in early 1985.

Possil Marsh
Balmoral Road, Maryhill, NW.
Scottish Wildlife Trust. 29ha.
A nature reserve since 1930, it has been owned and managed by the Scottish Wildlife Trust since 1982. The reserve consists of a shallow loch with extensive fringing fen swamp, damp grassland, dry meadow, birch and willow scrub. In addition to a number of uncommon plants, birds and invertebrates are also of interest. As described in the management plan, it represents a fragment of an extensive system of lochs and marshes which once extended throughout much of lowland west central Scotland. Over the centuries, drainage and reclamation have resulted in the elimination of many such sites. Those remaining have come under increasing pressure from encroaching development.

Forth and Clyde Canal
Running along the eastern edge of Possil Marsh and following the Kelvin valley, the canal divides at Maryhill, an eastern branch running towards the city centre and a western branch joining the Clyde among the Clydebank docks. Built for ocean-going ships rather than the barges of English canals, it offers a wide range of habitats in the water, in the waterland transition zone and on its banks – particularly those on the side opposite the towpath. Alongside its eight-mile length in Glasgow are several wildlife sites including a former clay quarry at **Hamiltonhill**, owned by BWB and managed by Scottish Conservation Projects. The *Forth and Clyde Canal Guidebook* containing a chapter on wildlife by Clive Morgan is available from BWB at the address below.

Cunningar Loop
Downiebrae Road, Rutherglen.
Private. 35 ha.
A classic wasteland site, it occupies a southern peninsula of the

Clyde and remains undeveloped because of former colliery workings and the possibility of subsidence or collapse (see, for example, the north-east of the site). Planning permission for industrial development granted after a public inquiry some years ago was not implemented, and, though interest has been expressed in its housing potential, it is among 29 sites identified as having significant wildlife value in the draft of the Second Review of the Strathclyde Structure Plan. A total of over 150 flowering plants have been recorded here, and 117 bird species with some 60 thought to breed on site. Even after the construction of a new road across the neck of the land some 27 ha will remain and it is hoped this can be designated as a nature reserve in a heavily built-up area with very few remnants of natural vegetation.

Pollok Country Park
2060 Pollokshaws Road, G43 1AT.
Glasgow DC. 146 ha. Ranger service (041-632 9299)
Glasgow's first country park, together with the surrounding privately owned golf courses and farmland (amounting to another 322 ha) provide wildlife-rich habitats within three miles of the centre of Glasgow. There are both semi-natural ancient woodlands and 19th century plantations, herb-rich grasslands, scrubby areas, ponds and a two-mile length of an important watercourse – the White Carr Water. Since 1983 there has been a countryside ranger service which organises a comprehensive range of wildlife-orientated activities. The ranger service also monitors the wildlife closely. After four years their biological records included: about 200 vascular plant species (including Scottish rarities like toothwort); 122 species of fungi; 8 species of odonata (including azure damselfly which is very scarce in Scotland); 72 species of lepidoptera; 70 species of birds (including kingfishers along the river and sparrowhawks in the woods); 20 mammal species. The mammal records include many foxes, a small population of roe deer and the exciting confirmation made in 1986 that otters live along sections of the White Carr Water flowing through the heart of Glasgow!

On the outskirts of Glasgow are a number of other sites of interest, including:

Woodend Loch

Townhead Road, Townhead, Monklands.

Monklands DC. 28 ha. Drumpellier Country Park.

Just outside the Glasgow city boundary, the loch lies within the Drumpellier Country Park. Also part of the park, the adjacent Lochend Loch has been developed for active recreation but retains natural features described in a nature trail leaflet.

Woodend, an SSSI, is described in a Glasgow College of Technology survey which reports: 'Despite the operation of intensive management systems on land surrounding the SSSI the site remains relatively undisturbed. Woodland and scrub provide some protection around much of the loch while on the exposed southern side steep banks inhibit easy access.'

55 per cent of the area is covered by the loch, the remainder consisting of reed swamp, wet meadow, carr, woodland and grassland. The open water constitutes the most important for wildfowl among the east Glasgow lochs. The marginal vegetation includes several species uncommon locally and supports abundant invertebrates, being a good site for molluscs.

Rouken Glen Park

Rouken Glen Road, Thornliebank.

Eastwood DC. 66 ha.

A private park until 1906, its origins stretch back to 1530 or earlier. The gorge is of national importance as a geological site and is designated as an SSSI. There are also small areas of land which have received minimal disturbance over the years, providing, in the main, the rich wildlife resources of the park. Its large bird population includes sparrowhawk, grey wagtail, redwing, long-tailed tit, treecreeper and brambling. Since its acquisition by Eastwood council in 1984, a ranger service figures among proposals for the park's future management, but so far only commercial enterprises such as a garden centre and exotic butterfly kingdom have been implemented.

Braidbar Quarries

Braidholm Road, Giffnock, G53.

4 ha.

Since sandstone quarrying ended in 1912 the site was used for the tipping of steelworks slag up to the late 1960s. While most of the former industrial land has been reclaimed and built on, the remainder includes a range of habitats, the most valuable being wetland, and includes a large variety of wildlife species, many of which are uncommon in urban environments. The authors of the Glasgow College of Technology Survey propose that its amenity and educational potential merit its designation as a Local Nature Reserve, but the local authority thinks otherwise and has refused to amend the local plan which identifies the site for housing.

Contacts

The Glasgow Urban Wildlife Group is c/o Countryside Rangers' Centre, Pollok Country Park, 2060 Pollokshaws Road, Glasgow 43 1AT (041-632 9299).
The surveys mentioned above can be found in the list of 'Occasional Publications' of the Department of Biological Sciences and available from: Glasgow College of Technology, Cowcaddens Road, Glasgow G4 0BA (041-332 7090).
The local 'Support Groups' of the Scottish Wildlife Trust cover: Allander and Kelvin (041-942 0867), Calder and Cart (041-644 1116), North Clydeside (0389-76231) and Paisley and Renfrew c/o Paisley Museum (041-889 3151).
Scottish Conservation Projects is at 54 Waddell Street, Hutchesontown, Glasgow (041-429 0919).
Forth and Clyde Project Office, British Waterways Board, Canal House, Applecross Street, Glasgow C4 9SP (041-332 6936).
Bellarmine Environmental Community Resource Centre, Bellarmine Secondary School, Cowglen Road, Glasgow G53 6EW.

EDINBURGH

Duddingston Loch
Old Church Lane, E16
Scottish Development Department. 8 ha.
At the base of Arthur's Seat, the loch is managed as a bird sanctuary. In addition to its breeding birds it attracts large numbers of water birds in winter. To the south of the loch is the **Bawsinch** (7 ha) reserve created by the Scottish Wildlife Trust from allotments and other derelict land. A number of small ponds have been excavated, each designed to support a distinctive fauna and flora.

Contacts

The Scottish Wildlife Trust is at 25 Johnston Terrace, EH1 2NH (031-2264602).

An energetic programme of environmental education projects is organised at the Environmental Resource Centre, Drummond High School, Cochran Terrace, EH7 4PQ (031-557 2135).

The Lothian Wildlife Group is c/o the Technical Block, Broughton Primary School, Broughton Road, Edinburgh EH7 4HD (031-556 1243).

Directory

Organisations and addresses additional to those in the gazetteer.

Government
Department of the Environment
2 Marsham Street
London SW1P 3EB
(01-212 3434)
including Central Unit on Environmental Issues

DoE – Wildlife Division
Tollgate House
Houlton Street
Bristol BS2 9DJ
(0272-218811)

Welsh Office
Cathays Park
Cardiff CF1 3NQ
(0222-825111)

Scottish Office
New St Andrew's House
Edinburgh EH1 3TD
(031-556 8400)

Department of the Environment for Northern Ireland
Countryside and Wildlife Branch
Calvert House
23 Castle Place
Belfast BT1 1FY
(0232-230560)

Agencies
Nature Conservancy Council
Northminster House
Peterborough PE1 1UA
(0733-40345)

Countryside Commission
John Dower House
Crescent Place
Cheltenham GL50 3RA
(0242-521381)

Groundwork Foundation
Bennetts Court
6 Bennetts Hill
Birmingham B2 5ST
(021-236 8565)

UK 2000
19/21 Rathbone Place
London W1P 1DF
(01-636 6901)

think green
Midland Business Centre
Temple House (room 303)
43-48 New Street
Birmingham B2 4LJ
(021-643 8899 x 303)

Voluntary Organisations
RSNC (Royal Society for Nature Conservation)
The Green
Nettleham
Lincoln LN2 2NR
(0522-752326)
including WATCH and Urban Steering Group

Fairbrother Group
c/o Urban Wildlife Group
11 Albert Street
Birmingham B4 7UA
(021-236 3626)

BTCV (British Trust for Conservation Volunteers)
36 St Mary's Street
Wallingford
Oxford OX10 0EU
(0491-39766)

TRUE (Trust for Urban Ecology)
South Bank House
Black Prince Road
London SE1
(01-587 1562)

BANC (British Association of Nature Conservationists)
c/o Urban Wildlife Group, Birmingham (*see* page 170)

References

References and further reading – by author and date of publication.

1940s – 1960s

Tansley, A G. *Our Heritage of Wild Nature: A plea for organised nature conservation* (CUP 1945).

Fitter, R S R. *London's Natural History* (Collins, 1945, paperback 1985).

Allsop, Kenneth. *Adventure Lit their Star* (Macdonald 1949, revised edition 1962).

Edlin, H L. *The Changing Wild Life of Britain* (Batsford 1952).

Hoskins, W G. and Stamp, Dudley. *The Common Lands of England and Wales* (Collins 1963).

Stamp, Dudley. *Nature Conservation in Britain* (Collins 1969).

1970s

Fairbrother, Nan. *New Lives, New Landscapes* (Architectural Press 1970, Penguin 1972).

Whitaker, Ben and Browne, Kenneth. *Parks for People* (Winchester Press, New York, 1971).

Mabey, Richard. *The Unofficial Countryside* (Collins 1973).

Taylor, Nicholas. *The Village in the City* (Temple Smith 1973).

Burton, John A. *The Naturalist in London* (David and Charles 1974).

Warren, A and Goldsmith, F B (eds). *Conservation in Practice* (Wiley 1974).

Sheail, John. *Nature in Trust: The History of Nature Conservation in Britain* (Blackie 1976).

Chinnery, Michael. *The Natural History of the Garden* (Collins 1977, Fontana 1978).

Owen, Denis. *Towns and Gardens* (Rainbird 1978).
Teagle, W G. *The Endless Village* (Nature Conservancy Council 1978).
Wilson, Ron. *The Back Garden Wildlife Sanctuary Book* (Astragal 1979, Penguin 1981).
Laurie, Ian (ed). *Nature in Cities* (Wiley 1979).
Ruff, Allan. *Holland and the Ecological Landscapes* (Deanwater 1979).

1980-85
Cole, Lyndis. *Wildlife in the City* (Nature Conservancy Council 1980).
Royal Society for Nature Conservation (eds). *Nature Conservation Goes to Town* (conference papers, 1980, unpublished).
Mabey, Richard. *The Common Ground* (Collins 1980).
Shoard, Marion. *The Theft of the Countryside* (Temple Smith 1980).
Brown, Jane. *The Everywhere Landscape* (Wildwood 1982).
Bornkamm, R, Lee, J A and Seaward, M R D. *Urban Ecology* (Blackwell 1982).
Davidson, Joan and MacEwan, Ann. *The Livable City* (1983).
Warren, A and Goldsmith, F B (eds). *Conservation in Perspective* (Wiley 1983).
Higgins, Sandra. *Green Towns and Cities UK/USA* (Dartington Institute 1984).
Hywel-Davies, Jeremy and Thom, Valerie. *The Macmillan Guide to Britain's Nature Reserves* (Macmillan 1984, paperback 1986).
Baines, Chris. *How to Make a Wildlife Garden* (Elm Tree 1985).
Conservation Foundation. *The Conservation Review* (Webb and Bower 1985).
Chinery, Michael and Teagle, W G. *Wildlife in Towns and Cities – gardens, parks and waterways* (Country Life 1985).
Harvey, Sheila and Rettig, Stephen (eds). *Fifty Years of Landscape Design 1934-1984* (Landscape Press 1985).

1986-
Tyldesley, David. *Gaining Momentum: An Analysis of the Role and Performance of Local Authorities in Nature Conservation* (Pisces 1986).
Emery, Malcolm. *Promoting Nature in Cities and Towns: A*

Practical Guide by the Ecological Parks Trust (Croom Helm 1986).

Baines, Chris. *The Wild Side of Town* (BBC 1986).

Weightman, Gavin and Birkhead, Mike. *City Safari: Wildlife in London* (Sidgwick and Jackson 1986).

Goode, David. *Wild in London* (Michael Joseph 1986).

Brooker, John and Corder, Matthew. *Environmental Economy* (Spons 1986).

Bradshaw, Tony, Goode, David and Thorpe, Ed. (eds). *Ecology and Design in Landscape* (Blackwell 1986).

Smyth, Bob. *City Wildspace* (Hilary Shipman 1987).

Index

Index does not include gazetteer entries

Mostyn, Barbara 44 – 5, 72

Nash, John (1752-1835) 14
National Parks and Access to the
    Countryside Act (1949) 10, 26
National Trust 10 – 11, 65, 70
Nature Conservancy Council (NCC) 2,
    4, 7, 10, 15, 16, 29, 31, 43 – 7,
    49, 62, 65, 81 – 2
'Nature conservation goes to town'
    conference (1980) 65
Newcastle 32, 45
Nicholson, Max 9, 11, 15, 21, 27, 71
North Tyneside 32
Norwich Wildlife Group 66

O'Connor, Brian 46
Owen, Jenny 71

Parkin, Ian 19
Patton, Dennis 67
Perring, Frank 61, 69
Phillips, Adrian 48, 56
Pye-Smith, Charlie 15

Ramblers' Association 10
Randall, David 24
Rawnsley, Hardwicke (1851-1920) 10
Regent's Park 14
Ridley, Nicholas – MP 81
Roberts, John 27
Robinson, Richard 64, 70
Rodgers, Bill 76
Rose, Chris 15, 64
Rotherham 31
Rothschild, Nathaniel 11
Rourke, Adrian 18
Royal Society for Nature
    Conservation (RSNC) 11, 16, 57,
    65 – 6, 69, 70 – 2
Royal Society for the Prevention of
    Cruelty to Animals (RSPCA) 10
Royal Society for the Protection of
    Birds (RSPB) 11, 70
Ruff, Allan 17 – 19, 22, 39
Rural Preservation Association – *see*
    Landlife

St Helens 30, 40, 49, 50
Scottish Conservation Projects 69
Scottish Wildlife Trust 68
Sheail, John 11, 17
Sheffield 31

Sheffield City Wildlife Group 67
Shirley, Peter 61
Social Democratic Party 75, 76
Socialist Environment and Resources
    Association (SERA) 75
Society for the Promotion of Nature
    Reserves – *see* RSNC
South Tyneside 32
South Yorkshire county council 7, 27,
    30
Southwark 6, 21, 34 – 6, 39, 80
Sparks, David 63
Stoke-on-Trent 14, 16, 21, 22, 45
Sukopp, H 20
Sunderland 32
Swansea 14, 45
Sydenham Hill Wood 36 – 8, 39

Teagle, Bunny 7, 43 – 4, 61
Thames Angling and Preservation
    Society 10
think green 58
Thomas, Janie 23
Thompson, Peter 54
Tregay, Rob 19 – 20
Trust for Urban Ecology (TRUE) 16,
    21, 33 – 4, 71
Turner, William (d. 1568) 7
Tyldesley, David 27, 84, 86
Tyne and Wear county council 7, 27,
    39

UK 2000 57 – 8
University College London 16, 64, 72

Victoria Park 10

Wakefield 32, 40
Waldegrave, William – MP 81
Warrington 19 – 21
West Midlands county council 7, 26,
    33, 39, 43
West Yorkshire county council 7, 27,
    31
White, Gilbert (1720 – 1793) 8
Wigan 40, 49
Wild, Mike 67
Wilde, Mike 55
Wildlife Link 84
William Curtis Ecological Park 8, 12,
    16, 21, 34
Wirral 29, 39
Wood, David 31